D1626575

A Daily Dose of MERCY

Don Stephens
with
Nancy Predaina

First published in Great Britain in 2018 by Hodder & Stoughton
An Hachette UK company

1

A CIP catalogue record for this title is available from the British Library

ISBN 978 1 529 33713 6
eBook ISBN 978 1 529 33714 3

Printed and bound in the UK by Clays Ltd, Elcograf S.p.A.

Hodder & Stoughton policy is to use papers that are natural, renewable and recyclable products and made from wood grown in sustainable forests. The logging and manufacturing processes are expected to conform to the environmental regulations of the country of origin.

Hodder & Stoughton Ltd
Carmelite House
50 Victoria Embankment
London EC4Y 0DZ

www.hodderfaith.com

Dedication

A *Daily Dose of Mercy* is dedicated to all the amazing Mercy Ships crew and staff—prior and present. Their compassion, commitment, and sacrifice wrote the stories on these pages.

Don Stephens

Contents

It's All About Mercy ...

I could say it all started with a hurricane, or reading a book about the famous SS *Hope*. I could say it started with meeting Mother Teresa, or with the birth of our special-needs son, John Paul. Or I could say it began with my parents' simple way with grace and mercy and dignity with their small-town helping hand. I could say all those things about the very beginning of the idea that became Mercy Ships, and they'd all be true.

A seed of an idea in the mind of a nineteen-year-old young man on a youth mission trip—an idea born from an overheard prayer in the midst of a hurricane in the Bahamas—was cultivated, watered, and pruned by a loving God who wants all of His people to have abundant life. The things He has done and the doors He has opened have humbled and awed me. And this idea of a hospital ship filled with volunteer crew members and offering free surgical care—this illogical business model that shouldn't work—*has* worked.

And the reason it has worked is because the heart of Mercy Ships is Jesus. Our staff and crew desire to model their lives upon His life. Those who serve on the hospital ship pay their own way, volunteering their time and skills to help those less fortunate than themselves.

Our work is far from over. The tragic truth is that more than five billion people worldwide have no access to safe surgical care. Please pray for our dedicated staff and crew as we sail ahead to offer even more hope and healing to the people of Africa.

These daily devotional readings are taken from the very best stories from our *Mercy Minute* radio program, which began in October 2000. Each one-minute script points to the need for mercy everywhere … across the ocean, down the street, next door, and even in our very own homes.

As you read *A Daily Dose of Mercy*, I hope you will "choose mercy" by showing kindness to someone every day.

Yes, it really *is* all about mercy.

—Don Stephens

About the Ships . . .

Since 1978, Mercy Ships has operated five ships—at various times and in various combinations: the *Anastasis*, the *Caribbean Mercy*, the *Island Mercy* (originally named the *Good Samaritan*), the *Pacific Ruby*, and the *Africa Mercy*. The first four have been retired after faithful and distinguished service. The *Africa Mercy* has a capacity equal to the other four ships combined. And a new (even larger) ship, the *Global Mercy*, is currently under construction. What powerful partners the two ships will be as they deliver hope and healing to the poorest countries in the world!

A Daily Dose
of
MERCY

January

"And what does the LORD require of you? To act justly and to love mercy and to walk humbly with your God."
(Micah 6:8)

January 1

Something that Matters

Becky Johns volunteered as a ward nurse onboard our hospital ship in the Republic of Congo. She shared this New Year's reflection:

"I love a new year ... it is a clean slate, a time of reflection, a fresh perspective. My favorite moment so far has been seeing our teenage patient Rovel's wounds heal enough that he could finally go home. It was so amazing to watch Rovel and his grandmother give hugs to all of us. 'Renewed hope for the future,' my friend called it. This is where my excitement for this year is rooted. For each of us is right where we need to be to do something that matters."

Start the New Year with something that matters—like finding a volunteer opportunity in your community. Helping others is *always* an act of mercy.

"It is God Himself who has made us what we are and given us new lives from Christ Jesus; and long ages ago He planned that we should spend these lives in helping others." **(Ephesians 2:10 TLB)**

"Shared joy is double joy; shared sorrow is half sorrow."
(Swedish Proverb)

⚓ Formerly the *Victoria*, the *Anastasis* was built in 1953 as an Italian passenger liner and served as the flagship of the Mercy Ships fleet from 1978 to 2007.

Mercy Minute Volume 62, Script 15; blog (1/21/2014) of Becky Johns submitted to Grace Antonini, staff writer; 2013-14 AFM Congo Field Service;

January 2

Catching Shadows

A volunteer crew member described a life-transforming moment on our hospital ship, the *Africa Mercy*:

"Yesterday I witnessed something incredible and amazing—a group of 15 children who have been blind since birth saw FOR THE FIRST TIME. As one little girl, four-year-old Fatmata, walked out the door, she stopped in front of me and reached down and curiously touched the floor. It was a split second before I realized what she was doing—she was trying to touch her shadow . . . that she had never seen before and didn't understand. Next time, I see my shadow, I know what I'll be grateful for."

This beautiful moment was created by the extravagant mercy of volunteers and donors … mercy that represented an investment of love, time, and commitment. And YOU can create a beautiful moment of extravagant mercy for someone today.

"Great crowds came to Him, bringing the lame, the blind, the crippled, the mute and many others; and laid them at His feet; and He healed them." **(Matthew 15:30 NIV)**

⚓ January 2, 1981: The Maltese flag was raised as the flag of registry for the *Anastasis*, the first Mercy Ship.

Mercy Minute Volume 52, Script 45; from blogpost by Catherine Murphy, AFM *staff writer; 1/13/13; used with permission; 2013* AFM *Guinea Field Service;*

January 3

Mother Teresa's 129 Lunches

"Excuse me," Mother Teresa said. *"How much does this meal cost?"*

The airline stewardess said, *"I don't know. Maybe a dollar."*

Mother Teresa responded, *"If I give up my meal, will you give me a dollar for the poor?"*

The stewardess consulted the pilot and returned. *"Yes, Mother,"* she said. Suddenly, *everyone* on the plane decided they weren't hungry, and Mother Teresa had $129.

Then Mother Teresa asked for the meals because they were going to be discarded. When the plane landed in Latin America, Mother Teresa was given the 129 lunches, as well as the loan of an airline truck. Thirty minutes later in a desperately poor neighborhood, 129 people enjoyed lunch, courtesy of Taca Airlines.

Mother Teresa was very resourceful and saw an opportunity for mercy—double mercy, in fact. So, look around, there may be an opportunity for kindness close at hand.

"God has given each of you a gift from His great variety of spiritual gifts. Use them well to serve one another." **(1 Peter 4:10 NLT)**

Mercy Minute Volume 28, Script 22; submitted by Larry Mast, Mercy Ships staff writer; based on Guideposts, *April 2006;*

January 4

A Crowd's Mercy for Edoh

In 1995 the Mercy Ship was in Togo, West Africa. Thousands of desperate people stood in line—hoping to receive an appointment card for surgery.

At the back of the line was a little nine-year-old girl named Edoh—slowly suffocating to death. A large tumor was literally stealing the breath of life from her.

But in the midst of that suffering crowd, mercy heard the gasping child and raised its head. Arms of compassion—some weak and some strong—lifted Edoh and passed her to the front of the line. And that day, Edoh received an appointment card … a ticket for life instead of death.

You see, mercy looks beyond its own needs to recognize the needs of others. Remember: *"Blessed are the merciful, for they shall receive mercy."* (Matthew 5:7 **ESV*)***

⚓ January 2002: The *Africa Mercy* held its first entry-level training course while in drydock in Newcastle, UK.

Mercy Minute Volume 40, Script 53; from 2003 Mercy Ships donor appeal letter; edited by Nancy Predaina, Special Projects Writer/Editor;

January 5

Spider-Man to the Rescue

An eight-year-old autistic boy faced his first day at a special-needs school in Bangkok, Thailand—and he was frightened. He began to cry, and then he climbed onto a third-floor window ledge.

When the teachers couldn't persuade him to come back inside, they called the fire department. Then someone mentioned that the boy loved comic superheroes. Fireman Yoosabai rushed back to the station and grabbed the Spider-Man costume he normally uses to liven up school fire drills.

The sight of Spider-Man holding a glass of juice for him made the boy smile. He immediately threw himself into the arms of his "superhero."

You see, mercy comes in all forms—even a Spider-Man in Thailand! Sometimes you have to be very creative to find a way to show mercy to someone.

***"There is no room in love for fear. Well-formed love banishes fear."* (1 John 4:18 MSG)**

⚓ *"The greatest healing therapy is friendship and love."* (President Hubert H. Humphrey)

Mercy Minute Volume 37, Script 48; adapted from "Thai 'Spider-Man' to the Rescue," http://news.bbc.co.uk 3/24/2009;

January 6

The Boy with the Backward Legs

Abel is a handsome, bright boy in West Africa. But for years, people didn't see his joyful spirit and contagious smile. They only saw his horrible deformity.

You see, when Abel was a baby, something went terribly wrong. His leg muscles quit growing, but his bones didn't. His legs bent backward at the knees, forcing his thighs out behind him. For ten years, his startling appearance made him the object of ridicule. But his father taught him to respond only with kindness. And Abel learned to walk and even played as a soccer goalie.

For three months Abel underwent free orthopedic surgeries and physical therapy onboard our hospital ship, the *Africa Mercy*. He's no longer the "boy with the backward legs"!

Abel experienced an amazing transformation because surgeons and nurses volunteered their skills to serve others. Everyone has some skill or talent that can be used to offer a dose of mercy to others.

> ***"So two good things happen as a result of your gifts—those in need are helped, and they overflow with thanks to God."***
> **(2 Corinthians 9:12 TLB)**

Mercy Minute Volume 42, Script 53; from patient story by Elaine Winn, staff writer; AFM *Field Service to Togo 2010;*

January 7

Bambay Forgives

Sierra Leone's civil war was brutal. Bambay was only 15 when rebel soldiers entered his village. They chopped off his hands and left him to bleed to death.

A nun found him and saved his life. One day she asked, "What would you do if you found your attacker?"

Bambay quickly answered, "I would kill him."

The nun told him that if he wanted a good future he must give up his anger and hatred. He must learn to forgive.

One day Bambay saw his enemy and caught him—but he just couldn't kill him. Instead, he forgave the man.

You see, Bambay received more than physical healing. He learned that forgiveness is the *greatest* act of mercy.

"Live out your God-created identity. Live generously and graciously toward others, the way God lives toward you."
(Matthew 5:48 MSG)

Mercy Minute Volume 47, Script 33; submitted by Elaine B. Winn, staff writer; from interview with Ken Winebark, April 18, 2011; AFM *2011 Sierra Leone Field Service;*

January 8

A Nurse and the Devil Child

In Freetown, Sierra Leone, a newspaper displayed a photo of a little girl with a facial deformity. The caption read "Devil Child." The girl was kept locked up in a cement chicken coup—alone and slowly starving to death.

Then someone brought her to our hospital ship, the *Africa Mercy*. She hesitated at the gangway—afraid of rejection. Despite the child's smell and filth, a Mercy Ships nurse gently picked her up and carried her onboard.

The girl received a free surgery to repair the deformity. But the love and kindness she experienced repaired her heart. It reminds us of the words of Francis of Assisi: *"Preach the Gospel always; use words when necessary."*

I think that also applies to showing mercy to others … "only use words when necessary."

"Follow God's example, therefore, as dearly loved children and walk in the way of love, just as Christ loved us and gave Himself up for us as a fragrant offering and sacrifice to God."
(Ephesians 5:1-2 NIV)

⚓ January 2000: Mercy Ships opened a land-based program called New Steps in Sierra Leone to help land mine victims and amputees, many of whom were injured in Sierra Leone's decade-long civil war.

Mercy Minute Volume 48, Script 27; based on an interview with volunteer Laura Coles by Nicole Pribbernow, staff writer; 2011 AFM *Field Service to Sierra Leone;*

January 9

Cobblestones of Gratitude

Underneath the paving on Bank Street in New London, Connecticut, are some very special cobblestones of gratitude.

When Germany invaded Belgium in World War I, they stopped all imports. Since Belgium imported 80% of its food, the people were starving. Help came from an American organization directed by Herbert Hoover, who later became president. Ships carried food to Belgium. Hoover guaranteed the Germans that the returning ships would carry no cargo to aid the Allies. So, the grateful Belgians ripped up some streets. Then they donated the cobblestones to provide ballast for the homeward-bound ships. Some of the stones eventually paved the streets of New London. You see, the by-product of your acts of kindness to others is gratitude.

"Carrying out this social relief work involves far more than helping meet the bare needs of poor Christians. It also produces abundant and bountiful thanksgivings to God."
(2 Corinthians 9:12 MSG)

⚓ *"If you want happiness for an hour, take a nap. If you want happiness for a day, go fishing. If you want happiness for a year, inherit a fortune. If you want happiness for a lifetime, help somebody."* (Chinese Proverb)

Mercy Minute Volume 47, Script 56; adapted from "Bank Street's Belgian Cobblestones," by Carol Kimball; www.theday;8/17/09;

January 10

Abisoye, a Light on the Ward

For thirteen years, Abisoye lived with a facial tumor. Many people—even in her own family—teased and avoided her. Her husband died, leaving her to care for their four young children. She baked and sold bread to survive.

Then our hospital ship, the *Africa Mercy*, came to Benin, West Africa. Abisoye received a free surgery to remove the tumor.

Now, you'd think that she would be angry or bitter about the hardships in her life. But Abisoye encouraged everyone around her. One of the nurses said, "*Abisoye was a light in the hospital ward. She would always say, 'God is so good.'*"

You see, a merciful heart looks beyond its own difficulties and encourages others. You can be the light of mercy in someone's life today because God *is* good!

"Since you have been chosen by God who has given you this new kind of life, and because of His deep love and concern for you, you should practice tenderhearted mercy and kindness to others."
(Colossians 3:12 TLB)

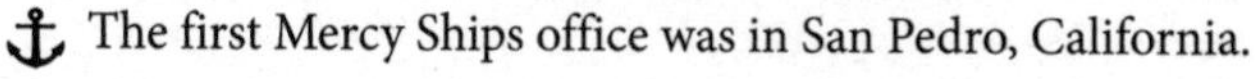

The first Mercy Ships office was in San Pedro, California.

Mercy Minute Volume 47, Script 6; based on patient interview by staff writer Megan Petock; 2009 AFM Field Service to Benin;

January 11

Five Children See

Five children, ages 6 to 15, sat silently on a long wooden bench. All five were from the same family. Despite the sunny day, they sat in darkness, blind from birth by cataracts. In the west, these children would have had restorative surgery before they spoke their first word.

But the harsh reality of West Africa is that no accommodation is made for disability. Mercy Ships was their only chance for a future.

Onboard the *Africa Mercy*, Mercy Ships volunteer doctors performed successful free surgeries for all five children. The horrible darkness was gone! It was replaced by the music of children's laughter. Their mother said, *"I am so happy, so thankful."*

You see, mercy always brings light into darkness … and that means **you** can brighten someone's life today.

"Love each other with genuine affection, and take delight in honoring each other." **(Romans 12:10 NLT)**

Mercy Minute Volume 51, Script 1; submitted by Catherine Clarke Murphy, staff writer; based on patient story by Nicole Pribbernow, staff writer; 2012 AFM *Togo Field Service;*

January 12

Malala Yousafzai

Malala Yousafzai is a courageous 15-year-old Pakistani girl. She is a vocal advocate for girls' education. She even wrote a blog for the BBC called "Diary of a Pakistani Schoolgirl."

On October 9, 2012, Taliban gunmen boarded her school bus and shot her in the head. They said they had to silence her extremist Western thinking.

Miraculously, she survived and recovered in a hospital in Britain. She's become an inspiration around the world. In fact, in 2014 she was given the Nobel Peace Prize. Her father says, "*When she fell, Pakistan stood*" because the nation rallied to her cause.

Mercy means standing up for what is right—even at great cost. Each one of us can make the world a better place by showing mercy to others.

***"Speak up for the people who have no voice, for the rights of all the down-and-outers. Speak out for justice!"* (Proverbs 31:8-9 MSG)**

⚓ January 12, 1983: The first Mercy Ship, the Anastasis, arrived in Guatemala to deliver $1 million U.S. in relief supplies for the Ixil Indians.

Mercy Minute Volume 52, Script 11; based on "Malala Yousafzai" by Howard Chua-Eoan, 11/26/12, www.time.com, and "Malala Yousafzai Should Win Nobel Peace Prize," www.globalpost.com; 11/9/12;

January 13

Memouna Laughs

When thirteen-year-old Memouna arrived onboard our hospital ship for surgery, she was scared. For years she had been teased about the tumor on her face. People even said she was cursed. But a free surgery onboard our *Africa Mercy* changed her forever. Mercy Ships ward nurse Lynne White described the transformation:

"Memouna was so quiet. I didn't think she could speak! But now that she has had surgery, she is so happy. A few nights ago, I walked into the room and found her laughing and painting her nails, just like any 13-year-old would. Memouna finally feels normal. And she won't be teased for the way she looks anymore."

Showing compassion to others is so powerful! Mercy completely transformed Memouna's life … physically and emotionally. And YOU can transform a life by showing mercy to someone.

"Here are My directions: Pray much for others; plead for God's mercy upon them; give thanks for all He is going to do for them."
(1 Timothy 2:1 TLB)

⚓ January 13, 2001: An earthquake estimated at 7.7 or 7.9 struck El Salvador, killing hundreds and leaving hundreds of thousands homeless. The *Caribbean Mercy* was docked in Guatemala. The ship's medical team sprang into action, and the crew assembled supplies and joined the relief efforts.

Mercy Minute, Volume 51, Script 47; based on patient story by Catherine Clarke Murphy, staff writer; 2012 AFM Guinea Field Service;

January 14

The Waving Man

In the Berkeley History Center in California, you'll find a pair of yellow gloves once owned by Joseph Charles. He was called the "waving man."

You see, every weekday morning for 30 years, Joseph stood on his porch, smiled, and waved his yellow-gloved hands at every passing car. If you lowered your car window, you'd hear him call out, *"Keep smiling"* or *"Have a GOOD day!"*

One person said, *"He embodied the spirit of unconditional giving."*

Charles died in 2002. Every year on March 22, his birthday, people of the community put on yellow gloves and stand in front of his old house from 7:30—9:00. They smile and wave at passing cars.

Yes, mercy gives happiness to others without requiring anything in return. Today would be a great day to show unconditional mercy to someone.

"*So encourage each other to build each other up, just as you are already doing.*" (1 Thessalonians 5:11 TLB)

⚓ *"Good works are the links that form a chain of love."* (Mother Teresa)

Mercy Minute Volume 55, Script 14; based on "Day 686: Tribute to the Waving Man,"4/3/13; http://gooddeedaday.wordpress.com;

January 15

The Witch of Freetown

Aminata was an energetic 19-year-old girl from West Africa. She had a fabric trading business in Freetown, Sierra Leone. The future looked bright—until one day she noticed a small lump inside her mouth . . .

"It was so small at first, but it grew and grew," said Aminata. "I watched my world fall apart. Over the next 10 years I lost everything—my husband, my job, my place in the community. I barely managed to live by selling oranges along the road. Many called me The Witch of Freetown.

"God, in His mercy, provided Mercy Ships doctors who removed the tumor. It was as big as a melon! Now, no one calls me a witch."

You see, Aminata's life was restored by the mercy of volunteers willing to offer their skills and time to help those less fortunate than themselves.

"I call on You, my God, for You will answer me; turn Your ear to me and hear my prayer. Show me the wonders of Your great love."
(Psalm 17:6-7 NIV)

Mercy Minute Volume 51, Script 60; submitted by Larry Mast, staff writer; from the Dec. 1993 Mercy Ships N.A. Newsletter;

January 16

Baby Wasti

Volunteer nurse Ali Chandra wrote this blog entry about one of her favorite patient stories:

"Wasti lived in Benin with his mama, his sister, and his papa's other wives and children. His sister had something wrong with her eyes. When Wasti was born with a cleft lip, his mama was thrown out because a woman who made 'broken babies' didn't deserve a place in the family.

But his mama heard about a ship that would operate for free. Wasti's surgery was the very last one we did that field service. A short half-hour in the operating room held out the promise of better things to come. He recovered perfectly."

Mercy embraces brokenness and offers a beautiful promise for a better tomorrow. You can brighten someone's future by showing mercy today.

"Through the heartfelt mercies of our God, God's Sunrise will break in upon us, shining on those in the darkness, those sitting in the shadow of death." **(Luke 1:78-79 MSG)**

⚓ January 16, 2006: Ellen Johnson Sirleaf was inaugurated as the President of Liberia—the first democratically elected female president of an African nation.

Mercy Minute Volume 54, Script 19; from blog of Ali Chandra, alirae.net, 8/7/2013; used with permission;

January 17

A Pilot Shows Mercy

Mark received the devastating news that his three-year-old grandson was dying. In 24 hours, the life support would be removed.

Mark immediately booked a flight with Southwest Airlines and arrived at the airport two hours early.

But bad weather had delayed the flights, and the airport was packed. Security officials wouldn't let Mark move to the front of the line. Finally, he ran to the gate and was surprised to see the pilot there. The pilot said, "*We are so sorry about the loss of your grandson. We held the plane for you. They can't go anywhere without me, and I wasn't going to go anywhere without you.*"

Risking the consequences, the pilot showed mercy and compassion. Now you go, take a chance and look for an opportunity to show mercy to someone today.

***"The generous will prosper; those who refresh others will themselves be refreshed."* (Proverbs 11:25 NLT)**

Mercy Minute Volume 47, Script 7; submitted by Vicki Gregg; adapted from TIME, *Sun, Jan 16,2011;*

January 18

Blessed Assurance

Songs of faith touch the soul. Scott Temple volunteered as a nurse onboard our hospital ship. He shared how a hymn encouraged his heart:

"A group of post-op ladies were walking up and down the hallway, singing 'Blessed Assurance.' The words were in their native language, but the melody is universal.

This beautiful hymn refocused me to our loving God. His love brought me across the world to serve as a nurse. His love enabled a group of ladies recovering from surgery to sing praise.

'Echoes of mercy, whispers of love' became part of the fabric of my heart, and it strengthened me."

It's such a privilege that God allows us to be the face of His love to others. It's truly a "foretaste of glory divine."

***"Let us draw near to God with a sincere heart and with the full assurance that faith brings ..."* (Hebrews 10:22 NIV)**

"The quality of mercy is not strain'd,
It droppeth like the gentle rain from heaven
Upon the place beneath: it is twice blest;
It blesseth him that gives and him that takes."
(William Shakespeare)

Mercy Minute Volume 66, Script 27; based on an article by Scott Temple sent to Kelly Grizzard; 2015-16 AFM *Madagascar Field Service; used with permission;*

January 19

Everybody Can Serve

Martin Luther King Jr. was an American pastor and leader in the African-American Civil Rights Movement. In one of his sermons, he said:

"Everybody can be great because everybody can serve. You don't have to have a college degree to serve. You don't have to make your subject and your verb agree to serve. You don't have to know about Plato and Aristotle to serve. You only need a heart full of grace, a soul generated by love."

Beautifully said! Mark 10:45 says, *"For even the Son of Man did not come to be served, but to serve."*

If you have "a heart full of grace and a soul generated by love," you can follow the model of Jesus by serving others.

"Never worry about numbers. Help one person at a time, and always start with the person nearest you." **(Mother Teresa)**

Mercy Minute Volume 58, Script 26; based on devotional in Our Daily Bread, *1/20/14;*

January 20

Good Job! Good Job!

Four-year-old Lee received a free orthopedic surgery onboard our hospital ship, the *Africa Mercy*. She has a round face, plump cheeks, twinkly eyes, and a lovely little-girl laugh. She loves to be tickled.

Morris is another child who also had a free orthopedic surgery. With a great deal of effort and persuasion, he managed to maneuver around the ward for the first time on crutches. Little Lee cheered him on, saying, *"Good job! Good job!"* in her sweet little-girl voice. That went on for almost ten minutes. Later, she did the same thing for another orthopedic patient.

You see, encouragement is a gift of mercy. Show mercy today by giving the gift of encouragement.

***"Here is a simple rule of thumb for behavior: Ask yourself what you want people to do for you; then grab the initiative and do it for them!"* (Luke 6:31 MSG)**

Mercy Minute Volume 33, Script 36; based on blog of Megan Petock, volunteer nurse; megisinafrica.blogspot.com 4/21/08; used with permission;

January 21

A Merciful Cab Ride

Listen to this moving story from a former cab driver:

"I took a fare at 2:30 a.m. A small, frail, elderly woman gave me an address and asked, 'Can we drive through downtown?'

'It's not the shortest way,' I answered.

'Oh, I don't mind,' she said. 'I'm on my way to a hospice.'

For the next two hours, we drove through the city. Sometimes she'd ask me to slow in front of a particular building or corner. Finally she said, 'I'm tired. Let's go.'

We drove in silence to the address. 'How much do I owe you?' she asked.

'Nothing,' I said.

'You gave an old woman a little moment of joy,' she said.

I don't think that I've done anything more important in my life."

It is important to be on the lookout for an opportunity to give someone a merciful moment of joy.

***"Yes, dear brother, give me joy with this loving act, and my weary heart will praise the Lord."* (Philemon 1:20 TLB)**

⚓ Jan. 21, 2015: Sambany, a patient with a 16.45 pound (7.46 kg) tumor arrived at the *Africa Mercy* in Madagascar. Five of his friends took turns carrying him on their backs for two days to reach the ship … and healing.

Mercy Minute Volume 58, Script 19; from "A Cab Ride I'll Never Forget," 3/28/08; www.kindspring.org

January 22

The View from the Hotel Ducor

Megan volunteered as a nurse for Mercy Ships. One day, she followed a guide up to the roof of what was once a five-star hotel. But now the hotel was just a concrete shell from years of civil war. The view from the roof revealed the overwhelming poverty of Liberia.

Megan was crushed by the sight as she returned to the street. But then she recognized a small boy with a large cast. He'd received a free surgery on the *Africa Mercy*. Using a pair of hand-crutches, he navigated through the crowds and over the uneven pavement. His determination and smiling face reflected his confidence and his hope for the future. Megan realized that life is a matter of perspective.

You see, Mercy Ships brings hope to seemingly hopeless patients. And YOU can speak words of encouragement and hope to someone who is feeling hopeless.

"... when dreams come true at last, there is life and joy."
(Proverbs 13:12 TLB)

"Love recognizes no barriers. It jumps hurdles, leaps fences, penetrates walls to arrive at its destination full of hope."
(Maya Angelou)

Mercy Minute, Volume 32, Script 37; from "Monument to Liberia's Destruction," by Megan Petock, volunteer nurse; Philadelphia Inquirer *9/23/2007;*

January 23

Queen Jaroben

Jaroben stood up, serene and beautiful, in the ward of the *Africa Mercy*. Her silvery hair added a regal touch. And this was her day to celebrate!

Jaroben, like many West African women, suffered a childbirth injury which left her incontinent. She was abandoned by her husband and shunned by her community. For 46 years she lived in humiliation and isolation!

But now, after a free surgery onboard the Mercy Ship, Jaroben was completely transformed. She had a new dress, a beautiful smile, and renewed hope. Jaroben joyfully said, *"I never imagined I would be able to stand amongst people or sit and talk with friends."*

You see, mercy really does transform lives. Find a way to show mercy to someone today.

***"Let me give you a new command: Love one another. In the same way I loved you, love one another."* (John 13:34 MSG)**

Mercy Minute Volume 32, Script 65; from patient report by volunteer Lu Mizen, 8/23/2007; 2007 AFM *Liberia Field Service;*

January 24

Surgery by Text Message

British vascular surgeon Dr. David Nott volunteered with Doctors Without Borders. One of his patients in Africa was a 16-year-old boy. His left arm had been ripped off by a hippopotamus. He needed a forequarter amputation, requiring the removal of the collarbone and shoulder blade. He also needed an intensive care unit and a blood supply.

Dr. Nott had only one pint of blood and an elementary operating room—and he had never performed that particular surgery. A colleague in London sent him step-by-step instructions by text message! Dr. Nott says, *"The boy was dying, so I took a deep breath and followed the instructions."* And the boy made a full recovery!

You may not be a surgeon, but you can still take a deep breath and find a way to show mercy to someone today.

"Never walk away from someone who deserves help; your hand is God's hand for that person." **(Proverbs 3:27 MSG)**

"What we say is important, but what we do is more important." **(Truett Cathy, founder of Chick-fil-A)**

Mercy Minute Volume 36, Script 37; adapted from "Surgeon Saves Boy's Life by Text," BBC News; news.bbc.co.uk; 12/3/08

January 25

A Party for Harris

One hundred excited friends and family lined the road. When the car appeared, they screamed, cried, and praised God. Harris was returning from a Mercy Ship where surgeons had removed his 6 ½-pound facial tumor. The man who had lived as an outcast for more than 10 years now shyly waved to the welcoming crowd.

Scott Harrison, a volunteer photojournalist, decided to throw a homecoming party for Harris. Fifty people attended, including some from the local radio station. They heard the story of Harris's faith in God, and the miracle that took the form of a Mercy Ship, a free surgery and volunteer surgeons. Now Harris was able to speak and to laugh with his friends.

You see, God will work miracles through you—if you're willing to show mercy to others.

"This is how everyone will recognize that you are My disciples—when they see the love you have for each other."
(John 13:35 MSG)

Mercy Minute Volume 24, Script 14; adapted from onamercyship.com, website of Scott Harrison, volunteer photojournalist; 2006 Anastasis *Liberia Field Service;*

January 26

A Good Memory and an Old Husband

Dr. Glenn Strauss is a gifted eye surgeon. He and his wife Kim often volunteer onboard our hospital ship the *Africa Mercy*. They have wonderful memories of patients who have had their eyesight restored—or, in some cases, see for the first time in their lives.

On one occasion, a man and his wife both had eye surgery. They had been blind for many years—just getting along as best as they could. When the eye patches were removed, the husband was so excited about his beautiful wife whom he hadn't seen in years. His wife, on the other hand, asked, *"How did my husband get so old?"*

Well, mercy does produce wonderful—and sometimes funny—memories. Now you go, create a memory by showing mercy to someone today.

"A happy heart makes the face cheerful ..." **(Proverbs 15:13 NIV)**

"If you have no joy, there's a leak in your Christianity somewhere."
(Billy Sunday)

Mercy Minute Volume 39, Script 32; from staff interview with Dr. Glenn Strauss; 2009 AFM *Field Service to Benin;*

January 27

Holocaust Hero

Sir Nicholas Winton was a Jewish stockbroker in London. During World War II, he abandoned everything to help Jewish refugees fleeing Nazi occupation.

He arranged for trains to carry Jewish children out of occupied Prague to Britain. He saved them from almost certain death and organized foster families for them.

Sir Nicholas was knighted by the Queen in 2003 for rescuing 669 children destined for Nazi concentration camps. He died on July 1, 2015, at the age of 106.

Lord Dubs, who was one of the saved children, says, *"His legacy is that where there is a need for you to do something for your fellow human beings, you have got to do it."*

That's a great definition of mercy … and we should all try to follow Sir Nicholas' example by showing mercy to someone today.

"For we are God's workmanship, created in Christ Jesus to do good works, which God prepared in advance for us to do." **(Ephesians 2:10 NIV)**

"Don't be content in your life just to do no wrong; be prepared every day to try and do some good." **(Sir Nicholas Winton)**

Mercy Minute Volume 62, Script 33; based on "Holocaust 'Hero' Sir Nicholas Winton Dies Aged 106," http://www.bbc.com/news/uk-england-33350880

January 28

Baby Francois

Ali Chandra has volunteered as a nurse on our hospital ship, the *Africa Mercy*. She tells this story:

"The ship was docked in Togo, West Africa. One evening someone said, 'There's a baby on the dock.' I ran outside and found Francois. He was tiny, just under 2 months old, and weighed only 5 pounds. His lip and palate were split wide. His mother didn't want a 'broken' baby and had planned to abandon him. But someone told her about the Mercy Ship.

I cuddled the fragile baby in my arms. Through the Mercy Ships Infant Feeding Program, he will gain weight. Then he'll have a free surgery to restore his life.

I wanted drums and dancing to announce that here on our dock a mother was choosing life for her baby."

And you can make a choice today … a choice to daily seek for opportunities to show mercy to others.

"If I speak with human eloquence and angelic ecstasy but don't love, I'm nothing but the creaking of a rusty gate."
(1 Corinthians 13:1 MSG)

Mercy Minute Volume 40, Script 18; alirae.net/blog, 2/11/2010; used with permission;

January 29

A Merciful Hot Water Bottle

The doctor's best efforts couldn't save the woman in labor. She left behind a tiny, premature baby. The South African clinic didn't have an incubator, and their only hot water bottle had burst. So, the doctor put the baby in a flannel-lined box to maintain warmth, praying for help.

The next day, the doctor went to an orphanage and told the newborn's story. Ten-year-old Ruth prayed, *"Please, God, send us a hot water bottle for the baby this afternoon."*

Well, that very afternoon a parcel arrived. It had been mailed 5 months before by the doctor's church back home. And—you guessed it—it contained a hot water bottle!

You see, sometimes God answers prayers through OUR acts of mercy. Just imagine—when you do something kind for someone, you may be the answer to someone's prayer.

"Generous hands are blessed hands because they give bread to the poor." **(Proverbs 22:9 MSG)**

"God has given us two hands, one to receive with and the other to give with." **(Rev. Billy Graham)**

Mercy Minute Volume 33, Script 23; based on ernestanderson.wordpress.com/2008/02/18;

January 30

Thank You, Sister

Adrienne Smalley volunteered as a nurse onboard our hospital ship. She wrote this beautiful blog about one of her patients:

"Tonight a woman told me she'd been an orphan, and now even her husband has abandoned her! And she walked right into my heart!

The woman received a free surgery to correct a childbirth injury. She brought her two-year-old son with her. And he was fussing and crying. I picked up the unhappy toddler. Gradually his tears subsided, his little body relaxed, and he went to sleep.

As I tucked him into bed beside his mother, she smiled and silently applauded my success. When I turned to go, she grabbed my hand and whispered, 'Thank you, Sister.'"

Acts of kindness unite us and inspire gratitude. When we are kind to someone, we are mirroring the love of Jesus.

"For I was hungry and you gave Me something to eat, I was thirsty and you gave Me something to drink, I was a stranger and you invited Me in, I needed clothes and you clothed Me, I was sick and you looked after Me, I was in prison and you came to visit Me."
(Matthew 25:35-36 NIV)

Mercy Minute Volume 39, Script 22; gilesandadrienne.blogspot.com, 7/1/2009; blog of Adrienne Smalley, RN on the AFM; 2009 Field Service to Benin;

January 31

The Milton Hershey School

In 1909 a successful candy manufacturer with only a fourth-grade education devoted virtually his entire fortune to low-income children. It's likely you've enjoyed Hershey's chocolate candy on more than one occasion. You may not know that when you buy Hershey products, you are supporting the Milton Hershey School.

The Milton Hershey School was established by Milton and Catherine Hershey. It is the largest, free private school for low-income children in grades Pre-K through 12. Milton said, *"One is only happy in proportion as he makes others feel happy."* And he made many graduates very happy. They continue his legacy as they contribute their talents to society.

Be determined to leave a legacy of mercy. You can start by showing mercy to someone today.

"Have two goals: wisdom—that is, knowing and doing right—and common sense. Don't let them slip away."
(Proverbs 3:21 TLB)

⚓ January 31, 2004: A BBC-TV documentary, *African ER*, aired in the UK. The presenter was Tash Monie, a glamorous south London girl, who visited the *Anastasis* in Sierra Leone.

Mercy Minute Volume 40, Script 54; by Nancy Predaina, Mercy Ships Special Projects Writer/Editor; based on thehersheylegacy.com;

February

"God is love. Whoever lives in love lives in God, and God in him. In this way, love is made complete among us so that we will have confidence on the day of judgment, because in this world we are like Him."

(1 John 4:17-18 NIV)

February 1

Curing Bad Days

Six-year-old Elina was recovering from surgery onboard our hospital ship. She didn't trust easily. You see, she'd been deliberately held in a fire as retaliation for a family argument. She'd suffered terrible burns.

But, over time, one stranger in particular worked his way into her heart. Ben worked in an office on the ship, but he went to the ward during breaks. He and Elina hit it off! They'd make funny faces and laugh. Ben pushed Elina in a little red car, while she smiled and squealed his name and demanded that he do it again—faster this time.

Ben said, *"She just made things better... with her big brown eyes and a laugh that cures bad days."*

Mercy IS a great cure for bad days! Now you go, cure someone's bad day by showing mercy today.

"On your feet now—applaud God! Bring a gift of laughter, sing yourselves into His presence." **(Psalm 100:1-2 MSG)**

⚓ The *Africa Mercy* was originally a Danish rail ferry. It was acquired in 1999 through an initial Balcraig Foundation donation and was renamed the *Africa Mercy* in April 2000.

Mercy Minute Volume 69, Script 21; submitted by Windsor Marchesi, staff writer; from interview with Ben Dumbacker and his blogpost; 2016-17 AFM *Benin Field Service*

February 2

Fly Fishing Mercy

Project Healing Waters is a nonprofit dedicated to the rehabilitation of disabled active military and veterans. They use fly fishing, which has a soft spot in my heart! Lew Duckwall founded the Healing Waters group in North Texas.

He served over 20 years as a Marine combat engineer, receiving 19 medals. He was injured in Iraq, suffering spinal cord injuries and partial paralysis. He came home angry and with post-traumatic stress. But he was blessed with a supportive wife, a good doctor … and fly fishing.

Lew says, "*There's just something about standing in the middle of a river that is physically and spiritually healing. I want other disabled vets to feel what I have felt.*"

Lew used his hobby as an avenue of mercy. And you can follow his example by finding a creative way to show mercy to someone.

***"He made the world and everything in it, and since He is Lord of heaven and earth … He Himself gives life and breath to everything, and satisfies every need there is."* (Acts 17:24-25 TLB)**

***"The moment you begin to delight in beauty, your heart and mind are raised."* (Basil Hume)**

Mercy Minute Volume 69, Script 17; http://www.projecthealingwaters.org/ and "Healing Waters Finds Lake Fork Success," by Larry Tucker; Wood County Monitor; *October 19, 2016;*

February 3

Scrubbing Together

A volunteer onboard our hospital ship wrote about visiting an OR in a hospital in Guinea, West Africa, in 2012:

"I was with a group of Canadians who teach Operating Room Sterilization. I asked a man who worked there, 'When was the last time this room was cleaned?'

He said, 'We don't have cleaning supplies. This OR hasn't been sterilized since I began working here in 1988.'

So … I put down my notebook and started scrubbing. Because I was born in 1988. We scrubbed that room all day. You know, when you're on your hands and knees with a toothbrush, trying to kill germs as old as you are, look up—you'll see that you're not the only one scrubbing."

Yes, together we CAN make a difference by taking advantage of opportunities to help others.

***"Then make me truly happy by loving each other and agreeing wholeheartedly with each other, working together with one heart and mind and purpose."* (Philippians 2:2 TLB)**

⚓ *"If you want to travel fast, travel alone. But, if you want to travel far, travel together."* (African proverb)

Mercy Minute Volume 69, Script 43; based on a speech by Catherine Murphy, (Mercy Ships staff)for a Medical Bridges gala; used with permission;

February 4

On God's Watch

Vidhya volunteered as a doctor onboard our hospital ship. She hoped that an emergency wouldn't happen on her watch—when she was the doctor on call.

But, late one night, a patient onboard our hospital ship had a complication—severe bleeding. He was rushed into the operating room, and Vidhya jumped into action. But her nervousness disappeared, and she felt calm—as if God was saying, *"It's always on* **My** *watch. It's never on* **your** *watch."* And, later that night, the patient was stabilized.

Vidhya says, *"It's never us. It's God that gives us talents. We're like boats in the ocean. God is the wind in our sails. Without Him, we sit there. But with Him, we soar."*

Now you go, remember everything happens on God's watch, and show mercy to someone today.

"For the Lord watches over all the plans and paths of godly men ..."
(Psalm 1:6 TLB)

⚓ The conversion of the *Africa Mercy* from a rail ferry to a hospital ship was completed at A & P Shipyard at Newcastle-upon-Tyne in March 2007. The refit was deemed the largest conversion project of its kind in the UK.

Mercy Minute Volume 69, Script 53; interview with Vidhya Nagaratnam by Anna Psiaki, staff writer; used with permission; 2016-2017 AFM *Benin Field Service*

February 5

An Airport Blessing

Alicia Kramer, a Mercy Ships staff member, wrote a blog about an unexpected blessing she received at an airport:

"I was still in a stupor from getting up at 4 a.m. I stood bleary-eyed in line to buy a coffee at the airport McDonalds. I heard a booming voice engaging customers with a cheery 'How are you doing this morning, my friend? You have a bless-ed day.'

I shifted to his line. And, as I fumbled for correct change, he said, 'Take your time. I am here to serve you and make your morning start off well.'

Wow! I've been inspired to wake up to the life around me—the common moments I have to be light, salt, and encouragement."

We all could take that lesson to heart. Take a moment to encourage others today.

***"Let Me tell you why you are here. You're here to be salt-seasoning that brings out the God-flavors of this earth. If you lose your saltiness, how will people taste godliness?"* (Matthew 5:13 MSG)**

***"Don't shine so others can see you. Shine so that, through you, others can see Him."* (C.S. Lewis)**

Mercy Minute Volume 65, Script 29; by Nancy Predaina, Special Projects Writer/Editor; based on blog by Alicia Kramer, staff member; used with permission

February 6

Stopping to Pray

Imagine walking down the hospital corridor onboard our hospital ship, the *Africa Mercy*, at 11:00 in the evening. The lights are dimmed, and things are quiet. You peek through the ward window to see the nurses beginning the night shift.

They stand shoulder to shoulder, heads bowed. Some hold hands. Others hold sleepy babies or patient charts or bandages. They have clearly stopped in the middle of whatever they were doing to come together—a circle praying in soft whispers for our patients. It is beautiful.

Ward Supervisor Kirstie Randall says, *"Love is stopping to pray for our patients because we realize here in God's hospital that is a powerful thing we can do as nurses."*

Yes, praying for others is a powerful act of mercy. Today, you can show mercy by lifting someone up in prayer.

"Make this your common practice: Confess your sins to each other and pray for each other so that you can live together whole and healed. The prayer of a person living right with God is something powerful to be reckoned with." **(James 5:16 MSG)**

Mercy Minute Volume 56, Script 12; personal observation by Catherine Murphy and comment by Kirstie Randall during AFM *Community Meeting, 10/24/13; 2013-14* AFM *Congo Field Service;*

February 7

Friends to the Rescue

Torrential rains hit East Texas, and many homes were flooded. Nancy had water in the basement of her house. She explains how mercy came to her rescue:

"One Sunday, just a few weeks after the death of my husband, I came home from church, walked down to the basement, and stepped into water. It was overwhelming! I just didn't know what to do!

But wonderful friends rushed to my rescue. They showed up with carpet-dryers and shop vacs, and they vacuumed up all the water. They even brought a tractor and dug a trench to carry water away from the house.

It was really unbelievable. I don't know what I would have done without them. They showed me what mercy really is!"

I agree! You can be a living example of mercy today by helping someone in need.

***"This is My command: Love one another the way I loved you. This is the very best way to love. Put your life on the line for your friends."* (John 15:13 MSG)**

***"Kindness is the language which the deaf can hear and the blind can see."* (Mark Twain)**

Mercy Minute Volume 64, Script 56; by Nancy Predaina, Special Projects Writer/Editor; personal experience; December 2015;

February 8

Aminata's Baby Girl

Cleft lips and palates are a serious problem in poor countries where medical care is largely unavailable. In fact, the condition can be life-threatening because the babies cannot nurse properly. This is Aminata's story:

"My baby girl was born with a cleft lip and palate. At eight months, she weighed only eight pounds.

My husband said she must be a 'demon-child.'

When I said, 'I will not kill my baby,' he abandoned us.

Then I took her to the hospital ship, the Africa Mercy. *They placed her in a baby feeding program to gain weight for a free surgery. They saved her life—and now she will have a beautiful smile like other children."*

Thanks to the mercy of a courageous mother and a dedicated volunteer crew, a life was changed. Take a moment of mercy to pray for the children who need medical care.

"Jesus said, 'Let the little children come to Me, and do not hinder them, for the kingdom of heaven belongs to such as these.'"
(Matthew 19:14 NIV)

Mercy Minute Volume 47, Script 44; interview with Aminata by Elaine B. Winn, staff writer; 2011 AFM *Sierra Leone Field Service;*

February 9

Emmanuel, Star of the Show

Something unusual was happening outside the refugee home in Liberia. A crowd of excited children were holding welcome signs scribbled in bright crayon. The "star" of the show wasn't a world-famous celebrity. It was ten-year-old Emmanuel, returning home!

Emmanuel had suffered the physical pain of having two clubfeet along with the emotional pain of rejection and ridicule. But two free surgeries onboard the Mercy Ship had changed everything!

Well, finally, the Mercy Ships Land Rover arrived. The children swarmed around it. They carefully lifted Emmanuel up high—like a returning hero. *Now*, he knew what acceptance felt like. Emmanuel said, *"I will tell Papa God thank you."*

You see, mercy changes everything for the better! And you can make someone's life better by showing mercy today.

"Her neighbors and friends heard that the Lord had shown her great mercy, and they shared her joy." **(Luke 1:58 NIV)**

⚓ The *Caribbean Mercy* was a Norwegian ferry acquired by Mercy Ships in 1994. During her 12 years of service, she conducted 56 field assignments in 13 nations.

Mercy Minute Volume 36, Script 3; based on story by crew member Megan Petock, 2008 AFM Liberia Field Service;

February 10

We Can Do Better Than That!

Seven-year-old Frank was dying of leukemia. He'd always wanted to be a fireman. So, his mother asked the local Phoenix fire department if Frank could ride on a fire truck. The response was: "*We can do better than that!*" Fireman Bob gave Frank a special made-to-order uniform, and the little boy went on calls with him. Months later, Frank's condition became critical. The nurse asked the fire department if they could send a fireman over.

And the response was: "*We can do better than that!*"

Minutes later, a fire truck extended its ladder to the hospital window, and five firemen climbed into the room.

Little Frank asked, "*Am I a real firefighter?*"

Fireman Bob responded "*Of course you are!*"

I encourage you to do your very best to show extra-special kindness to someone today.

***"The King will reply, 'Truly I tell you, whatever you did for one of the least of these brothers and sisters of mine, you did for me.'"* (Matthew 25:40 NIV)**

***"At the end of life we will not be judged by how many diplomas we have received, how much money we have made, how many great things we have done. We will be judged by 'I was hungry, and you gave me something to eat. I was naked and you clothed me. I was homeless, and you took me in.'"* (Mother Teresa)**

Mercy Minute Volume 60, Script 50; submitted by Larry Mast; based on http://www.huffingtonpost.com/2013/11/01/bopsy-fireman-make-a-wish_n_4181841.html,

February 11

Blowing Kisses

Carolina is a Mercy Ships volunteer who developed a special bond with a six-year-old patient named Ruth. The little girl had been severely burned, and her face was quite scarred. Carolina describes a special moment:

"I saw her in the hospital today and hollered, 'Hello Ruth!' She turned and looked at me and smiled and waved. In French, I said, 'You are very pretty!'

And she stopped still, ran her hand down the side of her face, and stared into my eyes. A smile came across her face, and she started to blow me kisses! I teared up ... this by far has been my favorite moment."

Now you go, create a special moment of mercy by encouraging someone today.

"The LORD does not look at the things people look at. People look at the outward appearance, but the LORD looks at the heart."
(1 Samuel 16:7 NIV)

Mercy Minute Volume 69, Script 20; submitted by Windsor Marchesi, staff writer; based on Carolina Hinds' Facebook Post; used with permission;

February 12

Treehouse

There's an amazing multi-generational community located in the heart of Easthampton, Massachusetts. It's called Treehouse, and it's the brainchild of Judy Cockerton.

There are 48 one-bedroom cottages for senior adults who are willing to help foster families. And there are 12 townhomes for families who are willing to adopt foster children.

A woman who adopted three siblings from foster care says, *"I thought to myself, 'How can I do this and still stay sane?'"* She found the answers by moving to Treehouse.

Pam, a senior adult who lives at Treehouse, says, "*We constantly look out for these kids. On prom night, they have a dozen grandmas taking pictures.*"

Now that's a community of mercy! And I'm sure you can come up with some creative ideas for showing mercy in your community.

"*God sets the lonely in families ...*" (Psalm 68:6)

"*We cannot always build the future for our youth, but we can build our youth for the future.*" (Franklin D. Roosevelt)

Mercy Minute Volume 66, Script 64; based on "One Big Happy Family," by Jennifer Wolff Perrine, Woman's Day, *May 2016;©2016 Mercy Ships, All Rights Reserved*

February 13

Gamaah's Good Husband

A West African woman named Gamaah suffered an injury during childbirth. As a result, she was incontinent. This condition, called an obstetric fistula, is common in poor countries in West Africa because of the lack of healthcare.

Sad to say, the overwhelming majority of these women are abandoned by their husbands. They are left destitute and isolated from society. However, happily, Gamaah's spouse stuck by his vows. He remained faithful both in sickness and health. Gamaah says, *"It was our secret because it was between me and my husband."*

The couple's prayers were answered when a Mercy Ship came to Liberia. You see, Gamaah received a free onboard life-changing surgery!

"Sticking by" loved ones and friends in good times and in bad times is a beautiful gift of mercy.

"Husbands, go all out in your love for your wives, exactly as Christ did for the church—a love marked by giving, not getting."
(Ephesians 5:25 MSG)

Mercy Minute Volume 31, Script 61; by Mike Osborne, staff writer; based on interview with Esther Biney, crew member; 2007 AFM *Liberia Field Service; ©2007 Mercy Ships, All Rights Reserved*

February 14

Seeing "I Love You"

On Valentine's Day, we think of love, candy, and flowers. But 26-year-old Zafiline had lost all hope of ever having those things. You see, she had a large tumor on her face. People shunned her. It also made eating and sleeping almost impossible. And there was no medical help in her remote village in Madagascar. But a radio announcement about Mercy Ships changed everything! After a four-day journey, she received a free surgery. And every day, the crew showered her with love and care. Every day, Zafiline saw the words, *"I love you"* lived out. And now the joy of that love is reflected in her eyes.

And, today, YOU can be a living example of the words *"I love you"* simply by showing kindness to someone.

"Little children (believers, dear ones), let us not love [merely in theory] with word or with tongue [giving lip service to compassion], but in action and in truth [in practice and in sincerity, because practical acts of love are more than words]."
(1 John 3:18 AMP)

⚓ The *Anastasis* was sometimes affectionately called the "love boat." During its service from 1978 until 2007, over 250 couples met as crew, and several weddings were held onboard.

Mercy Minute Volume 66, Script 46; based on patient interview by Tanya Sierra, staff writer; 2014-2015 AFM *Madagascar Field Service;*

February 15

Never Leave a Man Behind

Ben Baltz was diagnosed with bone cancer in his right leg when he was six years old. He learned to walk with a mechanical knee and a prosthetic leg.

When he was 11, he participated in a triathlon. Local Marines monitored the event. Ben completed the 150-yard swim and the 4-mile bike ride. But, during the one-mile run, a screw came loose, and his prosthetic leg broke in half.

His mom became worried when he didn't appear at the finish line. Suddenly, everybody began to cheer. Private First Class Matthew Morgan was running, carrying Ben on his back! His commanding officer said, *"It's great to see what Marines do—they don't leave anybody behind."*

And mercy doesn't leave anybody behind either. Show mercy by helping someone today.

"You have not deserted your brothers these many days to this day, but have [carefully] kept the obligation of the commandment of the Lord your God." **(Joshua 22:3 AMP)**

Mercy Minute Volume 60, Script 53; "Marines Help a Young Boy Finish a Triathlon," CNN iReport, 10/7/12;

February 16

Girl with a Stone in Her Ear

A 10-year-old girl and her mother came to the Mercy Ships outpatient clinic in West Africa. The child had an unusual complaint. She had a stone in her left ear. When asked how it got there, she said she put it there. She said it had been there for more than a year.

The little girl sat bravely while Dr. Sandra Lako used a syringe to flush out the ear. In only 10 minutes, the stone and some other debris came out.

The mother was surprised and thankful when she learned that there was no fee for the treatment. Dr. Lako explained, *"This is what we do; we're here to help."*

And that's why you're here and I'm here … to help one another. Now let's go show mercy to someone today.

***"Mercy to the needy is a loan to God, and God pays back those loans in full."* (Proverbs 19:17 MSG)**

***"We make a living by what we get, we make a life by what we give."* (Winston Churchill)**

Mercy Minute Volume 32, Script 25; sandralako.blogspot.com 12/20/07; used with permission;

February 17

Deb Louden

Deb Louden, from Australia, volunteered as a nurse onboard our hospital ship for over five years. She wrote a beautiful farewell blog:

"I think living on this ship and being in this community and loving on the people of Africa, has helped change me beyond anything I could imagine. I have experienced the deepest feelings of my life in this place. Loving so hard that it feels impossible to say goodbye. The tears have come more freely, sparked by little things like the singing of a song that reminds me of a patient I loved."

Most of our volunteers would agree that their experiences as mercy-givers have changed them as much—or even more—than they have changed others. And being a mercy-giver will change YOUR life!

"'What do you want Me to do for you?' Jesus asked him.

The blind man said, 'Rabbi, I want to see.'" **(Mark 10:51 NIV)**

⚓ On February 17, 1987, the first surgery was performed onboard the *Anastasis* during a field service to Mexico.

Mercy Minute Volume 66, Script 57; by Nancy Predaina, Special Projects Writer/Editor; blog of Deb Louden; used with permission; http://debsheartinafrica.blogspot.com 5/23/16; 2015-16 AFM *Madagascar Field Service;*

February 18

Seeing the Blind See

The Mercy Ships vision program addresses blindness caused by cataracts. Here's a Mercy Ships volunteer's description of one transformation:

"I watched a man open his eyes and see for the first time in three years! It might compare to watching a parent hold their newborn for the first time … or watching a family welcome home a loved one in the armed forces … or watching when the minister says, 'You may now kiss the bride.' These moments are so magical that your mind is delightfully wordless. But … you have to be able to see to experience them. So, when I got to see a man see, it was remarkable because now he doesn't have to miss those moments anymore."

And when you help others, you will witness delightfully wordless moments of mercy and joy.

"So the crowd was amazed when they saw the mute speaking, the crippled restored, the lame walking, and the blind seeing; and they praised and glorified the God of Israel." **(Matthew 15:31 AMP)**

⚓ In February 1978 Don Stephens located the Italian ocean liner, the *Victoria*, and began negotiations to purchase it for use as a Mercy Ship.

Mercy Minute Volume 52, Script 39; "To South Africa and Back," from blog "My Life Aquatic" by Catherine Murphy (staff writer); 3/8/13; ©2013 Mercy Ships, All Rights Reserved

February 19

Lincoln and a Dying Soldier

President Lincoln often visited hospitals during the Civil War. He asked a young soldier who was near death, *"Is there anything I can do for you?"* The soldier didn't recognize the President and asked him to write a letter to his mother.

President Lincoln graciously wrote the letter that the young man dictated and signed it *"Written for your son by Abraham Lincoln."* He showed the note to the soldier, who was astonished by the signature.

Then in the quiet room, the President held the boy's hand and spoke kind words of encouragement until death came.

Just taking time to ask, *"Is there anything I can do for you?"* is a great act of kindness. This is the perfect day to see what you can do in showing mercy to someone.

***"I can do all things [which He has called me to do] through Him who strengthens and empowers me [to fulfill His purpose—I am self-sufficient in Christ's sufficiency; I am ready for anything and equal to anything through Him who infuses me with inner strength and confident peace.]"* (Philippians 4:13 AMP)**

Mercy Minute Volume 62, Script 46; based on http://www.chickensoup.com/book-story/35261/an-act-of-kindness

February 20

Isatu: the Mystery of Mercy

The West African newspaper headline blared: *"Mystery! Thirteen-year-old girl turns into pig!"* The photo showed Isatu with a grossly swollen facial tumor. A Mercy Ships crewmember found Isatu locked in a chicken coop, covered with feces, abandoned, and starving to death. Relatives finally agreed to let Mercy Ships help. As Isatu painfully walked up the gangway of our *Africa Mercy*, a nurse descended toward her. In a heart-rending act of mercy, the nurse carried her onboard. Burkitt's Lymphoma, a form of childhood cancer, had ravaged her immune system. Even with treatment, she died just three months later . . . but she was not alone.

You see, compassion reached out to a love-starved child and showed her the mercy and love of Jesus in her last days.

"Love is patient, love is kind ... It always protects, always trusts, always hopes, always perseveres ... Love never fails."
(1 Corinthians 13:4-8 NIV)

⚓ A Newfoundland coastal ferry was donated to Mercy Ships in 1983. She sailed for 11 years as the *Good Samaritan*, serving the Caribbean, Central America and South America. In 1994 she was renamed the *Island Mercy* and redeployed to the South Pacific, where she served until 2001.

Mercy Minute Volume 52, Script 30; by Nancy Predaina, Special Projects Writer/Editor; based on interview with Mercy Ships staff, Kerry Peterson;

February 21

A Software Blessing

Dr. Richard Hipp developed a database called SQLite [S-Q-L Lite]. It's used by some of the biggest names in the computer industry, including Apple. But he receives no royalty for the millions of copies used. Why? He placed it in the public domain. He says, *"I never expected to make one penny. I just wanted to make it available to other people to solve their problem."*

You're probably familiar with the service agreements for online programs. But Dr. Hipp's agreement is actually a blessing that says:

"May you do good and not evil. May you find forgiveness for yourself and forgive others. May you share freely, never taking more than you give."

What a wonderful challenge to us all—and a great recipe for mercy!

> ***"Owe nothing to anyone except to love one another; for he who loves his neighbor has fulfilled the law."* (Romans 13:8 NASB)**

> ***"Constant kindness can accomplish much. As the sun makes ice melt, kindness causes misunderstanding, mistrust, and hostility to evaporate."* (Albert Schweitzer)**

Mercy Minute Volume 61, Script 4; adapted from "Size Isn't Everything for the Modest Creator of SQLite," by Tim Anderson, The Guardian, *6/20/07;*

February 22

The Little Pink Mirror

Dr. Glenn and Kim Strauss often volunteer with our Mercy Ships Eye Team. Recently, Kim described the remarkable transformation of one young woman:

"A beautiful young woman named Bountraby was missing one eye. It made her ineligible for marriage.

Glenn inserted several prosthetic eyes until he found one that fit. A nurse handed Bountraby a small, round, pink mirror to take a look. She looked in disbelief! Then a HUGE smile came and tears of joy!

When she returned for follow-up care two weeks later, she wore a beautiful shiny pink dress and her hair in pink bows. And . . . still in her hand . . . was that little pink mirror."

You see, God's love literally transforms lives. And He allows us the privilege of partnering with Him in these amazing acts of mercy!

***"For it is [not your strength, but it is] God who is effectively at work in you, both to will and to work [that is, strengthening, energizing, and creating in you the longing and the ability to fulfill your purpose] for His good pleasure."* (Philippians 2:13 AMP)**

Mercy Minute Volume 52, Script 62; from newsletter by Dr. Glenn and Kim Strauss; 2/16/13; used with permission; 2013 AFM *Guinea Field Service;*

February 23

The Best Touchdown Ever!

An eight-year-old was the star of a high school football game in Rhinelander, Wisconsin. First-grader Gabe White has Down Syndrome. His brother plays on the freshman team, and Gabe is the honorary captain.

The team lost their last game of the season, but they remained on the field. Then Gabe came out, wearing an oversized jersey, a helmet, and pads. The coach of the opposing side told his team, *"Run the kickoff and don't tackle him."*

And that's what they did! They kicked the ball. Then they leaped through the air with missed tackles as they carefully chased Gabe to the end zone.

It was a night that Gabe and the two teams will never forget!

You know, mercy is always unforgettable. And you can make someone feel special by showing mercy today.

"As each one has received a special gift, employ it in serving one another as good stewards of the manifold grace of God."
(1 Peter 4:10 NASB)

"I've learned that people will forget what you said, people will forget what you did, but people will never forget how you made them feel." (Maya Angelou)

Mercy Minute Volume 60, Script 63; based on "8-Year-Old Gets to Suit Up for High School Football Game," by Joey White, 0/17/14;http://twentytwowords.com

February 24

Sory Sings

Sory was an active little nine-year-old boy in Guinea, West Africa. Then, a tumor appeared on his face. His world shattered. People even whispered that it would be better if he died.

When he was 17, hope appeared in the form of our hospital ship, the *Africa Mercy*. A free surgery removed the tumor and restored Sory's life.

Mercy Ships volunteer Tori Hobson walked into the ward early one morning. Sory was singing and dancing on his bed—echoing the worship songs he had heard in the ward church service. Tori said, *"His joy was so contagious that I started dancing and singing with him."*

You see, a by-product of mercy is contagious joy!

***"I'm thanking you, God, from a full heart, I'm writing the book on your wonders. I'm whistling, laughing, and jumping for joy; I'm singing your song, High God."* (Psalm 9:1-2 MSG)**

Mercy Minute Volume 53, Script 17; by Nancy Predaina, Special Projects Writer/Editor; based on information from Catherine Murphy, staff writer; 2012/13 AFM *Guinea Field Service;*

February 25

Priest Peter Claver

In the 17th century, the port city of Cartagena, Spain, was a thriving center of the slave trade. But one brave Jesuit priest dared to show compassion.

Priest Peter Claver met every slave ship. He called each slave by name. He bandaged wounds. He provided food and drink. And he told them that they were people worth loving.

Peter became known as the "slave to the slaves." For 33 years he poured out his life in ministry to people who were labeled as worthless. He was ridiculed and died alone. But in those 33 years, 300,000 slaves came to know the loving God that Peter Claver served.

You see, mercy values everyone. Make it your mission to represent our loving God as you show mercy to others.

***"No one has* greater love *[nor stronger commitment] than to lay down his own life for his friends."* (John 15:13)**

***"To do more for the world than the world does for you—that is success."* (Henry Ford)**

Mercy Minute Volume 37, Script 34; adapted from "Peter Claver, Servant of Slaves, Jesuit, Priest," baptistbard.blogspot.com, 9/8/08;

February 26

A Lullaby of Love

A crewmember beautifully described a moment of mercy on our hospital ship, the *Africa Mercy*:

"As I walked down the hospital hallway, a nurse was in front of me holding a small baby with bandages on his upper lip.

She walked slowly, gently bouncing the baby up and down as she whispered, 'One, two, three—kiss!' Then she kissed him on the top of the head.

Then she began singing in her language—Norwegian. The baby didn't understand the words, but he recognized the soothing lullaby of love as he trustingly rested his head on her shoulder."

Yes, we all should strive to be fluent in God's international language of love and mercy.

***"And now these three remain: faith, hope and love. But the greatest of these is love."* (1 Corinthians 13:13 NIV)**

⚓ The *Good Samaritan* carried cargo and personnel to the Pan-American games for the U.S. Olympic committee in 1991 and became the first ship to legally sail from the United States to Cuba in 30 years.

Mercy Minute Volume 52, Script 13; based on personal experience of Catherine Murphy, staff writer; AFM 2013 Guinea Field Service;

February 27

Bone for Bone, Steps for Steps

A Mercy Ships supporter had to abandon her dream of serving onboard our hospital ship. Her osteoporosis had advanced to the point that her bones were fracturing. She sent us this note:

"I calculated the amount I intended to spend on coming to Texas for training and contributed that amount.

Delightfully, the amount allowed me to pay for one orthopedic surgery. My heart is laughing and lifted by the idea that, as my old bones are disintegrating, someone in Africa will be able to have his or her bones repaired.

Bone for bone, steps for steps! There's no doubt in my mind that this is meant to be!"

What a beautiful and joyful act of mercy, born out of heart-rending disappointment! Now you go—no matter what your circumstances—and find a way to show mercy today.

***"Live generously and graciously toward others, the way God lives toward you."* (Matthew 5:48 MSG)**

Mercy Minute Volume 56, Script 16; letter sent to Donor Services (name withheld at donor's request); 1/9/14;

February 28

Mercy for Otto

An elderly couple couldn't afford to pay the veterinary bills for their 14-year-old dachshund, Otto. So, they took him to a shelter, with a note explaining his medical problems and asking that he be put to sleep.

Otto was taken to an animal foster care organization called *Leave No Paws Behind*. They successfully treated him. Then they tracked down his owners and offered to provide free medical care for the dog for the rest of his life.

Henry James said, *"Three things in human life are important: the first is to be kind; the second is to be kind; and the third is to be kind."*

Simple kindness and a compassionate heart made an elderly couple very, very happy. Make kindness the hallmark of your life.

"Be kind and compassionate to one another, forgiving each other, just as in Christ God forgave you." **(Ephesians 4:32 NIV)**

⚓ Mercy Ships crew joined relief efforts in Greece after an earthquake rocked the country in 1981.

Mercy Minute Volume 62, Script 39; based on "Coffee News: Tyler South Edition," Vol. 6 No. 13, March 20, 2015;

February 29

George and Dieuveil

George and Dieuveil had a lot in common. They both lived in Congo. They were both three years old. And they both had a free cleft lip and palate surgery onboard our hospital ship.

Their surgeries took place one day apart, and they became great friends. The first boy used hand gestures and pointing to prepare the second boy for the post-surgery removal of the nasal packing.

They enjoyed admiring their new faces in a hand mirror. One crew member wrote on her blog, *"Dieuviel was so fascinated with his new look that he couldn't stop staring at his reflection. And neither could we."*

Yes, these two little boys experienced the vital ingredients in mercy—love, friendship, and hope.

"You use steel to sharpen steel, and one friend sharpens another."
(Proverbs 27:17 MSG)

Mercy Minute Volume 56, Script 18; based on presentation by Kirstie Randall, Ward Supervisor, at AFM *Community Meeting; quote from "My Life Aquatic," blog by Catherine Murphy, staff writer; 2013-14* AFM *Congo Field Service;*

March

"I was hungry and you fed Me,
I was thirsty and you gave Me a drink,
I was homeless and you gave Me a room,
I was shivering and you gave Me clothes,
I was sick and you stopped to visit,
I was in prison and you came to Me."
(Matthew 25:35-36 MSG)

March 1

Joseph Gets a Nose

A bacterial infection called *noma* is common in West Africa. It destroys soft tissue and leaves people disfigured for life. Joseph was such a victim. For 52 years, he lived without a nose. People teased him, calling him "No-Nose Joseph."

Then Joseph heard about our Mercy Ship. He traveled a long way to get to our hospital ship. But it was worth it! A successful free surgery reconstructed his nose.

Joseph simply described the experience, *"Forever, from a baby, I have no nose. I come here, and Dr. Gary gives me a nose. You see what God can do."*

It is amazing how God works through willing mercy-givers to change lives. Allow God to use you to show mercy to someone today.

***"And my God will meet all your needs according to the riches of His glory in Christ Jesus."* (Philippians 4:19 NIV)**

Mercy Minute Volume 36, Script 57;based on patient interview by Carmen Radley, staff writer; 2008 AFM *Liberia Field Service,*

March 2

Scene of No-Crime

Florida police office Bobby White responded to a complaint about youth playing basketball too loudly. But he didn't scold the kids or break up the game. Instead, he joined them and promised to come back for a re-match.

And he did come back—with a backup in the form of Shaq O'Neal, the former Miami Heat player. The sports star gave the kids basketball tips, doled out hugs and fist bumps, and encouraged them to follow their dreams.

The Gainesville Police Department stated: "*We're going to let kids be kids. We are going to focus on the ones that commit crimes. These kids will never forget the day Shaq rolled up to their house to play ball.*"

And I'm sure that's true! You can create an unforgettable day for someone by showing mercy and acceptance today.

***"Accept one another, then, just as Christ accepted you, in order to bring praise to God."* (Romans 15:7 NIV)**

Mercy Minute Volume 64, Script 21; http://www.cnn.com/2016/01/24/us/florida-shaq-police-officers-game/

March 3

Dr. Keith Thomson and Catherine Conteh

Eighteen-year-old Catherine Conteh suffered 5 days of obstructed labor. Then, doctors said she would die because her family couldn't afford the Caesarean section. But mercy arrived in the form of a Mercy Ships volunteer, Dr. Keith Thomson. He just happened to be visiting the hospital ashore. He paid the necessary $100 for the surgery on the spot.

Dr. Keith has stayed in touch with this family. Five years later, they met him at a neighboring nation's airport. Catherine's daughter held up a sign saying, *"Uncle Keith, thank you for saving my life and my mum's."* One faces decisions in life when we have choices, and we can choose to help someone or not.

You see, mercy always chooses to help. I encourage you to choose to help someone today.

"And whatever you do, whether in word or deed, do it all in the name of the Lord Jesus, giving thanks to God the Father through Him."
(Colossians 3:17 NIV)

⚓ One of the early mercy ships, the *Good Samaritan*, was affectionately known to her crew as the "Little Giant."

Mercy Minute Volume 32, Script 50; based on "You're Our Hero," by Emily Ann Elliott; Hampshire Today; *©2008 Mercy Ships, All Rights Reserved*

March 4

Burmese People Help One Other

A hurricane devastated Burma. But the Burmese government rejected foreign help. None the less, a London newspaper, *The Sunday Times*, organized food supplies.

They scrounged up a rickety old truck to carry the supplies and headed to the town of Bogale. However, the Burmese soldiers stopped them cold. Then three Burmese men volunteered to deliver the food. It was a dangerous mission, but they succeeded! These heroic men had lost their own homes in the hurricane. One of the men said, "*My heart is crying. The people are broken.*"

Yes, the merciful heart cries over the anguish of others. And it also takes risks to help relieve that pain.

What a privilege we have to soothe despair as we show mercy to others!

"What a wonderful God we have—He is the Father of our Lord Jesus Christ, the source of every mercy, and the one who so wonderfully comforts and strengthens us in our hardships and trials. And why does He do this? So that when others are troubled, needing our sympathy and encouragement, we can pass on to them this same help and comfort God has given us."

(2 Corinthians 1:3-4 TLB)

Mercy Minute Volume 36, Script 17; adapted from "My Mercy Mission into the Cyclone Zone," http://www.timesonline.co.uk 5/18/08;

March 5

"Mr. Serious" No More

Crew member Tanya Sierra shared a special memory about a lively eight-year-old boy:

"Libertho was nicknamed 'Mr. Serious' because of his constant serious face.

After Libertho had surgery to correct his clubbed foot, he was forced to stay in bed for a couple of days. Slowly the nurses began to win him over. A short game here. A tickle there. A warm embrace here. An encouraging smile there.

And then it happened! One day, Libertho let out the biggest laugh and hasn't stopped smiling since.

When we last saw Libertho, he was wearing a pair of shoes for the first time ever and a wonderful smile."

You see, mercy and love can bring a smile to even the most serious face. Give the gift of mercy today by making someone smile.

"Shout for joy to the Lord, all the earth. Worship the Lord with gladness; come before Him with joyful songs."
(Psalm 100:1-2 NIV)

Mercy Minute Volume 61, Script 31; Personal observation of Tanya Sierra, staff writer; 2014-2015 AFM *Madagascar Field Service;*

March 6

A Tale of Two Men

When Roger Gonzalez was just a boy, he saw a child with only one leg. His father told him it was only by God's grace that he had two good legs. Roger never forgot that statement.

Across the world in West Africa, rebels raided Gibrilla's village. They cut off his foot with a machete. Later, the infected leg had to be amputated.

Years later, Gibrilla was given a new prosthetic leg. The special knee was created specifically for developing countries. It was designed by—you guessed it—Dr. Roger Gonzalez and one of his students at Le Tourneau University in Longview, Texas. Gibrilla simply states, *"It's a beautiful leg."*

The lives of two men—worlds apart—were united by mercy. I encourage you to find a way to use your skills and talents to show mercy to others.

***"God has given each of you some special abilities; be sure to use them to help each other, passing on to others God's many kinds of blessings."* (1 Peter 4:10)**

⚓ In March 2017, Graça Machel, the widow of Nelson Mandela, visited the *Africa Mercy* in Benin. She's a champion of women's and children's rights. She said, "This expression of service … of goodness to others … it's something which is more and more missing in our world."

Mercy Minute Volume 36, Script 21; adapted from "Group Hopes Prosthetics Foster Independence," by Jim Landers, Dallas Morning News, *7/6/2008;*

March 7

Josue and the Nerf Gun

Bethany, the Mercy Ships Eye Team Coordinator, befriended a patient named Josue. Everyone fell in love with this lively little boy with the huge smile.

One day, Bethany and Josue walked the halls so he could sneak up on crew members. Then he'd shoot his sock monkey at them.

But Josue got a taste of his own medicine when he sneaked into Esther's office. She immediately reached into her desk and pulled out her Nerf gun.

Josue turned and ran, laughing and squealing. Bethany says, "*The moment was priceless and one we will all remember.*"

Yes, mercy can even lessen the scariness of a medical procedure! And you can create a priceless moment as you take the time to give attention and kindness … perhaps accompanied by giggles … to someone today.

***"A cheerful disposition is good for your health; gloom and doom leave you bone-tired."* (Proverbs 17:22 MSG)**

Mercy Minute Volume 61, Script 20; Catherine Murphy and Nancy Predaina, Special Projects Writer/Editor; from interview with Bethany Kremer, Eye Team Field Coordinator, 2013-14 AFM *Congo Field Service;*

March 8

Lucrech and the Yellow Ball

Josh is a videographer onboard our hospital ship and sees some amazing transformations . . . like this five-year-old little boy:

"I was filming the rehab exercises Lucrech was doing with Courtney. He was trying to grip a yellow ball and lift it up—a difficult task considering he hadn't been able to grip with that hand at all before surgery. Slowly he lifted it up. His reaction of pure excitement and joy caused the group around him to erupt with cheers. That moment is burned into my memory and fills my heart to this day."

These moments of mercy are created by thousands of people around the world who lend their support to make Mercy Ships work.

And I believe YOU can create an amazing moment ... a moment of mercy, hope and healing . . . for someone today.

***"Let each one give [thoughtfully and with purpose] just as he has decided in his heart, not grudgingly or under compulsion, for God loves a cheerful giver [and delights in the one whose heart is in his gift]."* (2 Corinthians 9:7 AMP)**

Story submitted to Catherine Murphy, staff writer, by Josh Callow, videographer. 2013-14 AFM *Congo Field Service;*

March 9

The Ugly Blanket

A volunteer in Canada was sorting donated items. She retrieved an ugly green and orange blanket from the discard box. It was in good shape, except for one small hole. So, she sat on the warehouse floor patiently repairing the damage. Then the blanket was loaded in a container for Uganda.

Several months later, a photo arrived in the mail. The ugly blanket was wrapped around a woman dying of AIDS. That now "beautiful blanket" was an answer to her prayers. You see, in her culture, a person must own a blanket to die with dignity.

Mercy can transform the ordinary—and even the ugly—into something beautiful. Transform an ordinary day into a beautiful one by finding a way to show kindness to someone.

"He has made everything beautiful in its time."
(Ecclesiastes 3:11)

"Lord, give me an open heart to find You everywhere, to glimpse the heaven enfolded in a bud, and to experience eternity in the smallest act of love." **(Mother Teresa)**

Mercy Minute Volume 36, Script 26; adapted from "Beautiful Blanket," by Dell Marie Wergeland, Reflecting God *(devotional book), Dec/Jan/Feb 2009;*

March 10

A Lesson in Kindness

Edmond Kaiser founded Terre des Hommes in 1960 to help children in need. He aptly described noma as *"an illness devouring both beauty and life."* And for Rovelle, a 14-year old boy who came to our hospital ship in Congo, that's exactly what it did.

The terrible bacteria left behind a boy with a broken heart and a hole in his face. He learned a lesson about human cruelty. People didn't even want to look at him.

But then Rovelle came onboard our ship and learned another lesson . . . about kindness. In fact, a group of crew members saw his potential and put together a school program just for him while he recovered.

It's amazing what love can do!

Now, in Congo, there's a boy who absolutely loves to go to school to fulfill his dreams.

And YOU can teach a lesson in kindness by showing mercy to someone today.

"Little children, let us stop just saying we love people; let us really love them, and show it by our actions." **(1 John 3:18 TLB)**

Mercy Minute Volume 61, Script 25; from interview with Scott Reed, Hospital Supply Coordinator, by Eunice Hiew; story recounted from 2013-2014 AFM *Congo Field Service;*

March 11

Hery Matters

In the poorest regions of Madagascar, eating once a day is a luxury. Lack of nutrition and healthcare provides a perfect environment for an enemy called noma. It's a flesh-destroying bacteria that strikes in Africa. A crew member described one of its victims:

"Twenty-six-year-old Hery is among the survivors of noma. We found him hiding his face with a baseball cap—ashamed to show us his scars.

Then Dr. Gary Parker, Chief Medical Officer for the Africa Mercy, *said the words to Hery that changed his life, 'You matter. We can do this surgery.'*

Hery's twenty-year journey of rejection and disappointment was over! His life was transformed in an instant!"

Thanks to the mercy of doctors and volunteers, Hery's life was transformed. Take a moment today to let someone know that they really do matter.

> ***"O my soul, why be so gloomy and discouraged? Trust in God! I shall again praise Him for his wondrous help; He will make me smile again, for He is my God!"*** **(Psalm 43:5 TLB)**

Mercy Minute Volume 61, Script 36; personal observation of Tanya Sierra, staff writer; 2014-2015 AFM *Madagascar Field Service;*

March 12

A VIP Funeral

More than 300 people crowded into the funeral service to honor a very special person. The deceased was not a famous celebrity. She was just another widow who had lived in the area. Her major accomplishment was walking through the neighborhood, delivering "cookies of love." She even gave cookies to utility workers and the garbage collectors.

During the service, people spoke about her care and love. They told stories of how she impacted their lives with her prayers. And they expressed how much they were going to miss her.

You see, the impact of a life is not measured in wealth, but by the compassion and love shown to others. Invest your life in showing mercy and kindness to others.

"Love God, your God, with your whole heart: love Him with all that's in you, love Him with all you've got! Write these commandments that I've given you today on your hearts. Get them inside of you and then get them inside your children. Talk about them wherever you are, sitting at home or walking in the street; talk about them from the time you get up in the morning to when you fall into bed at night."

(Deuteronomy 6:5-7 MSG)

Mercy Minute Volume 36, Script 41; adapted from "With Her Mite, She Changed Her World," By Dell Marie Wergeland, Reflecting God *(devotional book), Dec/Jan/Feb 2009;*

March 13

Sainey

As a small child, Sainey continuously felt grit in his right eye. Then a small lump formed on his right eyelid. By the time he reached his mid-twenties, the obvious tumor in his eyelid caused great pain. Only medication to relieve the daily headaches made it possible for him to continue his job.

With hope in his heart, Sainey went to a screening at the Mercy Ship. With gratitude he acknowledged God's intervention. He said, *"God Almighty took me into the hands of Mercy Ships."* After seeing himself just after surgery, an almost speechless Sainey could only utter, "Wow!"

Often, the response to mercy is a humble, grateful heart.

Find a way to bring joy by showing kindness to someone today.

"God's love is meteoric, His loyalty astronomic, His purpose titanic, His verdicts oceanic. Yet in His largeness nothing gets lost; not a man, not a mouse, slips through the cracks." **(Psalm 36:5-6 MSG)**

"The greatest use of life is to spend it for something that will outlast it." **(William James)**

Mercy Minute Volume 27, Script 11; patient story; 2007 Anastasis *Liberia Field Service;*

March 14

Shouting Hallelujah!

Imagine being a parent of a child with a disability that could be surgically fixed—but there's no help available. Imagine the hopelessness. Then a hospital ship arrives, and your child gets a free surgery. Imagine the joy! Crewmember Aisling Russell explains:

"Two kids came out of the cast today, which is just the best thing. The mom quickly called the papa straight afterwards and was on the phone going 'arahrahrahrah' because they were so excited. And as soon as I told them—even though they didn't understand what I was saying—they celebrated, just shouting 'Hallelujah!' Which is great."

Mercy is great and makes you want to shout, "Hallelujah!" Give someone a reason to shout for joy by showing mercy today.

"Jesus said, 'Love the Lord your God with all your passion and prayer and intelligence.' This is the most important, the first on any list. But there is a second to set alongside it: 'Love others as well as you love yourself.'" **(Matthew 22:37-39 MSG)**

"For centuries the Bible's emphasis on compassion and love for our neighbor has inspired institutional and governmental expressions of benevolent outreach such as private charity, the establishment of schools and hospitals, and the abolition of slavery."
(Ronald Reagan)

Mercy Minute Volume 70, Script 28; by Nancy Predaina, Special Projects Writer/Editor; from interview with Aisling Russell by AFM *Communications Team; 2016-17* AFM *Benin Field Service;*

March 15

The Green Lion

Volunteers at a Canadian warehouse were packing medical supplies destined for a developing country. A stuffed animal, a green lion, was used as packing material.

Months later, a doctor in that developing country lifted the equipment out of the donation box. The stuffed toy dropped onto the floor. The doctor's eyes filled with tears as he grabbed it and ran down the hall to the ward.

He reached the bed of a little girl dying of AIDS. He gave her the toy. The little girl hugged it, and said, *"I told you Jesus loves me and would send me a green lion."*

You see, Jesus will use your acts of mercy to answer the prayers of others. Ask God to bless your actions as you show mercy to someone today.

> ***"But you, Lord, are a compassionate and gracious God, slow to anger, abounding in love and faithfulness."*** **(Psalm 86:15 NIV)**

Mercy Minute Volume 36, Script 53; adapted from "I Told You Jesus Loved Me," by Dell Marie Wergeland, Reflecting God *(devotional book), Dec/Jan/Feb 2009;*

March 16

Fandresena's Encouragement

Worship time in the ward onboard our hospital ship is noisy. It's a beautiful time—everyone sings and many dance. During one worship time, five-year-old Fandresena noticed a female patient who wasn't singing. She'd just come back from surgery. So, Fandresena gently took her by the hand and helped her clap through the songs. After a little bit, she began singing very softly. She even offered a small smile to Fandresena. As the last song ended and everyone broke into applause, Fandresena leaned in and whispered into her ear, *"Good job!"*—the phrase the nurses said to him when his bandages were changed.

You know, sometimes it's the smallest things that have the greatest impact. Now you find a way—small or big—to show mercy to someone today.

***"Pleasant words are like a honeycomb, sweet and delightful to the soul and healing to the body."* (Proverbs 16:24 AMP)**

⚓ In March 2011, the *Africa Mercy* crossed the Equator between Durban and Cape Town. In Crossing the Line, the crew graduated from "Pollywogs" to "Shellbacks"—a tradition celebrated by the Royal Navy, U.S. Navy, and other navies.

Mercy Minute Volume 61, Script 48; by Tanya Sierra, staff writer; personal observation; 2014-2015 AFM *Madagascar Field Service;*

March 17

A Merciful Cup of Coffee

Sascha struggled to get through airport security. It was an early morning. And a busy toddler, an armful of coats, and carry-on bags made it daunting. Finally, she arrived at the gate.

Sascha looked longingly at the Starbucks just 15 yards away. But she couldn't juggle the bags, her son, and the cup of coffee.

Then an attractive, well-dressed woman walked toward her. And she asked, *"How do you take your coffee?"* Sascha told her *"cream and sugar."* A few minutes later, the woman handed her a large cup of life-saving coffee. The entire morning was suddenly brightened up by an unexpected act of kindness.

You see, a cup of coffee for a stressed parent—it's a simple act of mercy. Brighten someone's day with a little dose of unexpected mercy.

***"And if anyone gives even a cup of cold water to one of these little ones who is My disciple, truly I tell you, that person will certainly not lose their reward."* (Matthew 10:42 NIV)**

Mercy Minute Volume 32, Script 28; adapted from "How to Make Someone's Day," by Sascha Zuger; Woman's Day *10/2/2007;*

March 18

Amy's Bucket List

Volunteers of different nationalities and ages serve onboard our hospital ship, the *Africa Mercy*. Amy, our assistant purser, described how her "bucket list" was completed by a mercy moment.

"I was a teenager when I went on my first mission trip. I started saying, 'If I'm still single when I turn 30, I'm going to move to Africa and work in an orphanage.'

Years later I learned about Mercy Ships. I applied to serve. One day, I was in an orphanage in Guinea, holding a two-week old baby. I suddenly realized, 'I'm thirty, single, living in Africa! And I am in an orphanage!' His plan for me is so much more amazing than I could have ever imagined!"

How about adding moments of mercy not just to your *bucket list*, but also to your *to-do* list every day?

> ***"I know what I'm doing. I have it all planned out—plans to take care of you, not abandon you, plans to give you the future you hope for."*** **(Jeremiah 29:11 MSG)**

Mercy Minute Volume 63, Script 1; by Sharon Walls, staff writer; interview with Amy Moser, Assistant Purser; 2014-2015 AFM *Madagascar Field Service;*

March 19

The Presidential Medal of Freedom

The Presidential Medal of Freedom is the highest award granted by the U.S. government to civilians. In 2007, President Ellen Johnson Sirleaf of Liberia, West Africa, received this award. She was honored for her unwavering commitment to build a more hopeful future for her homeland.

Mercy Ships is honored to partner with this remarkable woman and the people of Liberia. President Johnson Sirleaf wants to be remembered for getting children back in school and for providing the basics of life—electricity, water, good housing. She says, *"I now see hope in the eyes of children in Liberia. They are smiling because they now believe there is a future."*

You see, acts of mercy give hope to others and help for the future. And you can make someone smile by showing kindness today.

***"May the God of hope fill you with all joy and peace as you trust in Him, so that you may overflow with hope by the power of the Holy Spirit."* (Romans 15:13 NIV)**

Mercy Minute Volume 32, Script 30; by Nancy Predaina, Special Projects Writer/Editor; www.maysville.com 10/25/2007; www.allAfrica.com 10/29/2007 and 10/30/2007;

March 20

Hope on My Horizon

It was 1983. Peter Woolston stood dejected, leaning over the ship's railings. The eighteen-year-old musician-in-the-making had just toured the Mercy Ship *Anastasis* in his home port in New Zealand.

He was captured by the vision to take free medical care to people in the greatest need. But he thought, *"God, I'm not a doctor or an engineer. What can I do to help heal the poor?'*

Peter nurtured the vision that mercy had planted in his heart. And, more than 30 years later, he released *Hope On My Horizon*. The song's sales are dedicated to Mercy Ships. Each time the song is sold, funds are generated to help sponsor surgeries for people in desperate need.

What skill has God placed in your hand that you can use to show mercy to others?

"There are different kinds of service, but the same Lord. There are different kinds of working, but in all of them and in everyone it is the same God at work."
(1 Corinthians 12:5-6 NIV)

⚓ Mercy Ships Mission Statement: Mercy Ships follows the 2000-year-old model of Jesus, bringing hope and healing to the world's forgotten poor.

Mercy Minute Volume 63, Script 5; by Sharon Walls, staff writer; interview with Peter Woolston, 10/18/14; 2015-16 AFM Madagascar Field Service;

March 21

Palliative Care Team

Our Mercy Ships Palliative Care Team shows God's love by giving practical care and support to patients with terminal illness. When asked why they do what they do, here's what they say:

"There's nobody else to be there. They've never heard of the concept of palliative care. The most powerful part of what we do is just going there. Somebody listening. It's, you know, the little things—bringing them medication, holding their hand, letting them tell us things they've never told anybody before.

We can show the love of Christ because they're valued. Their life still matters and means something."

It may be that the greatest gifts of mercy we can give are our time and a sympathetic, listening ear. Offer your time and attention to someone today.

"Ears that hear and eyes that see—the Lord has made them both."
(Proverbs 20:12 NIV)

Mercy Minute Volume 63, Script 35; by Nancy Predaina, Special Projects Writer/Editor; from interview with the Mercy Ships Palliative Care Team by Eunice Hiew, staff writer; 2014-15 AFM *Madagascar Field Service;*

March 22

Flood Victim Helps Relief Worker

July floods devastated northeastern Oklahoma in 2007. Nancy, a Red Cross volunteer, walked through the neighborhoods to assess the damage. As she charted the water levels in the houses, she visited with the homeowners.

The heat and humidity were intense. Nancy's reddened face signaled her discomfort. Suddenly, she felt a tap on her shoulder. Mr. Marquez was standing there with a smile and a cold bottle of water from an ice chest. He said, *"I think you need this."*

Nancy was amazed that a man with over three feet of water in his house, in desperate need of mercy, would take time himself to show mercy!

Sometimes it's hard to put aside our own concerns to focus on helping others ... but it's always a good thing to do.

***"Be devoted to one another in love. Honor one another above yourselves."* (Romans 12:10 NIV)**

Mercy Minute Volume 31, Script 2; by Nancy Predaina, Special Projects Writer/Editor; personal experience, July 2007;

March 23

Captain's Day Off

What does the volunteer Captain of a Mercy Ship do on his day off? He finds ways to express God's mercy, of course!

Every second Saturday, Captain Jan, his wife Elizabeth and their daughter Isabella packed bags full of balloons, crayons and other fun-stuff for kids. Then they gathered a bunch of fellow crew members and headed out to a Madagascan village.

The local pastor and his wife run a village school. But every second Saturday was packed full of fun—Jesus-style! Between games, crafts, laughter and songs, the Gospel was shared with about 60 noisy village children.

Mother Teresa said, "*We shall never know all the good that a simple smile can do.*"

Take a few minutes today to offer a smile, a hug … a moment to show you care.

***"A twinkle in the eye means joy in the heart, and good news makes you feel fit as a fiddle."* (Proverbs 15:30 MSG)**

***"Laughter is the most beautiful and beneficial therapy God ever granted humanity."* (Chuck Swindoll)**

Mercy Minute Volume 63, Script 44; by Sharon Walls, staff writer; from interview with Captain Jan Tuinier, 23/09/2015, 2015-16 AFM *Madagascar Field Service;*

March 24

Bridge of Mercy

Crispin Valeri was deeply troubled. He was a missionary to Zambia and had adopted Africa as his home. His purpose there was to *help* the people of Zambia. But when five people drowned while crossing the Zambezi River enroute to his mission station, he was burdened. They could have been saved if there had been a bridge!

Crispin was haunted by the idea. But he wasn't an engineer and had very few resources. None the less, he began poring over books and scavenging discarded cable from the mines.

After five long years and with the help of local people, a suspension bridge was finally finished. A 1,000-foot-long suspension bridge stands today as a monument to one man's creativity, persistence and mercy.

You can follow Crispin's example by being persistent and creative in building a bridge of mercy to someone.

"I can do all things through Him who strengthens me."
(Philippians 4:13 NASB)

Mercy Minute Volume 23, Script 12; by Larry Mast; adapted from National Geographic, *September 2005;*

March 25

75 Goats

It was a quiet African evening in the hospital ward of the Mercy Ship. Khalisile, a 76-year-old cataract patient scheduled for surgery, sat with his head in his hands. Crewmember Warrie sat down beside him and told him about God's love.

Khalisile was overwhelmed with her kindness. He said, *"Never before has a white person gone out of their way to help me."*

Following his successful surgery, Khalisile offered eye-surgeon Dr. Bob Dyer a 75-goat dowry to marry Warrie. Well, Warrie declined Khalisile's offer. And today, Warrie and her husband Brian still work for Mercy Ships.

You know, mercy is simply showing kindness to others. And that's something all of us can do.

***"Never walk away from someone who deserves help; your hand is God's hand for that person."* (Proverbs 3:27 MSG)**

⚓ We chose to fly Malta's flag for the *Anastasis*. The Maltese flag displays the Maltese cross, a cross developed by the knights of St. John, who were called the Hospitalers. During the Middle Ages, they developed what they called "hospices" throughout the Middle East, where they would care for weary and sick travelers. It seemed the perfect flag for the very first Mercy Ship.

Mercy Minute Volume 64, Script 12; by Larry Mast, Mercy Ships staff;

March 26

Bishop John Rucyahana

Anglican Bishop John Rucyahana stood before those who were responsible for the 1994 genocide in Rwanda. Nearly a million people had been slaughtered in 100 days. Bishop John told the prisoners to close their eyes and see the faces of their victims. Many of them began to cry. Bishop John said, *"Now that which made you cry, you must confess."*

Bishop John started a project to bring together tens of thousands of perpetrators and victims—providing opportunity for confession and forgiveness. The Bishop himself lost the majority of his family in the genocide. He simply says, *"We must forgive now, like Jesus did."*

You see, we are most like Christ when we forgive. Is there someone in your life who needs your gift of forgiveness?

***"Be kind and compassionate to one another, forgiving each other, just as in Christ God forgave you."* (Ephesians 4:32 NIV)**

Mercy Minute Volume 36, Script 31; adapted from "Love Your Enemies," by Chuck Colson; www.virtueonline.org; 1/30/09;

March 27

Mioty Winks

Volunteer nurse Heather Morehouse shared the story of a special little patient who came to our hospital ship, the *Africa Mercy*:

"Mioty was five years old. When she was just a week old, a rodent had bitten her in the face. She came to us missing part of her nose; her eye did not function and was scarred over.

Mioty had spent her entire life fighting to live. And so she fought with us. Every medicine included screaming. She wouldn't interact with any of us. She hid behind her mama, and my heart broke.

After seven weeks, I caught Mioty singing in her bed. And then she winked at me. What a transformation!"

Yes, mercy and love really do transform lives. Show mercy and love to someone today … and watch the transformation!

"Shout your praises to God, everybody! Let loose and sing! Strike up the band!" **(Psalm 98:4 MSG)**

Mercy Minute Volume 64, Script 20; from crew interview by Tanya Sierra, staff writer; 2014-2015 AFM *Madagascar Field Service;*

March 28

Mercy at the Toll Booth

Lynda often passes through toll booths in Chicago. One day she decided to use it as an opportunity for kindness.

Lynda gave the toll booth worker some extra money to pay the toll for the driver behind her. She asked the worker to tell the driver that his toll was paid and to have a great day.

Why did she do this? She explains: *"Maybe that person is having a bad day. My small gesture might turn their day around . . . the cost is just a buck or two, so it's worth it."*

You see, small acts of kindness **can** turn around someone's day. Give it a try!

"He has told you, O man, what is good; and what does the Lord require of you but to do justice, to love kindness, and to walk humbly with your God?" **(Micah 6:8 NASB)**

"Life's most urgent question is: What are you doing for others?" **(Martin Luther King Jr.)**

Mercy Minute Volume 36, Script 34; adapted from "The Kindness of Strangers," by Gina Roberts-Grey; Woman's Day, *11/11/08;*

March 29

X's and O's

Sharon, a staff writer on our hospital ship, shared her observations of the children's orthopedic ward:

"It's full of children's laughter and giggles. Some children arrive with severely knocked-knees. Their legs make a definite 'X' shape. Other children have bowed legs. Their legs are shaped like an 'O.'

They receive free surgeries onboard our hospital ship to straighten their legs. And each morning, these brave little souls line the hallway with their walkers to exercise their 'new' straight legs. Their speedy recovery is aided by physical therapy, a healthy diet, and by our heartfelt prayers."

To many of us, X's and O's represent kisses and hugs. But the next time you see X's and O's, say a little prayer for these children. It's true: "When prayers go up, blessings come down!"

"Here are my directions: Pray much for others; plead for God's mercy upon them; give thanks for all He is going to do for them."
(1 Timothy 2:1 TLB)

Mercy Minute Volume 64, Script 63; by Sharon Walls, staff writer; personal observation; 2015-16 AFM *Madagascar Field Service;*

March 30

Nurse Jenica and Alice

Nurse Jenica Gammie volunteered onboard our hospital ship, the *Africa Mercy*, in the Republic of Congo, and shared this special memory:

"Alice was the first patient I took care of in Africa. At first, we were doing twice-a-day dressing changes on her eye. She would stare downcast at the floor and not make a peep.

The constant love and attention slowly began to extract Alice from her shell. I still remember the first real smile I saw creep across her face—the way it lit up her face. It was amazing! The first time she laughed, the first time she ran up to me saying, 'Jenny!!!!'—these are moments I will remember and cherish forever."

Yes, merciful moments are cherished both by the giver and the receiver. Create a merciful moment for someone today.

***"Don't panic. I'm with you. There's no need to fear for I'm your God. I'll give you strength. I'll help you. I'll hold you steady, keep a firm grip on you."* (Isaiah 41:10 MSG)**

Mercy Minute Volume 64, Script 28; by Nancy Predaina, Special Projects Writer/Editor; from the crew blog: http://zupkefamily.blogspot.co.uk/2014/02/alice-post-one.html

March 31

Wrong Bus, Right Place

Casimiro was homeless on the streets of McAllen, Texas. His family had kicked him out because of his addiction to drugs and alcohol. He decided to escape it all by getting on the first bus he could find.

Well, it turned out to be the city bus. And the bus driver insisted on taking him to the Salvation Army. Casimiro says, *"I'm grateful because I reached out my hand for help, and The Salvation Army gave it to me."*

Two months later, he transferred to a residential rehabilitation program at The Salvation Army Center of Hope in Tyler, Texas. It transformed his life.

You see, the wrong bus took him to the right place … all because of a merciful bus driver.

Keep your eyes open for opportunities to show mercy to someone today.

"Many plans are in a man's mind, but it is the Lord's purpose for him that will stand (be carried out)." **(Proverbs 19:21 AMP)**

"God, the master artist … wants to paint a beautiful portrait of His Son in and through your life. A painting like no other in all of time." **(Joni Eareckson Tada)**

Mercy Minute Volume 64, Script 3; adapted from Spring Lone Star eNewsletter by Salvation Army; Spring 2016;

April

"Love is patient, love is kind … It always protects, always trusts, always hopes, always perseveres … Love never fails." (1 Corinthians 13:4-8 NIV)

April 1

Jeremy's Egg

Jeremy was born with severe learning problems and a terminal illness. He was a 12-year-old in a second-grade classroom. At Easter, his teacher, Mrs. Miller, gave her 19 students plastic eggs to fill with something that showed new life. The next day, the children put their eggs in a basket. Mrs. Miller opened each one and found things like a flower and a plastic butterfly. Then she opened an egg that was empty and moved on.

Jeremy said, *"Aren't you going to talk about my egg?"*

Mrs. Miller replied, *"But, Jeremy, your egg is empty!"*

He answered softly, *"Yes, but Jesus's tomb was empty, too."*

Sadly, just three months later, Jeremy died. There were 19 empty plastic eggs on top of his casket. Jeremy was right! At Easter we celebrate the empty tomb—the greatest example of mercy!

"Who then will condemn us? Will Christ? No! For He is the one who died for us and came back to life again for us and is sitting at the place of highest honor next to God, pleading for us there in heaven."
(Romans 8:34 TLB)

⚓ We christened our first Mercy Ship the *Anastasis*, the Greek word for "resurrection."

Mercy Minute Volume 55, Script 25; by Nancy Predaina, Special Projects Writer/Editor; adapted from "An Inspirational Easter Story," http://yooperpage.com/easter.html;

April 2

Anita and Baby Faith

Baby Faith was born with a cleft palate. Her mother had given birth to 6 children, *all* with cleft palates. All six had been abandoned and died in the African bush. Sadly, that's not uncommon in West Africa. The babies are believed to be cursed. Shortly after Faith was born, her mother left the hospital *without* her newborn daughter.

But Anita, the midwife, felt compassion for the rejected infant. She had her own family to support. But she and her husband took Baby Faith into their home. Anita and Faith traveled for three days to reach the *Africa Mercy*. There, Faith received a free, life-changing surgery. And the beautiful baby girl went home with a gorgeous smile.

A compassionate heart of mercy changed a life … and broke a cultural taboo in the process. Your compassion can change lives today.

***"The Christian who is pure and without fault, from God the Father's point of view, is the one who takes care of orphans and widows, and who remains true to the Lord—not soiled and dirtied by his contacts with the world."* (James 1:27 TLB)**

Mercy Minute Volume 32, Script 9; adapted from "Keeping the Faith," by Megan Petock; http://nursing.advanceweb.com Vol.9 Issue 24;

April 3

Purple Nail Polish

Chelsea Rasmussen volunteers as a nurse onboard our hospital ship, the *Africa Mercy*. Chelsea shared a story about a small patient hiding under a hospital bed:

"I found her crying silently—no whimpers, no sobs, just silent tears. Without a common language, how could I comfort her? Got a bottle of pink nail polish, and she snatched it and began painting my nails. Then I got a bottle of purple polish.

She immediately started painting my other hand with the purple. Then she wanted her nails to match mine. Finally she ran off to play, having forgotten why she was under the bed.

These are the moments I live for as a pediatric nurse."

Yes, mercy can even express itself through purple nail polish. I challenge you to find a creative way to show mercy to someone today.

"What a wonderful God we have—He is the Father of our Lord Jesus Christ, the Source of every mercy, and the One who so wonderfully comforts and strengthens us in our hardships and trials. And why does He do this? So that when others are troubled, needing our sympathy and encouragement, we can pass on to them this same help and comfort God has given us."

(2 Corinthians 1:3-4 TLB)

Mercy Minute Volume 65, Script 62; by Nancy Predaina, Special Projects Writer/Editor; based on interview (via email) of Chelsea Rasmussen by Pauline Rick, Mercy Ships U.S. Public Relations Coordinator; 5/21/15;

April 4

Hope in the Hall

Emotions ran high on the *Africa Mercy*, our Mercy Ships floating hospital. Ten women patients walked down the hall, singing, *"I have hope, I have hope, I have hope in Jesus."* What did they have in common? All lived in West Africa. All had suffered a childbirth injury called obstetric fistula. This injury results in incontinence, often causing rejection by friends and family. And all ten women had received a free, corrective surgery. Now, they had something else in common—HOPE! Hope of acceptance … of being reunited with family. Hope of a bright future. The corridor was illuminated by their brilliant smiles, and it resonated with their joyful song.

You can give others hope and a joyful song by showing mercy today.

"Yet this I call to mind and therefore I have hope: Because of the Lord's great love we are not consumed, for His compassions never fail. They are new every morning; great is Your faithfulness."
(Lamentations 3:21-23 NIV)

⚓ In April 2003, onboard the *Caribbean Mercy*, docked at the Dominican Republic, Dr. Glenn Strauss performed a procedure known as conductive keratoplasty for the first time ever in a developing nation. It is a revolutionary painless and quick way to remove cataracts.

Mercy Minute Volume 33, Script 5; by Nancy Predaina, Special Projects Writer/Editor; based on crew blog; used with permission;

April 5

Carrying the Torch

Ibrahim is a Syrian refugee. His dream of swimming in the Olympics came to an abrupt end when he lost his leg in a bombing raid.

But he got to participate in another way. He was chosen to carry the Olympic torch for a few hundred meters in Athens, Greece. He was surrounded by hundreds of children as he carried the torch through the refugee camp that was home to 1600 people.

The 27-year-old torchbearer said, *"The opportunity I have had today has been unique and a great honor. I wish that all wars would end and that everyone can go back to their homes in peace."*

And to that I say, "Amen!" Don't let anything stop you from showing mercy to someone today.

***"I have told you all this so that you will have peace of heart and mind. Here on earth you will have many trials and sorrows; but cheer up, for I have overcome the world."* (John 16:33 TLB)**

Mercy Minute Volume 65, Script 61; based on "Syrian Refugee Carries Rio 2016 Olympic Torch," https://www.rio2016.com

April 6

Joanna's Circle of Mercy

The Liberian mother was holding her 7-month-old baby, Joanna. Her child had received a free surgery onboard our Mercy Ship to repair a cleft lip and palate. Suddenly, the mother became distraught—her baby had stopped breathing.

Our emergency medical team instantly sprang into action. The baby was stabilized and placed in the ICU. Doctors gathered around her bed—an extraordinary circle of mercy! The group of five represented four nations and three specialties. They were all volunteering their medical skills to take care of a sick child in Liberia—a country with little healthcare and certainly no second opinions.

And little Joanna recovered—all because others were willing to use their skills to help the world's poor.

Find a way to use your skills to help those who cannot help themselves. You'll find your own life greatly enriched in the process.

"For we are His workmanship, created in Christ Jesus for good works, which God prepared beforehand so that we would walk in them." **(Ephesians 2:10 NASB)**

⚓ The Mercy Ships Los Angeles office relocated to Garden Valley, Texas, in 1989. The property was purchased in 1995.

Mercy Minute Volume 34, Script 19; from "Adapting," by Megan Petock; Advances for Nurses, *Vol.10, Issue 3, Feb. 2008;*

April 7

Suah and a Drawer Full of Eyes

Suah is beautiful—truly stunning. But for most of her life, people rejected her. You see, she lost an eye when she was two years old.

Suah studied hard, and she passed the entrance exam for nursing school. But her dreams died when she was not allowed to attend because she had only one eye.

Then, our Mercy Ship arrived in Liberia. Suah received a free surgery and a prosthetic eye. She laughs when she recalls seeing a drawer full of eyeballs! She said, *"The nurse took much care in choosing an exact match. It was a miracle!"*

Now, with two beautiful eyes, Suah has the confidence to pursue her dream of helping others.

You can demonstrate your desire to help others by showing mercy to someone today.

***"May He give you the desire of your heart and make all your plans succeed."* (Psalm 20:4 NIV)**

Mercy Minute Volume 33, Script 14; by Nancy Predaina, Special Projects Writer/Editor; from patient story by Lu Mizen, 2007 AFM *Liberia Field Service;*

April 8
Vulnerable Adults

Volunteering onboard our hospital ship often brings unexpected experiences. A volunteer nurse describes one:

"Working with children, you expect them to be vulnerable. Seeing vulnerability in an adult is something different.

My first encounter like this on the ship was when a patient, fearful she would never recover, broke down in my arms, clinging to me and crying. It was one of the most raw and humbling experiences of my life.

She did recover and was discharged last week. She hugged me again on her way off the ship and cried for the second time in my arms."

Tears of distress became tears of joy … all because of mercy. And you can change sorrow into joy by showing kindness to someone today.

***"Then He turned my sorrow into joy! He took away my clothes of mourning and clothed me with joy."* (Psalm 30:11 TLB)**

Mercy Minute Volume 65, Script 65; by Nancy Predaina, Special Projects Writer/Editor; from interview (via email) of Chelsea Rasmussen by Pauline Rick, Mercy Ships U.S. Public Relations Coordinator; 5/21/15;

April 9

Rescuing Hope

Anja Loven found a little two-year-old boy wandering the streets of Nigeria. He was starving and riddled with worms. His family threw him out because he was born with a congenital birth defect.

Anja took the tiny child to a hospital where doctors removed the worms and administered blood transfusions. She shared the story on social media, and one million dollars poured in to cover medical bills, including surgery to correct the birth defect.

Anja is the founder of African Children's Aid Education and Development Foundation. She named the little boy Hope—what an appropriate name! Anja says, *"He is safe and getting a lot of love."*

In this case, mercy really did deliver hope. And YOU can offer hope as you show mercy to others.

> ***"I was hungry and you fed Me, I was thirsty and you gave Me a drink, I was homeless and you gave Me a room, I was shivering and you gave Me clothes, I was sick and you stopped to visit, I was in prison and you came to Me.***
>
> ***... Whenever you did one of these things to someone overlooked or ignored, that was Me—you did it to Me."***
> **(Matthew 25:35-36, 40 MSG)**

Mercy Minute Volume 65, Script 30; by Nancy Predaina, Special Projects Writer/Editor; from http://www.9news.com.au/world/2016/04/01/09/41/starving-toddler-who-was-labelled-a-witch-and-left-to-die-makes-incredible-recovery

April 10

Dr. Jerry in Sierra Leone

After retiring from a successful practice, Dr. Jerry Putnam and his family packed up and moved to Africa to help start a new fistula hospital in Sierra Leone for Mercy Ships. He specializes in treating women who have childbirth injuries.

Dr. Jerry loved his job! He's an early riser and was always available for his patients. Most days, you could see him wearing sandals with his scrubs and a surgeon's cap with chili peppers on it. He didn't make a fashion statement, but his work changed lives. In fact, it made his patients . . . and Dr. Jerry himself . . . smile.

And that's what mercy does! You can bring smiles to others and to yourself through your acts of kindness.

"Do your best. Work from the heart for your real Master, for God, confident that you'll get paid in full when you come into your inheritance. Keep in mind always that the ultimate Master you're serving is Christ." **(Colossians 3:23 MSG)**

Mercy Minute Volume 29, Script 47; interview with Jerry Putman at the Aberdeen New Steps Centre, Sierra Leone, by Justin Hane, staff writer;

April 11

Camaraderie

The patients onboard our Mercy Ships receive mercy from our crew … and from each other. A volunteer nurse explains:

"The camaraderie developed among our patients was unlike anything I'd ever seen before. These men, women, and children—complete strangers only weeks before—came from all over the country and all walks of life, but their individual experiences created a sweet and unshakeable bond that was understood only by those who shared their years of pain, disfigurement, and separation from society.

For some, their time in the hospital was the first time they had ever experienced love and acceptance like they received from hospital staff and fellow patients."

Yes, you'll find mercy in all directions onboard our hospital ship. And you can develop a special bond with others through your own acts of mercy.

> ***"Oil and perfume make the heart glad; so does the sweetness of a friend's counsel that comes from the heart."*** **(Proverbs 27:9 AMP)**

Mercy Minute Volume 65, Script 19; by Nancy Predaina, Special Projects Writer/Editor; adapted from article by Sarah Strickland, volunteer nurse, for Reach Out Columbia, *local magazine in Columbia, SC ; 2015-16* AFM *Madagascar Field Service;*

April 12

Design to Fill a Need

An instructor at the College for Creative Studies in Detroit issued a challenge: "design to fill a need." So, student Veronika Scott designed an insulated overcoat that could double as a sleeping bag. She made 25 of them and gave them to homeless people in the city park. People were grateful, but one woman said, "*We need jobs, not coats.*"

So, Veronika found someone to teach two homeless women to sew and hired them to assemble the coats. She paid them with donations she received through her blog.

Later, she moved the shop into an old warehouse and founded a nonprofit called the Empowerment Plan. Now she employs 20 people, mostly single moms.

I challenge you to follow Veronika's example and find a creative way to show mercy and fill a need.

"Dear brothers, what's the use of saying that you have faith and are Christians if you aren't proving it by helping others? Will that kind of faith save anyone? If you have a friend who is in need of food and clothing, and you say to him, 'Well, good-bye and God bless you; stay warm and eat hearty,' and then don't give him clothes or food, what good does that do? ... Faith that doesn't show itself by good works is no faith at all—it is dead and useless."

(James 2:14-17 TLB)

Mercy Minute Volume 65, Script 4; by Larry Mast; adapted from "She Invented a Coat to Help the Homeless," by Beth Dreher and Michele Wojciechowsi, Reader's Digest, *December 2015;*

April 13

Ward Church

Every Sunday morning, patients voluntarily gather in a ward onboard our hospital ship, the *Africa Mercy*, for church. It's a congregation of the transient—short-term volunteers and short-term patients.

A man who had a massive tumor removed is sitting next to a man who almost died from a dental infection. Others are scarred by burns or bandaged beyond recognition. Yet, in spite of the crutches, the wrappings, and the casts—they rejoice! They dance, even missing limbs. They sing, voiceless. They smile, even though they're scarred.

And it's a beautiful tribute to the mercy they've received onboard our hospital ship—in the free, life-restoring medical care.

And your acts of kindness give others a reason to rejoice. That's a great motivation, isn't it?

"The Lord is my strength and my shield; my heart trusts in Him, and I am helped; Therefore my heart exults, and with my song I shall thank Him." **(Psalm 28:7 NASB)**

⚓ In 2016 Mercy Ships introduced the Ambulatory Surgical Project. Patients with minor surgical needs not warranting general anesthesia received surgeries onboard and were discharged on the same day for follow-up care through Outpatient Services.

Mercy Minute Volume 33, Script 54; adapted from mercyinafrica.blogspot.com by Mark Shrime; 5/25/08; used with permission; ©2008 Mercy Ships, All Rights Reserved

April 14

Panda Cares

Panda Cares is the philanthropic arm of Panda Restaurant Group. Since 1999, they've donated nearly 50 million dollars for underserved children and disaster relief.

In May 2013 at Panda's Leadership Conference, the employees received a raffle ticket if they made a contribution to Panda Cares. The prize was an iPad. The man who won it donated it back. Then it was auctioned off again and donated back … and a tidal wave of giving began. Everyone forgot about the iPad! The founders of Panda, the Cherng family, matched the donations. The end result . . . one million dollars for Panda Cares!

Aaron Wang, General Manager, said, *"I get chills just thinking about it."*

I challenge you to get caught up in giving. Start by showing mercy and kindness to someone today.

"For if you give, you will get! Your gift will return to you in full and overflowing measure, pressed down, shaken together to make room for more, and running over. Whatever measure you use to give—large or small—will be used to measure what is given back to you."
(Luke 6:38 TLB)

Mercy Minute Volume 64, Script 26; adapted from http://www.pandacares.org/ and https://www.youtube.com/watch?v=ac0cZEXbHf8

April 15

Kenneth's New Father

Kenneth had disfiguring burn scars on his face. The boy was abandoned at Redemption Hospital in Liberia.

The hospital was hosting a Mercy Ships dental clinic, and Kenneth became a friend of the team. Dr. Keith Chapman contacted a local orphanage, and Kenneth was accepted. Then a family in the U. S. decided to adopt the boy.

The adoptive father came to Liberia, and Kenneth was amazed to see that they had something in common—the man had scars on his face! The new dad said that when he saw the pictures of Kenneth, he knew that was the boy he would adopt.

You see, mercy looks beyond the superficial and sees the heart. And that's exactly what we should do as we show mercy to others.

***"But the Lord said to Samuel, '... The Lord does not look at the things people look at. People look at the outward appearance, but the Lord looks at the heart.'"* (1 Samuel 16:7 NIV)**

***"True humility is not thinking less of yourself; it is thinking of yourself less."* (C.S. Lewis)**

Mercy Minute Volume 64, Script 26; adapted from http://www.pandacares.org/ and https://www.youtube.com/watch?v=ac0cZEXbHf8

April 16

Celine's Bright Future

Four-year-old Celine was born with cataracts in both eyes. Her days were spent in cloudy darkness. Her father's heart broke every time she tripped and fell. He says, *"I feared that she would not have a job—or a future."*

Then Celine received a free surgery onboard our Mercy Ship in Benin, West Africa. The next day the bandages were removed. Celine stared at a toy train. One little finger traced the sharp black line on the red wheel. And she walked with confident steps down the gangway as she and her delighted father returned home.

Mercy restored Celine's vision. Her future is as bright as the colors she's seeing for the very first time! And YOUR acts of kindness brighten the lives of others.

***"Beware that you don't look down upon a single one of these little children. For I tell you that in heaven their angels have constant access to my Father."* (Matthew 18:10 TLB)**

Mercy Minute Volume 37, Script 1; by Carmen Radley, staff writer; patient interview; 2009 AFM Benin Field Service;

April 17

A Day on the Ward

Volunteering as a nurse onboard our hospital ship, the *Africa Mercy*, often involves more than just medical care. Nurse Sarah Strickland described a day on the ward:

"Every day when I arrived to work on the ward, I was greeted with faces that radiated joy from underneath heavy bandages.

My days were spent not only on the usual nursing roles, but also ministering to the fun and practical needs of patients: painting fingernails, coloring pictures, and playing soccer on the deck with the children—which sometimes ended sadly with the cry of 'Ball Overboard!' I think we may have introduced a new sport!"

Yes, volunteering onboard our hospital ship offers unusual and heartwarming opportunities to use skills. Check out opportunities to volunteer your skills in your community.

***"God has given each of you some special abilities; be sure to use them to help each other, passing on to others God's many kinds of blessings."* (1 Peter 4:10 TLB)**

⚓ Former UK Prime Minister John Major traveled to East Texas in spring 2001 to dedicate the newly-built Mercy Ships International Support Center.

Mercy Minute Volume 65, Script 1; by Nancy Predaina, Special Projects Writer/Editor; from article by Sarah Strickland, volunteer nurse, for Reach Out Columbia, *local magazine in Columbia, SC ; 2015-16 AFM Madagascar Field Service;*

April 18

A Liver for Jorge

Jorge Castro is a Los Angeles County Sheriff's deputy. He was diagnosed with a rare disease that attacks the liver. He needed a liver transplant … quickly. He was put on a transplant list, but the outlook was grim.

He told his friend and co-worker, Javier Tiscareno, about his problem. And Javier said, *"Let's do it this Saturday."*

Jorge thought his friend was joking, and he said, *"I'm not fooling around. This is serious."*

Javier answered, *"I'm not fooling around either."*

Well, Javier turned out to be a perfect match and donated a portion of his liver! The human liver can regenerate itself from healthy tissue. So, both men's livers returned to normal size within about two months.

You know, friendship and mercy often go hand-in-hand. Do you have a friend who needs a special act of kindness today?

***"A true friend is always loyal, and a brother is born to help in time of need."* (Proverbs 17:17 TLB)**

Mercy Minute Volume 64, Script 24; adapted from http://snip.ly/7ndc9?utm_content=bufferd70e4&utm_medium=social&utm_source=twitter.com&utm_campaign=buffer#http://www.keckmedicine.org/the-keck-effect-more-friendship/

April 19

Esther's New Hand

Little Esther was only three years old when rebel soldiers in Liberia stuck her hand into a fire.

When Esther was 14, her father brought her to our Mercy Ship for a free surgery. The next two months were a journey of free surgeries, dressing changes and physical therapy. But Esther is a spunky girl. She learned to swing dance, and she taught one of the nurses to carry things on her head like a proper African woman.

Finally the bandages were removed for good. Esther held a red ball in her hand—the first time in 11 years she'd been able to hold anything. Her purple dress and flowered backpack were as bright as her future as she left the ship.

And YOU can brighten the lives of others simply through acts of kindness.

***"But those who hope in the Lord will renew their strength. They will soar on wings like eagles; they will run and not grow weary, they will walk and not be faint."* (Isaiah 40:31 NIV)**

Mercy Minute Volume 33, Script 61; adapted from "Surgery a Godsend," by Megan Petock; Philadelphia Inquirer *11/21/07;*

April 20

Genevieve's Children See

Genevieve's first child was born with cataracts in both eyes. Four years later, her second child—a little girl—was born with the same problem. Another two years passed. A third child arrived—also blind. And people in her small village whispered, "*What terrible thing has this family done to deserve such difficulty?*"

With renewed hope, Genevieve traveled five hours to take her children to our Mercy Ship in Benin. *All three children* had their cataracts removed free of charge.

With a bright smile on her face, Genevieve looked at her children. They *saw* their mother for the first time. And the delightful sound of laughter rippled through the ward.

Mercy inspires joy. You can bring joy into the lives of others when you show them kindness.

"Walking down the street, Jesus saw a man blind from birth. His disciples asked, 'Rabbi, who sinned: this man or his parents, causing him to be born blind?'

***Jesus said, 'You're asking the wrong question. You're looking for someone to blame. There is no such cause-effect here. Look instead for what God can do.'"* (John 9:1-3 MSG)**

Mercy Minute Volume 37, Script 57; by Carmen Radley, staff writer; personal observation;2009 AFM *Benin Field Service;*

April 21

Held Hostage by Pirates

In 2009 the cargo ship, *Maersk Alabama*, was attacked off the coast of Somalia. As four heavily armed pirates boarded the ship, Captain Richard Phillips ordered his crew to lock themselves in the engine room. Then he faced the pirates alone.

Later, his crew used brute force to retake the ship. The pirates fled in a lifeboat with Captain Phillips as hostage. A five-day standoff ended dramatically on Easter Sunday. In a daring nighttime rescue, Navy SEALS liberated Captain Phillips. They gave him a note from his wife that said, *"Your family is saving a chocolate Easter egg for you."*

Captain Phillips offered his own life to save his crew. And Easter is a special time of remembering that Jesus sacrificed His life for us.

***"No one has greater love [nor stronger commitment] than to lay down his own life for his friends."* (John 15:13 AMP)**

***"God proved His love on the Cross. When Christ hung, and bled, and died, it was God saying to the world, 'I love you.'"* (Rev. Billy Graham)**

Mercy Minute Volume 47, Script 15; by Nancy Predaina, Special Projects Writer/Editor; from "Maersk Alabama Kidnapping," Wikipedia; and "Captain Freed After Snipers Kill Somali Pirates," 4/13/09, msnbc.com;

April 22

What Hope and Healing Look Like

Kirstie Randall serves as the Medical Capacity-Building Director onboard our hospital ship, the *Africa Mercy*. She wondered what hope and healing really looks like and wrote this beautiful response:

"It's more than just the surgery itself. What about hope restored? What about meeting eyes with someone who cares? To see a love that is unconditional.

I often find myself wondering how it felt for some of our patients to walk up the 'corridor of hope.' Yes, that's the place where the OR and wards are—but it's also the place where hands are held, and life is spoken, and hope begins to blossom again."

Kirstie has painted a beautiful word-picture of the power of mercy. And it begins with something as simple as the touch of a hand.

***"Moved with compassion, Jesus stretched out His hand and touched him."* (Mark 1:41 NASB)**

***"Hope is being able to see that there is light despite all of the darkness."* (Desmond Tutu)**

Mercy Minute Volume 66, Script 37; by Nancy Predaina Special Projects Writer/Editor; from "What Happened to the Patients in 2009, blog posted by Kirstie Randall on Navigator, August 2016;

April 23

Gifty Smiles and Plays Again

Two year-old Gifty yawned as she peeked over her mother's shoulder. It was early morning, but already long lines had formed at the Mercy Ships screening site in Liberia. Her mother told the surgeons her sad story.

Gifty was asleep when someone torched their house. Burns covered the child's entire body. Deep scars developed, restricting movement in her knee and her elbow.

But a free surgery onboard our Mercy Ship corrected the problem. Two weeks later, little Gifty was chasing a ball across the deck of the ship. Her large brown eyes were dancing. Her big smile reflected the joy on her mother's face.

You see, mercy brings freedom and joy to others. And we have the privilege of showing kindness to someone today.

***"Let us then approach God's throne of grace with confidence, so that we may receive mercy and find grace to help us in our time of need."* (Hebrews 4:16 NIV)**

⚓ Mercy Ships Vision Statement: Mercy Ships uses hospital ships to transform individuals and serve nations one at a time.

Mercy Minute Volume 33, Script 1; by Rosalie Schlichting; from patient story, 2005-06 Anastasis *Liberia Field Service;*

April 24

A Trip to Rio

Liz Willock missed her flight and took a later one. It turned out to be an opportunity for mercy. Ellis Hill was her Uber driver for the trip from the airport to the hotel.

Their conversation turned to the Olympics in Rio. Hill's son was competing in the men's shot put final. But he wasn't going because he couldn't afford it.

Liz says, *"It just made me sad because any loving parent would want to see their child compete in the Olympics."*

So, she started a GoFundMe campaign. In two days, it surpassed the goal of $7500 for flights, hotel, and meals.

So, Ellis Hill got a trip to the Olympics ... and a new friend ... all because of mercy!

Keep an eye and ear open for an opportunity to show mercy to someone today.

***"And do not forget to do good and to share with others, for with such sacrifices God is pleased."* (Hebrews 13:16 NIV)**

Mercy Minute Volume 66, Script 12; adapted from "Her Uber Driver Couldn't Afford the Trip to Rio ...," www.washingtonpost.com 8/6/16;

April 25

The Touch of a Hand

Many of the West Africans who come to our free medical screenings have terrible deformities that imprison them in a world of isolation. Here's one woman's story:

"I was so afraid. I stayed far away from everyone. A giant scarf hid the ugly tumor on my head. But the scarf could not hide the terrible smell.

At the screening, a Mercy Ships crew member sat down beside me. She put her arm around me and encouraged me. It was the first time in 10 years that another human being had touched me.

This stranger's kindness and love gave me courage to have surgery."

The incredible power of mercy can be found in a gentle touch. Extend your hand in mercy to someone today.

"Do nothing out of selfish ambition or vain conceit. Rather, in humility value others above yourselves, not looking to your own interests but each of you to the interests of the others."
(Philippians 2:3-4 NIV)

"The purpose of life is not to be happy. It is to be useful, to be honorable, to be compassionate, to have it make some difference that you have lived and lived well." **(Ralph Waldo Emerson)**

Mercy Minute Volume 48, Script 12; by Nancy Predaina, Special Projects Writer/Editor; adapted from blog written by Marty Schwebel on Jan. 25, 2012; used with permission;

April 26

Selvin's Plus-13 Eyeglasses

Somewhere in the United States, a used pair of "plus 13" eyeglasses were placed in a donation box. Members of the Lion's Club sorted and catalogued all the glasses and sent them to a Mercy Ship, then in Guatemala.

Thirteen-year-old Selvin Lopez traveled seven hours across Guatemala to the ship. He stared expectantly at the medical personnel examining him, his eyes looming behind the "coke bottle" lenses. The optician noticed his badly scratched oval lenses glued into square frames.

Well, those "plus 13" eyeglasses and Selvin were a matched pair! He left with a huge smile … and with new glasses that fit his needs and his youthful face perfectly.

You see, mercy gives others vision for a future. Check with service organizations in your community for ways to show mercy to people in need.

***"'If you have two coats, give one away,' He said. 'Do the same with your food.'"* (Luke 3:11 MSG)**

Mercy Minute Volume 33, Script 10; by Larry Mast, staff writer, Shipmate Letter 5/19/98;

April 27

Biddy Mason

Biddy Mason was born in 1818 as a slave on a plantation in Mississippi. In 1851 her owner moved his household to California, where slavery was forbidden. So Biddy petitioned the court and won freedom for herself and her children. She worked as a nurse and bought and developed real estate, accumulating a fortune of almost $300,000. Most of all, she was devoted to helping others—providing food and shelter for people of all races. She and her son founded the First African Methodist Episcopal Church in Los Angeles.

Biddy once said, "*The open hand is blessed, for it gives in abundance even as it receives.*" And she's right! Follow Biddy's example and devote your life to showing mercy to others.

"In everything I did, I showed you that by this kind of hard work we must help the weak, remembering the words the Lord Jesus himself said: 'It is more blessed to give than to receive.'"
(Acts 20:35 NIV)

⚓ Motivated by a desire to change the alarming maternal mortality rate in Africa, Mercy Ships initiated the development of one of the few specialized fistula hospitals in Africa. The Aberdeen and West Africa Fistula Centre is located in Freetown, Sierra Leone.

Mercy Minute Volume 66, Script 17; adapted from http://www.aaregistry.org/historic_events/view/slavery-entrepreneur-biddy-mason and "An Open Hand," Our Daily Bread, *7/17/16;*

April 28

I Can Help You

Marie Angele is a single mother struggling to raise two children in Madagascar. But life was even more difficult because of a large tumor on the right side of her face. Her husband abandoned her. Friends rejected her. Work was hard to find.

Marie sought help from local doctors, but no one could help her. Then she heard that Mercy Ships had come to Madagascar and could treat tumors like hers!

She gathered her courage, went to the patient screening, and heard some amazing news—the tumor could be removed, for FREE! Marie says, *"I have waited so long for someone to say, 'Yes, I can help you.'"*

Some of the most beautiful words are *"I can help you."* Say those words to someone in need this week.

***"Feed the hungry! Help those in trouble! Then your light will shine out from the darkness, and the darkness around you shall be as bright as day."* (Isaiah 58:10-11 TLB)**

***"Doing nothing for others is the undoing of ourselves."* (Horace Mann)**

Mercy Minute Volume 65, Script 5; by Tanya Sierra, staff writer; from patient interview; 2014-2015 AFM Madagascar Field Service;

April 29

Dinner with a Mugger

Julio Diaz ended his subway commute to the Bronx one stop early—just so he could eat at his favorite diner. But this night took a surprising turn. Suddenly, a teenage boy approached and pulled a knife. Julio handed over his wallet.

But as the mugger walked away, Julio called him back. He gave the teen his coat and invited him to join him for dinner. Of course, when the bill came, the teen had to return the wallet. So, Julio gave the boy $20 … in return for the knife.

Dr. Martin Luther King, Jr., said, "*Darkness cannot drive out darkness; only light can do that. Hate cannot drive out hate; only love can do that.*"

I think Julio—and all of us—would agree with that! Determine to drive out darkness by showing mercy and love to others.

***"Listen, all of you. Love your enemies. Do good to those who hate you."* (Luke 6:27 TLB)**

Mercy Minute Volume 66, Script 26; by Nancy Predaina, Special Projects Writer/Editor; adapted from http://www.npr.org/2008/03/28/89164759/a-victim-treats-his-mugger-right;

April 30

Lovetee's Beautiful Toes

A huge smile lit up Lovetee's face as she admired her beautiful, straight toes. The 14-year-old girl was born with a foot deformity. Walking was very difficult—and very painful.

Then the *Africa Mercy* came to West Africa. Lovetee received a free surgery onboard our floating hospital. Volunteer surgeons inserted screws into the small joints of her toes to correctly align them. She learned to walk first with a walker, and then with crutches. Now she walks very well—and without pain. She says, *"Thank you to all the people at Mercy Ships. May God bless you all."*

Lovetee, God DOES bless us all! And acts of mercy produce thankful hearts.

***"The Lord bless you, and keep you; the Lord make His face shine on you, and be gracious to you; the Lord lift up His countenance on you, and give you peace."* (Numbers 6:24-26 NASB)**

***"Within the covers of the Bible are the answers for all the problems that face us today, if we'd only look there."* (Ronald Reagan)**

Mercy Minute Volume 33, Script 42; by Nancy Predaina, Special Projects Writer/Editor; from email from Gerry O'Connor, ship physiotherapist, 5/9/2008;2008 AFM *Liberia Field Service;*

May

"For I am the Lord, your God, who takes hold of your right hand and says to you, 'Do not fear; I will help you.'"
(Isaiah 41:13 NIV)

May 1

Gabriel's Angels

The little boy was wearing a Spider-Man shirt and crying. He'd just been admitted to Crisis Nursery in Phoenix. It's a shelter that takes in young children who are victims of abuse and neglect.

Pam Graber brought her dog Gabriel to the shelter. The sobbing little boy nuzzled the dog, then started to smile, and then laughed. And Pam said, *"I was watching an animal reach a child in a way no adult could."*

So Pam got Gabriel registered as a therapy dog, and they became regular visitors at the Crisis Nursery. She established a nonprofit called *Gabriel's Angels* to provide free pet therapy to abused and at-risk children. Now she coordinates about 175 therapy teams.

What a great idea! If you have a heart for children, look around your community and use your creativity to find a way to help.

"But Jesus knew their thoughts, so He stood a little child beside him and said to them, 'Anyone who takes care of a little child like this is caring for Me! And whoever cares for Me is caring for God who sent Me. Your care for others is the measure of your greatness.'" **(Luke 9:47-48 TLB)**

"To say there are too many children in the world is like saying there are too many beautiful flowers." **(Mother Teresa)**

Mercy Minute Volume 66, Script 28; adapted from "Puppy Love," by Kellie B. Gormly; Family Circle; *December 2015;*

May 2

Webs of Friendship

Mercy Ships is truly a global organization, and our crew members come from over 40 nations. Dr. Gary Parker describes this multicultural community of mercy-givers:

"In all the years that I've worked with Mercy Ships, I realize the importance of webs of friendship and relationship that cross the world. And we can work together and do things together that we can never do by ourselves. If that's not one of the great lessons that I've learned from all these years on the ship, that's a big one—it's tremendous what we can do together."

Yes it IS tremendous what we can do together. I challenge you to find a way to join with others in making a difference in your community.

"Instead, we will lovingly follow the truth at all times—speaking truly, dealing truly, living truly—and so become more and more in every way like Christ who is the Head of His body, the Church. Under His direction, the whole body is fitted together perfectly, and each part in its own special way helps the other parts, so that the whole body is healthy and growing and full of love."
(Ephesians 4:15-16 TLB)

Mercy Minute Volume 62, Script 16; by Nancy Predaina, Special Projects Writer/Editor; from interview with Dr. Gary Parker; 2014-15 AFM Madagascar Field Service;

May 3

A Hand of Mercy

Passengers riding public transit in Vancouver witnessed an amazing act of mercy and courage. A large man obviously suffering from some type of mental health issue became very aggressive in his train car. He was moving erratically, cursing and shouting … until mercy entered the picture.

A 70-year-old woman reached out her hand and grabbed his hand. The sweet gesture calmed the man. He sank to the floor, and tears filled his eyes.

The woman said that she was afraid but felt it was more important that the man didn't feel alone. She said, *"I'm a mother, and he needed someone to touch."*

Sometimes a simple, compassionate touch is a wonderful act of mercy. Why don't you extend a hand of mercy to someone today?

"As a mother comforts her child, so will I comfort you …" **(Isaiah 66:13 NIV)**

"Dare to reach out your hand into the darkness, to pull another hand into the light." **(Norman B. Rice)**

Mercy Minute Volume 69, Script 41; by Nancy Predaina, Special Projects Writer/Editor; adapted from http://www.huffingtonpost.com/entry/woman-holds-train-passengers-hand_us_56bb5cbbe4b08ffac1236598

May 4
Zakael

Zakael can run like the wind. The seven-year-old says, "*I want to be a soldier, just like my grandfather.*" But something stood in his way . . . a tennis ball-sized cyst that had been slowly growing since birth.

The situation seemed hopeless until Zakael's father heard that Mercy Ships had arrived in Madagascar. Just imagine—a hospital ship staffed with volunteer surgeons that offer free surgeries!

The family sold their two treasures—a goose and a chicken—to pay for the two-day journey to the ship. It was a great investment … it purchased a new life for Zakael.

Now Zakael proudly wears his surgical scar—a symbol of where he's been and where he's is going.

You know, one of the most priceless investments you can make is to help someone achieve their dream.

***"Behold, children are a gift of the Lord, the fruit of the womb is a reward. Like arrows in the hand of a warrior, so are the children of one's youth."* (Psalm 127:3-4 NASB)**

⚓ On May 4, 2007, the *Africa Mercy* began its inaugural sail from England to Liberia, with a stop in the Canary Islands (for refueling and for divers to check the bottom of the ship for the surveyors).

Mercy Minute Volume 60, Script 25; by Nancy Predaina, Special Projects Writer/Editor; from patient interview by Tanya Sierra, AFM *staff writer; 2014-2015* AFM *Madagascar Field Service;*

May 5

Little Davilov Sleeps

Some problems—like getting a toddler to go to sleep—are the same no matter where you live. I'm sure you can sympathize with volunteer nurse Natalie's story:

"Little Davilov had been fighting sleep for hours. 'Give it up,' I thought. 'You'll be asleep in two minutes if you just let someone hold you.'

Later, among the loud drumming, clapping, and singing of African worship, I felt a tug on my scrubs and saw two tiny arms reaching up to me—as if to say, 'Okay, now I'm ready. Now I trust you.'

In the loudest moment possible, he dozed off. I held that peaceful, sweaty toddler and wondered how often God is saying to us, 'Give it up, little one! Stop fighting! I know what's best.'"

That's great advice for all of us. If you're struggling with something, show mercy to yourself by giving it to God—He really does know what's best for you.

"O my people, trust Him all the time. Pour out your longings before Him, for He can help!" (Psalm 62:8 TLB)

Mercy Minute Volume 58, Script 50; adapted from story submitted by Natalie Bullock, AFM ward nurse, to Catherine Murphy, staff writer; 2013-14 AFM Congo Field Service;

May 6

Saving Fitia

Fitia is a rambunctious two-year-old. But one day, she tripped over a pot of boiling soup and suffered burns to her neck and chest. In a nation like Madagascar with limited medical care, burns can lead to death.

Traditional healers told Fitia's parents to spit into the wounds. Of course, this caused life-threatening infection. Her parents prayed for miracle.

And a miracle came in the form of our big white hospital ship. Fitia's mother asked our Mercy Ships volunteer surgeons one simple question: *"Can you save my daughter's life?"*

And the answer was, "Yes!" A heavy dose of antibiotics, good nutrition, love, a free surgery, and physical therapy saved Fitia's life and restored hope to her family.

Every time you show kindness to others—through prayers, kind words, thoughtful actions—you're restoring hope.

***"... taking the little girl's father and mother and His three disciples, He went into the room where she was lying. Taking her by the hand He said to her, 'Get up, little girl!' (She was twelve years old.) And she jumped up and walked around!"* (Mark 5:40-42 TLB)**

Mercy Minute Volume 64, Script 55; based on crew interview by Tanya Sierra, staff writer; 2014-2015 AFM *Madagascar Field Service;*

May 7

Truman's Letter File

A well-known childhood saying is *"Sticks and stones may break your bones, but words will never hurt you."* Well, it's not true. The pen is truly mightier than the sword when it comes to inflicting emotional damage.

President Harry Truman understood the danger of words. So he followed a clear policy. Any letter written in anger had to sit on his desk for 24 hours before it could be mailed. At the end of his life, he had a large desk drawer full of unmailed letters.

In our day of instant communication, we all need to follow President Truman's example and think before we write, blog, post on Facebook, tweet, or text.

Yes, words do have the power to hurt or to help. Resolve to use your words to show encouraging mercy to others.

***"Kind words heal and help; cutting words wound and maim."* (Proverbs 15:4 MSG)**

"Kind words are short and easy to speak, but their echoes are truly endless." (Mother Teresa)

Mercy Minute Volume 66, Script 51; https://www.postcontrolmarketing.com/24-hour-rule-what-harry-s-truman-can-reach-us-about-social-media/

May 8

Winning Aicha's Heart

A house fire burned the side of Aicha's face and much of her body. Without proper treatment, the skin contracted, immobilizing her arms. A free surgery onboard our hospital ship restored her mobility … but the four-year-old girl was scarred by grief and fear. You see, the fire had killed her mother.

Sometimes winning over a broken heart means victory comes, in time, in shattered pieces. We gave her space. We waited until she smiled at our silly faces. We pretended not to notice when she took a little step away from her father's side.

Then the day came when she fell into our arms. Winning Aicha's heart was worth the wait.

Sometimes mercy takes patience and space … but the result is always worth the wait.

***"The Lord is close to the brokenhearted and saves those who are crushed in spirit."* (Psalm 34:18 NIV)**

Mercy Minute Volume 58, Script 62; based on story written by Catherine Murphy, staff writer; 2013-14 AFM *Congo Field Service;*

May 9

Angels on the Atlantic

Vince Hubach buys and sells restaurant equipment. One summer he was setting up a pizzeria in a poor section of Philadelphia. He says, *"Kids would be hanging around. I'd say 'Why don't you go to the beach?' They'd just look at me like, 'The beach?'"*

Vince and his wife Jeanie founded a nonprofit called *Angels on the Atlantic.* Then they bought two acres of beachfront property in Ocean City, New Jersey. In their first five years they hosted over 4,800 inner-city kids. Vince and Jeanie love watching children build sandcastles for the first time, find seashells, or run laughing into a flock of seagulls.

Their efforts were rewarded the day Vince overheard one boy say, *"I don't think we're gonna hear any gunshots today."*

You know, you can make life much better for others just by showing kindness to them.

"God's Message, from the God who lights up the day with sun and brightens the night with moon and stars, who whips the ocean into a billowy froth, whose name is God-of-the-Angel-Armies:"
(Jeremiah 31:35 MSG)

Mercy Minute Volume 69, Script 30; by Larry Mast; based on Reader's Digest, *May 2009;*

May 10

The Baby Box, Part 1

A large mail drop box is set into the wall of Pastor Lee's laundry room in South Korea. When the buzzer sounds, he rushes to the box and lifts out …a baby. The Baby Box is a place of rescue for unwanted and disabled infants.

Pastor Lee's own son was born with severe deformities and brain damage. Lee and his wife have adopted nine babies and personally take care of 15 more. Pastor Lee says, "*These babies were not born by accident. God sent them to the earth to use them.*"

Since 2009, over 600 children have been left in the Baby Box. They've received care and a home.

What an inspiring story of mercy!

"Beware that you don't look down upon a single one of these little children. For I tell you that in heaven their angels have constant access to my Father." **(Matthew 18:10 TLB)**

"No man stands so tall as when he stoops to help a child." **(Abraham Lincoln)**

Mercy Minute Volume 66, Script 56; adapted from http://lifebeautifulmagazine.com/departments/a-chance-at-life and http://thefederalist.com/2015/03/16/the-drop-box-where-disabled-babies-go-to-live/

May 11

The Baby Box, Part 2

Brian Ivie was a film student when he heard about Pastor Lee's Baby Box—a large mail box that was a rescue place for unwanted babies.

Brian got Lee's permission to do a short film. And he learned about love. He says, *"It was the way he lived his life in complete and utter sacrifice. That went against everything I thought love was."*

The project became a full-length documentary. Brian donated $50,000 to Pastor Lee and used the rest to start a nonprofit called Kindred Image to support Lee's ministry.

Oh, by the way, Brian was also adopted—into the family of God.

You know, mercy and love are powerful forces … and you and I can choose to show mercy and love to others.

"So here's what I want you to do, God helping you: Take your everyday, ordinary life—your sleeping, eating, going-to-work, and walking-around life—and place it before God as an offering."
(Romans 12:1 MSG)

⚓ Mercy Ships Values: Following the model of Jesus, we seek to love God, love and serve others, be people of integrity, and aim for excellence in all we say and do.

Mercy Minute Volume 66, Script 58; Adapted from http://lifebeautifulmagazine.com/departments/a-chance-at-life and http://thefederalist.com/2015/03/16/the-drop-box-where-disabled-babies-go-to-live/

May 12

A Mother's Model of Mercy

My mother, Jean Stephens, clearly taught me about mercy. I remember many occasions when she asked her three children to help her load our Chevy station wagon with groceries, clothes, and toys for others in need.

And Mom always made us go along to deliver the gifts. I confess that I was sometimes reluctant.

Over forty years later, I met a woman who shared with me how she came to faith in God. My mother's unconditional acceptance and friendship served as the catalyst that led her to a deeper relationship with our Creator. She **saw** Jesus in my mother's actions. She heard Jesus in my mother's words.

Now I challenge you to be a role model of mercy in your family. The results will reach farther than you can imagine.

***"She is a woman of strength and dignity and has no fear of old age. When she speaks, her words are wise, and kindness is the rule for everything she says. She watches carefully all that goes on throughout her household and is never lazy. Her children stand and bless her; so does her husband."* (Proverbs 31:25-28 TLB)**

Mercy Minute Volume 47, Script 40; by Nancy Predaina, Special Projects Writer/Editor; personal experience of Don Stephens;

May 13

A Mother's Prayer for Cyrus

Mary's baby son, Cyrus, developed a very large facial tumor. By the time Cyrus was 18 months old, he could no longer hold his head up. The doctors in Liberia said there was nothing they could do. In desperation, Mary asked God to send a surgeon who could help.

Her prayers were answered when our Mercy Ship came to Monrovia. Mary says, "*When I first saw the hospital ship, I was overcome with joy.*" Cyrus received a free surgery on the ship.

With the tumor removed, Cyrus happily crawled around the ship and constructed endless block towers. Cyrus was healed through the mercy of wonderful volunteers. His delighted mother said, *"Praise God! Praise God!"*

When we use our skills to help others, we are following the model of Jesus and giving glory to God.

"Praise the Lord. Praise the Lord, my soul. I will praise the Lord all my life; I will sing praise to my God as long as I live."
(Psalm 146:1-2 NIV)

"The highest form of worship is the worship of unselfish Christian service." **(Rev. Billy Graham)**

Mercy Minute Volume 33, Script 30; by Beth Herndon; from patient story, "Cyrus Manslen: Now He Has A Future;" Liberia 2007 AFM *Liberia Field Service;*

May 14

A Mutual Touch

Mercy Ships crew member Marissa Hall was the first person to touch Julien when he came to the *Africa Mercy* for surgery. He had suffered for years with a melon-sized tumor on his chin. But, as Marissa explained, Julien also touched her:

"I remember he used to wear a pink shirt wrapped around his tumor. He was so quiet. He never looked me in the eye, and he hardly spoke.

Now, after surgery, Julien has thrown away that shirt. And to see him each day is just awesome. He's happier and happier. He told me I was the very first one to touch him and to care for him. And I know what we do here really matters—it matters to him and it matters to God."

I challenge you to touch someone's life with mercy today. It really does matter!

"You are the light of the world. A town built on a hill cannot be hidden. Neither do people light a lamp and put it under a bowl. Instead they put it on its stand, and it gives light to everyone in the house. In the same way, let your light shine before others, that they may see your good deeds and glorify your Father in heaven."
(Matthew 5:14-16 NIV)

Mercy Minute Volume 69, Script 1; by Anna Psiaki, staff writer; from interview with Marissa Hall; 2016-2017 AFM *Benin Field Service;*

May 15

Showers on Wheels

San Francisco has been called the homeless capital of the U.S. In 2013, an estimated 4,300 people lived on the streets. One of their many problems is lack of access to showers.

Doniece Sandoval decided to change that. She started Lava Mae to provide showers on wheels. Old city buses are converted into shower stations. They plug into fire hydrants, and Lava Mae pays for the water with donations. Each bus has two shower stations.

A city official said, *"Doniece has done an incredible job as a citizen who cares about helping the poor."*

You know, caring for others—and finding a way to help them—is what mercy is all about.

> ***"Whoever oppresses the poor shows contempt for their Maker, but whoever is kind to the needy honors God."*** **(Proverbs 14:31 NIV)**

⚓ Mercy Ships has national offices in Australia, Belgium, Canada, Denmark, France, Germany, The Netherlands, South Korea, New Zealand, Norway, South Africa, Spain, Sweden, Switzerland, and United Kingdom. The Mercy Ships International Operations Center is in Garden Valley, Texas.

Mercy Minute Volume 68, Script 48; adapted from http://abcnews.go.com/blogs/headlines/2013/11/lava-mae-creating-showers-on-wheels-for-the-homeless/

May 16

Walkers for Tiny Patients

The children undergoing physical therapy at our Mercy Ships dockside rehab center needed miniature walkers. There were only five available, and we needed five times that number.

Word spread to crewmember Tom, who was in charge of maintenance projects. He and his wife came up with a very creative way to use some excess materials that were destined to be discarded. The result was an abundant supply of miniature walkers.

Of course the rehab team and the tiny patients were thrilled.

Isn't it amazing what a merciful heart mixed with God-given creativity and God-given talents can do?

Mother Teresa said, *"Good works are the links that form a chain of love."* Start forging a chain of love by showing kindness to someone today.

> ***"Let every skilled and talented man among you come, and make everything that the Lord has commanded:"*** **(Exodus 35:10 AMP)**

Mercy Minute Volume 68, Script 43; by Windsor Marchesi, staff writer; from interview with Physical Therapist Dean Hufstedler; 2016-17 AFM *Benin Field Service;*

May 17

EMT to OR3

Carron Meney volunteers as a physician onboard our hospital ship, and she wrote a blog about an amazing experience:

"An announcement came over the PA: 'Attention, all crew: Emergency Medical Team to Operating Theater 3.'

When we arrived in the OR, it was pretty obvious something was very, very wrong. One of the main blood vessels in the patient's neck had ruptured.

The on-call doctor was applying abdominal pressure. I started squeezing units of fluid and blood through the IV as quickly as possible. Crew with B-positive blood rushed to donate. And surgeons packed the wound to prevent more bleeding.

The patient was stabilized.

And God reminded me again that He is sovereign. And He is the Great Physician."

Merciful hearts, plus God, always make an unbeatable team.

> ***"Yes, I will bless the Lord and not forget the glorious things He does for me. He forgives all my sins. He heals me. He ransoms me from hell. He surrounds me with loving-kindness and tender mercies."*** **(Psalm 103:2-4 TLB)**

Mercy Minute Volume 68, Script 38; by Nancy Predaina, Special Projects Writer/Editor; from "From EMT to OR3," blog of Carron Meney, 10/30/16; used with permission;

May 18

Traveling on Kindness

Leon Logothetis used to be a broker—sitting at a desk, working 12-hour days. Something had to change.

So, he designed a mission with two goals in mind: to travel the world on nothing but the kindness of strangers and to raise funds for Make a Wish International.

He got on his yellow motorcycle and set out—no money, no food, nowhere to stay—just a belief in the generosity of people.

Compassionate people gave him assistance. In Pittsburgh, after a dozen people turned him down, a homeless man offered him food and shelter. Leon says, *"That's where the magic is—connection, heart to heart."*

So, how far can kindness take you? Leon would say "a long, long way!" Connect heart-to-heart with someone today.

"Do not forget to show hospitality to strangers, for by so doing some people have shown hospitality to angels without knowing it."
(Hebrews 13:2 NIV)

Mercy Minute Volume 68, Script 58; https://gma.yahoo.com/blogs/abc-blogs/far-kindness-man-traveling-world-strangers-generosity-135537242.html?vp=1

May 19

Firsts

Eight-year-old Valentin suffered severe burn injuries. He was the first surgery patient during our hospital ship's 2016 field service in Benin, West Africa.

The crew of the Mercy Ship is a "walking blood bank." Volunteer nurse Elizabeth was the first in line to donate, hoping her blood would be a perfect match for the patient.

Elizabeth was assigned to care for Valentin. She learned that her blood donation had been used during his surgery. Elizabeth says, *"I was his nurse for the first three days, which made it all the more personal and special for me. The first blood donor, taking care of the first surgical patient, who was the first to need blood ... my blood. Pretty cool, if you ask me!"*

It IS cool! Be the first in line to show mercy to someone today.

"But a Samaritan, as he traveled, came where the man was; and when he saw him, he took pity on him. He went to him and bandaged his wounds, pouring on oil and wine. Then he put the man on his own donkey, brought him to an inn and took care of him." **(Luke 10:33-34 NIV)**

"One of the secrets of life is that all that is really worth doing is what we do for others." **(Lewis Carroll)**

Mercy Minute Volume 69, Script 33; by Windsor Marchesi; from interview with Elizabeth Harter;2016-2017 AFM Benin Field Service;

May 20

Officer Paul

Juliana, age 14, and her brother Fabian, age 12, locked their bikes to a post outside a Walmart in Albuquerque, New Mexico. But, when they came out, only a broken lock was left there! How were they going to go home? Then a policeman named Officer Paul walked by. He knew the neighborhood, and he knew the kids' parents had worked hard to buy the bikes. Now, normal procedure was just to take a statement. But Officer Paul took the kids into the store to a display of new bikes. He said, *"You can't get around without a bike. Pick your favorite. I'm buying!"* So the two kids left the store with new bikes, big smiles, and a favorite policeman.

You know, mercy is often the correct procedure. And YOU can brighten someone's day by showing mercy today.

***"If you see some brother or sister in need and have the means to do something about it but turn a cold shoulder and do nothing, what happens to God's love? It disappears. And you made it disappear."* (1 John 3:17 MSG)**

***"The greatest single cause of atheism in the world today is Christians who acknowledge Jesus with their lips and walk out the door and deny Him by their lifestyle."* (Brennan Manning)**

Mercy Minute Volume 69, Script 25; adapted from "Hero in Uniform," by Bill Holton; Woman's World, *9/5/16;*

May 21

Josh Young

The dedicated crew onboard our hospital ship, the *Africa Mercy*, represent all walks of life. Josh Young, the Food Services Manager, describes his job:

"Here on the ship I can use the gifts, talents and abilities that God has supplied me with to further the work of this community. I'll never be able to do surgery on a patient with a large tumor or rebuild a dental clinic, but I can plan, supply, cook, serve and clean up after a meal that gives others the ability to do that. I know an army marches on its stomach, and the level of food served can make a big difference on the morale of the crew."

Yes, every job is vitally important. And mercy is often a group effort. I challenge you to join with others and find a way to make a difference in your community.

"He creates each of us by Christ Jesus to join Him in the work He does, the good work He has gotten ready for us to do, work we had better be doing." **(Ephesians 2:10 MSG)**

⚓ The *Africa Mercy* and the *Anastasis* docked side-by-side in the port of Monrovia, Liberia, in May 2007 for a Passing of the Torch ceremony. The torch was made from wood from three Mercy Ships: the *Caribbean Mercy*, the *Anastasis*, and the *Good Samaritan (Island Mercy)*.

Mercy Minute Volume 66, Script 32; by Nancy Predaina, Special Projects Writer/Editor; from questionnaire from Church Relations completed by Josh Young; 2015-16 AFM *Madagascar Field Service;*

May 22

Faharoa and Elina

Five-year-old Faharoa had a benign tumor that made her lips large and purple. Six-year-old Elina had severe burns that welded her right arm to her body. The girls received surgery and physical therapy onboard our hospital ship over several months. And they also received love and acceptance from the nurses. Fingernails were painted, songs were sung and stories were read.

And something wonderful happened! The girls' true personalities began to emerge. They giggled, they played, and they were healed. It was amazing to watch the newfound hope in their eyes.

As the wise sage Dr. Seuss wrote, *"Unless someone like you cares a whole awful lot, nothing is going to get better. It's not."*

Make the world a better place by proving YOU care "a whole awful lot."

***"Do not merely look out for your own personal interests, but also for the interests of others."* (Philippians 2:4 AMP)**

Mercy Minute Volume 66, Script 41; from story by Sharon Walls, AFM *staff writer; 06/06/2016, 2015-16* AFM *Madagascar Field Service;*

May 23

Surgery in a Cave

Dr. Paul McMaster volunteers with Doctors Without Borders. He said, *"I've worked in a lot of difficult situations before, but none like my emergency assignment in the conflict zone in northwest Syria."* Inside a dusty chalk cave, they created a fully-equipped sterile environment. The team set up an inflatable operating tent and six emergency beds.

It was definitely well-used. They treated a man who had been shot in the chest. They removed shrapnel from the faces of two babies. They treated diabetics and children with asthma. They even performed Cesarean sections.

It's amazing what hearts of mercy can accomplish in difficult situations!

Look around your community and—even if it's a difficult situation—find a way to show mercy today.

"For I am convinced that neither death, nor life, nor angels, nor principalities, nor things present, nor things to come, nor powers, nor height, nor depth, nor any other created thing, will be able to separate us from the love of God, which is in Christ Jesus our Lord."
(Romans 8:38-39 NASB)

Mercy Minute Volume 69, Script 2; from promotional mailing received from Doctors Without Borders, September 2016;

May 24

Bowed No More

Romino is a three-year-old bundle of energy. And he doesn't let his bowed legs stop him from having fun! But he does hear the whispers of the other children calling him "*bancale*," the French word for bowed legs.

Romino's family lives in the developing country of Madagascar and survive on less than two U.S. dollars a day. How could they afford the surgery their son needed?

The answer is our hospital ship, the *Africa Mercy!* The Mercy Ships orthopedic program straightened Romino's legs—for free!

Now Romino can go to school knowing that he is no longer "*bancale*." His mother says, "*His legs have a story, and now I want to build his future.*"

A new future—thanks to mercy. And you can help someone start building a new future by showing mercy today.

"'For I know the plans and thoughts that I have for you,' says the Lord, 'plans for peace and well-being and not for disaster, to give you a future and a hope.'" **(Jeremiah 29:11 AMP)**

Mercy Minute Volume 64, Script 19; from patient interview by Tanya Sierra, AFM *staff writer; 2014-2015* AFM *Madagascar Field Service;*

May 25

Dr. Gary and Paul

Dr. Gary Parker, a skilled maxillofacial surgeon, is chief surgeon onboard our hospital ship. He described the transformation of a patient named Paul:

"His nose had been lost when he was just 15 years old. For the next 16 years, without a nose, Paul didn't fit people's understanding of 'normal.'

So, we were able to create living tissue where his nose had been and graft a shaped nose back onto his face.

I saw the return of hope for Paul—the light that came back into his eyes. He started to laugh, to smile. He engaged with people.

I see the seeds of hope planted every day in people like Paul."

Every time you show love and kindness to someone, you're planting seeds of hope.

***"Hope deferred makes the heart sick; but when dreams come true at last, there is life and joy."* (Proverbs 13:12 TLB)**

Mercy Minute Volume 61, Script 13; from letter from Dr. Gary Parker for January 2015 newsletter;

May 26

New Life, New Home

William knew his home was in grave disrepair. He could sense the uneven flooring. He even felt the raindrops penetrating his roof. But he couldn't *see* the problems because he was blinded by cataracts.

His five-year-old son had to be his guide, and his wife had to earn the income.

But everything changed when Mercy Ships arrived in Madagascar. A simple, free, 20-minute surgery restored William's sight within 24 hours!

William was able actually to see the state of his home. He immediately went to work to rebuild it. And eight months later, he and his family were enjoying their new house! William says,
"I have a better life, a life of happiness."

Yes, mercy provided a new life and a new home for William. And you can help repair someone's life by showing mercy.

"For with God nothing [is or ever] shall be impossible."
(Luke 1:37 AMP)

***"You don't choose your family. They are God's gift to you, as you are to them."* (Desmond Tutu)**

Mercy Minute Volume 65, Script 10; by Tanya Sierra, staff writer; from patient interview; 2015-2016 AFM *Madagascar Field Service;*

May 27

Chief Master Sgt. Richard Etchberger

During the Vietnam War, Chief Master Sergeant Richard Etchberger and 18 other men manned a tiny radar station on top of one of the tallest mountains in Laos. It was a secret mission.

North Vietnamese troops attacked the station. Most of Dick's crew were killed. Single-handedly, he held off enemy forces with an M-16 while directing air strikes to the area. He further risked his life to place three wounded soldiers in the rescue sling hanging from a helicopter. As he climbed into the sling himself . . . sadly, he was mortally wounded.

Forty-two years later, the files were declassified. Dick Etchberger's three sons received the Medal of Honor from President Obama on behalf of their father.

During May, we celebrate Memorial Day, and I encourage you to pay tribute to those who have served our country so bravely.

***"Greater love has no one than this: to lay down one's life for one's friends."* (John 15:13 NIV)**

⚓ On May 27, 1986, Don Stephens, Alan Williams (another crew member), and Costas Macris (a friend in Athens) were acquitted of charges of proselytizing in Greece. The "Athens III" trial set a precedent in Greek religious freedom.

Mercy Minute Volume 47, Script 51; by Nancy Predaina, Special Projects Writer/Editor; from "Awarding Chief Etchberger the Medal of Honor," www.whitehouse.gov.blog; 9/21/2010;

May 28

Arlington Ladies

As many as 30 service personnel and veterans are laid to rest in Arlington National Cemetery on any given weekday. Each funeral includes an honor guard, a rifle volley, taps, a folded American flag … and one more thing … comforting words from an Arlington Lady. She also presents an envelope with a condolence card from the Chief of Staff and her personally handwritten note.

Arlington Ladies began in 1948 when the Air Force Chief of Staff and his wife Gladys noticed that sometimes the military chaplain was the only person at a funeral. Groups later formed for the Navy and the Army. One member says, *"We do it from our hearts. My heart breaks at every funeral."*

What a patriotic act of mercy! Please say a special prayer for all our service personnel and their families.

***"The Lord is close to the brokenhearted and saves those who are crushed in spirit."* (Psalm 34:18 NIV)**

Mercy Minute Volume 69, Script 45; from "A Personal Touch at Duty's End," by Marsha Mercer; AARP Bulletin; *November 2016;*

May 29

Priscilla's Tickles

One day, Nurse Noel Grant was working at her desk on our hospital ship, the *Africa Mercy*, when she had an unexpected visitor! Four-year-old Priscilla was recovering from leg surgery and wanted to play. So, she began to poke the side of a very ticklish Noel. To Priscilla's delight, Noel would giggle out loud.

Noel says, *"I think we did it for about 30 minutes . . . she kept poking me, I would laugh, and it just went on and on."*

Noel's and Priscilla's giggles were infectious. Soon the laughter spread through the ward as other recovering patients enjoyed the entertainment.

You know, sometimes laughter really is the best medicine … and a fun way to show kindness to someone.

***"Our mouths were filled with laughter, our tongues with songs of joy … The Lord has done great things for us, and we are filled with joy."* (Psalm 126:2-3 NIV)**

Mercy Minute Volume 62, Script 12; by Tanya Sierra, staff writer; from crew interview; 2014-2015 AFM *Madagascar Field Service;*

May 30
Wally

Showing mercy to others provides opportunities for special moments and special friendships. Rehab Team Leader Courtney shared a special memory of a little boy named Wally:

"Wally was my orthopedic patient and friend. He had surgery to correct his bowed leg.

While he was in the hospital, he'd frequently yell out, 'Courtney! Come here!' or 'Look at this!' He had an infectious, snaggle-toothed grin.

One day he called for me as I passed by. He presented me with a paper chain necklace and said, 'I made this for you.'

My heart melted, and from then on, he was my kiddo."

Yes, mercy binds hearts together in warm friendships. Show heart-to-heart mercy to someone today.

***"You have put gladness in my heart, more than when their grain and new wine abound."* (Psalm 4:7 NASB)**

Mercy Minute Volume 61, Script 65; from story submitted to Catherine Murphy, staff writer, by Courtney Waldron, Rehab Team Leader; 2013-14 AFM Congo Field Service;

May 31

Futbol Project

Soccer is the most popular sport in the world. But many of the world's children make soccer balls out of whatever they can find—rags, for example.

In 2010 Tim and Lisa founded One World Futbol Project. They took a cheap, indestructible plastic and turned it into a ball that will survive anything—including punctures and being driven over by a car. An investment by superstar Sting really got the ball rolling—literally.

For every ball they sell, one is donated. They've donated over one million balls to kids in 170 countries.

Tim says, *"The beauty of it is that they know what to do with it the minute it gets into their hands ...and in front of their feet."*

Bringing joy to children is a wonderful act of mercy. Perhaps there's a way you can help children in your community.

"When you help the poor you are lending to the Lord—and He pays wonderful interest on your loan!" **(Proverbs 19:17 TLB)**

"You can find Calcutta anywhere in the world. You only need two eyes to see. Everywhere in the world there are people that are not loved, people that are not wanted nor desired, people that no one will help, people that are pushed away or forgotten. And this is the greatest poverty." **(Mother Teresa)**

Mercy Minute Volume 68, Script 54; adapted from https://www.oneworldplayproject.com/benefits-of-play/power-of-play-story/

JUNE

"Words kill, words give life; they're either poison or fruit—you choose." (Proverbs 18:21 MSG)

June 1

The Next Step

Imagine being eight years old and having legs so badly bowed you could bounce a beach ball through them. Imagine going onboard a big white hospital ship to have a free surgery. Sounds wonderful, doesn't it?

But it's also hard work and often painful. You have to spend hours every week strengthening your beautiful legs. You practice walking down the hospital hallway and lifting your legs. And it hurts.

But the physical therapists, nurses and mothers cheer you on. They say, *"You can do it! You can make it to the end of the hall."* So, you stop crying, you look up … and you take the next step … and the next step.

That's a great picture of what happens on our Mercy Ships. And you can help someone take the next step just by being an encouraging voice today.

"So speak encouraging words to one another. Build up hope so you'll all be together in this, no one left out, no one left behind. I know you're already doing this; just keep on doing it."
(1 Thessalonians 5:11 MSG)

Mercy Minute Volume 69, Script 55; by Anna Psiaki, staff writer; personal experience; 2016-2017 AFM Benin Field Service;

June 2

Recycled Cycles

Paul Watson remembers how happy he was to get a handed-down bike. So, the 15-year-old restores damaged bikes and donates them to needy children.

It all started when the vice-principal at his high school brought in a damaged bike for him to work on in his life skills class. Since then, he's refurbished and donated 50 bicycles to elementary school children. The school even converted a storage room for a workshop for Paul. His new goal is to refurbish 100 bikes.

He says, *"It makes me feel so good to see the smiles on kids' faces. They can't believe it's right in front of them—their own bike!"*

Paul found a great way to use his skills and show God's love in helping others. I challenge you to find a way to use YOUR talents to help others.

***"Whatever you do, work at it with all your heart, as working for the Lord, not for human masters, since you know that you will receive an inheritance from the Lord as a reward. It is the Lord Christ you are serving."* (Colossians 3:23-24 NIV)**

***"It is one of the beautiful compensations in this life that no one can sincerely try to help another without helping himself."* (Ralph Waldo Emerson)**

Mercy Minute Volume 69, Script 56; adapted from "Ride On," https://parade.com/553699/lharris-2/kids-helping-kids-inspiring-stories-from-young-people-who-are-giving-back/

June 3

Aissa's Transformation

Noma is a terrible flesh-eating bacteria that destroys soft tissue, leaving its few survivors terribly deformed. Crew member Ali described the emotional transformation of seven-year-old Aissa:

"We saw her suffering in her hunched shoulders and defiant anger.

I'll never forget the day she tripped and fell. She immediately curled into a ball on the floor, ready for the beating she anticipated for being clumsy.

Her wonder at being picked up and comforted was profound, and I think that's the day her heart really started to heal along with her face.

She blossomed into a little girl who would throw her arms around our necks and declare in her loudest voice, 'I lub you!'"

Mercy and love profoundly transform lives. And you can choose to be a part of that by showing mercy and love to others every day.

"There is no room in love for fear. Well-formed love banishes fear. Since fear is crippling, a fearful life—fear of death, fear of judgment—is one not yet fully formed in love."
(1 John 4:18 MSG)

Mercy Minute Volume 55, Script 60; adapted from blog of Ali Chandra; http://alirae.net 8/4/13; used with permission;

June 4

Hotel Employee Returns Money

Essa Khan is the father of five children. He cleans rooms at a hotel in Pakistan. Guest often leave items behind. He was shocked to discover $50,000 left in one guest's room.

Now, Mr. Khan earned only $235 per month. Imagine how his family could have benefited from $50,000. But Mr. Khan immediately reported his discovery, and the money was returned to its very relieved owner.

When asked about his honesty, Mr. Khan explained, *"My family upbringing teaches me nothing else. All I want the world to know is that there are many good people in Pakistan. Everybody is not a terrorist here."*

You see, honesty and compassion spring from a merciful heart that does the right thing! And honesty and kindness are always the right thing.

***"To do what is right and just is more acceptable to the Lord than sacrifice."* (Proverbs 21:3 NIV)**

Mercy Minute Volume 42, Script 24; from "Cleaner Wins Acclaim after Handing in Cash," by Syed Hasan; www.bbc.co.uk/news July 12, 2010;

June 5

Bernadette and Her Mom

Bernadette packed her bags, lied to her mother, and bought a train ticket to the coast of Congo . . . to the *Africa Mercy*, our hospital ship.

You see, Bernadette had a large tumor covering one eye. No one would touch her, except her mother. But she knew her mother would worry about this trip.

Well, a free surgery removed the unsightly tumor, and Bernadette headed home, hoping her mother wouldn't be angry. After all, she was old enough to make her own decisions . . . she was 54! But, if you would ask her if you're ever too old to spare your mother from worrying, she'll say, *"No!"*

Yes, a mother's love is a wonderful reflection of God's unconditional love. And you reflect God's love when you show mercy to others.

***"Honor your father and mother. This is the first of God's Ten Commandments that ends with a promise. And this is the promise: that if you honor your father and mother, yours will be a long life, full of blessing."* (Ephesians 6:2-3 TLB)**

Mercy Minute Volume 55, Script 40; from "The Truth about Bernadette," patient story by Catherine Murphy, staff writer, 2013-14 AFM *Congo Field Service;*

June 6

A Cow for Wasti's Mama

Volunteer nurse Ali recently wrote this blog entry about hope and healing . . . and a cow:

"Baby Wasti's mama sold the only thing she had—a cow—to pay for the journey to our Mercy Ship so her baby could have his cleft lip repaired.

Mercy Ships talks a lot about bringing hope and healing. This time, it was hope, healing . . . and a new cow. When they left the ship, Wasti's mama had a little pouch tied around her neck. It contained money collected from all the nurses and doctors for the purchase of a new cow. Now she would have a way to provide for her children."

Yes, mercy comes in all forms—even a cow! Meeting a practical need is a wonderful way to show mercy.

***"Never walk away from someone who deserves help; your hand is God's hand for that person."* (Proverbs 3:27 MSG)**

***"The very fact that God has placed a certain soul in our way is a sign that God wants us to do something for him or her. It is not chance; it has been planned by God. We are bound by conscience to help him or her."* (Mother Teresa)**

Mercy Minute Volume 54, Script 37; from blog of Ali Chandra, alirae.net, 8/7/2013; used with permission;

June 7

Audie Murphy's Heroic Widow

Audie Murphy was an actor and the most decorated World War II hero. But he wasn't good with money. His widow, Pamela, was left with large debts. So, in 1971 she took a job as a clerk at a VA Hospital … and became an angel of mercy.

Pamela Murphy walked the hallways with a clipboard in hand—making sure "her boys and girls" got the care they needed. One vet said, *"She was our angel."* She helped veterans for 35 years—until she was 87 years old. She passed away at the age of 90—leaving a legacy of courage and mercy.

Mrs. Murphy turned a difficult situation into an opportunity to show mercy. Be on the lookout for every opportunity to show kindness to others.

"Open your mouth for the mute, for the rights of all who are unfortunate and defenseless; open your mouth, judge righteously, and administer justice for the afflicted and needy."
(Proverbs 31:8-9 AMP)

"The ultimate measure of a man is not where he stands in moments of comfort and convenience, but where he stands at times of challenge and controversy." **(Martin Luther King Jr.)**

Mercy Minute Volume 44, Script 12; from "Pam Murphy Was Veterans' Friend and Advocate," by Dennis McCarthy; www.dailynews.com 4/14/10;

June 8

Pulcherie Sees Her Baby

Ask any mother, and she will you about the first time she saw her baby. She'll describe counting fingers and toes.

Pulcherie lost the vision in her left eye in a childhood accident. Later, she lost the sight in her right eye due to a cataract.

Pulcherie had free cataract surgery onboard the *Africa Mercy* in Congo. When she saw her 11-month-old baby girl for the first time, she exclaimed, *"She's so beautiful! She's so beautiful!"*

Now Pulcherie can describe counting her baby's fingers and toes. And she can tell you how she fell in love with her baby all over again—truly love at first sight!

You know, Pulcherie's moment of mercy and joy was made possible by compassionate volunteers and donors. Consider volunteering some of your time and resources to a worthy cause.

"But we behaved gently when we were among you, like a devoted mother tenderly caring for her own children."
(1 Thessalonians 2:7 AMP)

⚓ The *Anastasis* sailed to Madagascar in 1996 for the first Mercy Ships field service in East Africa.

Mercy Minute Volume 56, Script 10; from patient story by Catherine Murphy, staff writer; 2013-2014 AFM *Congo Field Service;*

June 9

Mercy at a Coffee Shop

Nancy, a Mercy Ships writer and editor, was enjoying lunch at a coffee shop when she witnessed a wonderful Mercy Minute.

A young woman entered. It was obvious by the scarf covering her head, her lack of eyebrows, and her ashen complexion that she was battling cancer. She looked exhausted and discouraged.

Then an older woman approached her. She was a cancer survivor, and she immediately recognized the younger woman's despair. She spent a great deal of time encouraging her new friend.

The young woman left the coffee shop with a quicker step and a lighter heart. Nancy says, *"Opportunities to show mercy surround us every day. We just have to look for them."*

So … pay attention and take advantage of every opportunity to show encouraging mercy to others!

"What a wonderful God we have—He is the Father of our Lord Jesus Christ, the source of every mercy, and the One who so wonderfully comforts and strengthens us in our hardships and trials. And why does He do this? So that when others are troubled, needing our sympathy and encouragement, we can pass on to them this same help and comfort God has given us."
(2 Corinthians 1:3-4 TLB)

Mercy Minute Volume 44, Script 62; by Nancy Predaina, Special Projects Writer/Editor; personal observation 12/3/10;

June 10

Please Look Up!

A variety of dialects are spoken in the African countries. A crew member told of a surgeon's experience with the language issue:

"When volunteer surgeon Lord Ian McColl was in Togo, he was trying to communicate with a patient. He wanted her to look up so he could put drops in her eyes. So, he asked the translator to teach him how to say, 'Please look up' in the Ewe dialect. In that language, it translates as 'Lift your eyes up to God.'

Now, whenever Lord Ian sees a Togolese crew member, they say in unison, 'Lift your eyes up to God.'"

What a wonderful greeting—and what a great reminder that God is the source of all mercy!

"I will lift up my eyes to the mountains; from where shall my help come? My help comes from the Lord, Who made heaven and earth."
(Psalm 121:1-2 NASB)

Mercy Minute Volume 54, Script 48; by Nancy Predaina, Special Projects Writer/Editor; based on email from Catherine Murphy, staff writer; 9/5/13; 2013-14 AFM Congo Field Service;

June 11

A Dose of Love

Acetaminophen, commonly known by the brand name Tylenol, is a mild pain reliever and fever reducer. It became the focus of an interesting discussion. A Mercy Ships nurse described the encounter:

"Some local nurses commented to Mercy Ships nurses that they were surprised about how little pain medication we need to give our patients. They speculated, 'Maybe it's because the surgery is done more carefully. Or maybe it's because when the medicine is given with love, it has double the effect!'"

I think both explanations are correct. You know, there's a song that says, "a spoonful of sugar helps the medicine go down." But maybe it should say, "a heart full of mercy helps the medicine go down." Why don't you give a generous dose of mercy to someone today?

***"Let everything you do be done in love [motivated and inspired by God's love for us]."* (1 Corinthians 16:14 AMP)**

***"Thank You, Lord, for the grace of Your love, for the grace of friendship, and for the grace of beauty."* (Henri J.M. Nouwen)**

Mercy Minute Volume 56, Script 1; by Catherine Murphy; based on presentation of Kirstie Randall, Ward Supervisor, to AFM Community Meeting, 10/24/13; 2013-14 AFM Congo Field Service;

June 12
Mother Robin

Outside an Indonesian hospital, two women have waited all night. You see, the hospital is holding their newborn babies until the medical bills are paid. Meanwhile, they can visit twice a day. But if they can't pay, they may have to give their children up for adoption.

Midwife Robin Lim, affectionately called "Mother Robin," has opened two free birthing clinics. Since the average family earns only $8 per day, most women give birth without a skilled attendant. Robin says, *"My sister died of a complication of pregnancy ... I decided not to get angry. I decided to become part of the solution."*

Mercy is always part of the solution. And you can be part of the solution by showing mercy to someone today.

"If you are angry, don't sin by nursing your grudge. Don't let the sun go down with you still angry—get over it quickly; for when you are angry, you give a mighty foothold to the devil."
(Ephesians 4:26-27 TLB)

Mercy Minute Volume 48, Script 22; adapted from "Mother Robin Delivers for Poor Women in Indonesia," www.cnn.com; 3/10/2011;

June 13

Bernadette

Bernadette courageously made the long train journey from her village to the coast of Congo. A large tumor covered her right eye for more than 20 years. She had to lift it up to see her steps, her path, and, finally, her destination . . . our hospital ship.

Bernadette is only 5 feet tall. But what she lacks in height, she makes up for in spunk.

Thanks to a free surgery, her tumor is gone. In response, sometimes she erupts in loud, happy laughter. Sometimes she jumps up and down. She says her new look *"is going to be good for business"* as she sells her homemade peanut butter. She might even expand by selling pastries.

Yes, mercy **is** always good for business. And you can brighten someone's future by showing mercy today.

***"May the favor of the Lord our God rest on us; establish the work of our hands for us—yes, establish the work of our hands."* (Psalm 90:17 NIV)**

Mercy Minute Volume 56, Script 5; from "The Truth about Bernadette," patient story by Catherine Murphy, staff writer, 2013-14 AFM *Congo Field Service;*

June 14

A Pink Bow

Nurse Natalie Bullock described an encounter with Alice, a nine-year-old patient from Uganda who suffered serious burns:

"After I changed the dressing on her eye, I told her I had a surprise for her. So, I made her close her uncovered eye. When she opened it, I handed her a mirror. I had added flowers and a pink bow to her bandage.

She stared in the mirror, grinning from ear to ear, and then suddenly came alive—dancing, singing, laughing and prancing around the ward. Everyone told her how beautiful she was.

I love my job! Transformations happen daily!"

Yes, mercy really does transform lives. And when you show kindness to others, **you** are part of the transformations.

"He has made everything beautiful in its time. He has also set eternity in the human heart; yet no one can fathom what God has done from beginning to end." **(Ecclesiastes 3:11 NIV)**

Mercy Minute Volume 56, Script 3; by Catherine Murphy, staff writer; from Natalie Bullock's Facebook post on October 20, 2013; used with permission; 2013-14 AFM Congo Field Service;

June 15

A Father's Heart

Jeni Stepien's father was murdered. His heart was donated to a man named Arthur Thomas. Over the years, the two families kept in touch by letters and calls.

So, when Jeni was planning her wedding 10 years later, she asked Thomas to walk her down the aisle. They met face-to-face for the first time the night before the wedding. Thomas placed Jeni's hand on his wrist so she could feel her father's heartbeat. Jeni said, "*The whole family is here now. It's like everybody is here.*"

Thomas was delighted to be a part of the wedding. He said, "*What greater honor could a person have than walking the daughter of the man who's given his heart to me.*"

Now you go, give honor to your heavenly Father's heart of mercy as you help someone today.

"*Watch over your heart with all diligence, for from it flow the springs of life.*" (Proverbs 4:23 AMP)

Mercy Minute Volume 66, Script 42; adapted from "Bride Is Walked Down the Aisle by Man who Received Her Dad's Heart," by Christopher Dawson; www.cnn.com 8/8/16;

June 16

A Son Carries His Father

A long line of people stretched down the street and around the corner. It was medical Screening Day in Benin, West Africa. Our Mercy Ship had come to offer free surgeries to those in need.

A young man stood patiently in line, with his father on his *back*. He'd carried his father all the way from their distant village. And, although he didn't look it, he was very heavy.

Mercy Ships crew member Kelly Grizzard said, *"I had to put him in a wheelchair to bring him inside. It touched my heart."*

Thanks to his son's love, this father received the life-changing surgery he desperately needed.

Love and mercy go to great lengths to help those in need.

"But anyone who won't care for his own relatives when they need help, especially those living in his own family, has no right to say he is a Christian. Such a person is worse than the heathen." **(1 Timothy 5:8 TLB)**

"It is easy to love the people far away. It is not always easy to love those close to us. It is easier to give a cup of rice to relieve hunger than to relieve the loneliness and pain of someone unloved in our own home. Bring love into your home for this is where our love for each other must start." **(Mother Teresa)**

Mercy Minute Volume 37, Script 3; by Richard Brock, staff writer; personal observation; 2009 AFM Benin Field Service;

June 17

Helping Daddy

A man was installing large stone steps in his backyard. His five-year-old daughter begged to help. He suggested that she sing a song to encourage him. She said, *"No. I want to* HELP*!"*

So, he carefully let her put her hands on the rocks while he moved them. It took much longer to get the job done. But, at the end of the day, he had his new steps … and a daughter who was very proud of their accomplishment. She announced at dinner, *"Me and Dad made steps!"*

This earthly father allowed his little daughter to help him with a task. In the same way, our heavenly Father allows us to help—including helping those less fortunate than ourselves.

***"Just as a father loves his children, so the Lord loves those who fear and worship Him [with awe-filled respect and deepest reverence]."* (Psalm 103:13 AMP)**

Mercy Minute Volume 64, Script 4; adapted from "Me and Dad," by Philip Yancey; Our Daily Bread 90-Day Sample Edition; *Devotional for Day 25;*

June 18

John's Merciful Reunion

John lived in Liberia, West Africa. He had prospered enough to send three of his children to be educated in Monrovia, the capital city. Then a 14-year-long civil war destroyed his livelihood. It also cut him off from his children, 300 miles away. For years, he didn't know if they were dead or alive.

To make matters worse, John developed a tumor on his jaw. The Red Cross flew him to Monrovia for a free surgery onboard our *Africa Mercy*. While there, he found his children and discovered that he had 12 grandchildren!

He said, "*When I die, my children will be able to say, 'We got to see our father one last time.'*"

You see, mercy provided healing—and a family reunion!

***"Don't you see that children are God's best gift? The fruit of the womb His generous legacy? Like a warrior's fistful of arrows are the children of a vigorous youth. Oh, how blessed are you parents, with your quivers full of children!"* (Psalm 127:3-5 MSG)**

***"Nothing can bring a real sense of security into the home except true love."* (Rev. Billy Graham)**

Mercy Minute Volume 34, Script 60; from Mercy Ships Liberia Report 2007; Mike Osborne, staff writer;

June 19

Christine's Funeral

A volunteer writer on our hospital ship wrote about a funeral she attended for her friend Christine:

"*Words like* inspiring, caring, loving, radiant—*I've never heard these words repeated so many times in one day! This woman was full of love for God and His people.*

Whenever doctors fussed over her, she wished they'd fuss over 'others who needed it more.' She made these bright, fluffy 'chemo hats' for other cancer patients. She cooked and baked endlessly for other people. You know, she even recorded herself reading children's stories for her two soon-to-be-born grandchildren.

She saw every day as an opportunity to show love to someone."

What a wonderful legacy of mercy! We should all follow Christine's example and consider every day an opportunity to show mercy to someone.

> ***"These commandments that I give you today are to be on your hearts. Impress them on your children. Talk about them when you sit at home and when you walk along the road, when you lie down and when you get up."* (Deuteronomy 6:6-7 NIV)**

Mercy Minute Volume 69, Script 49; by Eunice Hiew, staff writer; AFM *2014-15 Madagascar Field Service; used with permission from Christine's husband;*

June 20

Lauren Serves

Lauren served as an army nurse for five years before leaving the military. But her husband was still serving and was deployed to Afghanistan. She said, *"I decided I'd rather strengthen myself spiritually and use my skills as a nurse than sit around for months on end waiting for my husband to return."*

So, Lauren served as a pediatric ICU nurse onboard our hospital ship. She felt pain for those who were suffering. And she felt satisfaction and joy for those who walked away healed. She said, *"I am thankful I made the decision to volunteer on the Mercy Ship. It has changed me for the better and has restored meaning and purpose in my life."*

Volunteering to help others is always a great decision!

***"God is not unjust; He will not forget your work and the love you have shown Him as you have helped His people and continue to help them."* (Hebrews 6:10 NIV)**

***"The best way to find yourself is to lose yourself in the service of others."* (Mahatma Gandhi)**

Mercy Minute Volume 69, Script 57; by Nancy Predaina, Special Projects Writer/Editor; from Mercy Ships Media Questionnaire of Lauren Blake Ritchie; 5/11/16; 2015-16 AFM Madagascar Field Service;

June 21

Daniel Walks

Daniel was born in Benin, West Africa, with deformities in the muscles and tendons of his legs. His mother, Odette, told the story:

"When Daniel was two years old, we wanted to help him stand and walk. But we could see that his legs wouldn't straighten. We went to many hospitals and tried many things, even traditional healers. But nothing helped.

So for eight years, I carried him everywhere. I carried him to the table to eat. I carried him to bed at night. And I worried. What would happen to Daniel if I died? He needed me for everything!

Then the Mercy Ship arrived. Wonderful surgeons operated on Daniel—for free! When he took his first steps, I was overjoyed. I couldn't believe it!"

Daniel's life was completely transformed, and his mother's anxiety was relieved … all because of mercy!

> ***"I will tell of the kindnesses of the Lord, the deeds for which He is to be praised, according to all the Lord has done for us—yes, the many good things He has done for Israel, according to His compassion and many kindnesses."* (Isaiah 63:7 NIV)**

⚓ Mercy Ships offers a Nutritional Agriculture Course to train agriculturalists in the countries we serve. Then the new trainers return home to train others. Good nutrition is essential to good health.

Mercy Minute Volume 39, Script 23; from patient story by Carmen Radley, staff writer, AFM 2009 *Benin Field Service;*

June 22

A Birthday for Mercy

Lynne Golodner decided to celebrate her 40th birthday by doing 40 things during the year to make a difference in the world.

For example, she raised money for the Leukemia and Lymphoma Society. She taught a poetry class at her worship center. She used her marketing skills to help a small business get publicity.

One day at the supermarket, she saw a veteran and thanked him for his service. Then she left a gift card with the cashier to pay for his groceries. Lynne says, *"The mission has truly changed the way I approach my family, my business and my life ... I want to keep this momentum going."*

Follow Lynne's example, which happens to be the example of Jesus, and set out on a mission of mercy today.

"Tell those who are rich not to be proud and not to trust in their money, which will soon be gone, but their pride and trust should be in the living God who always richly gives us all we need for our enjoyment. Tell them to use their money to do good. They should be rich in good works and should give happily to those in need, always being ready to share with others whatever God has given them."
(1Timothy 6:17-18 TLB)

***"No one has ever become poor by giving."* (Anne Frank)**

Mercy Minute Volume 48, Script 46; adapted from "Making a Difference," Woman's Day, *March 2012;*

June 23

Marthaline

A colorful washcloth hung from Marthaline's mouth to hide her huge tumor. The humiliation and separation caused by the growth had stolen her life. The tumor had grown for three years and was beginning to suffocate her. She walked through three neighboring countries to get to the ship as her last shred of hope. Then she stood in line for the screening for a possible free surgery onboard a Mercy Ship.

Marthaline was chosen, and Dr. Thurman Crocker removed the tumor. Then Marthaline went to the Mercy Ships dental clinic for replacement of her teeth destroyed by the tumor. Crew members even raised money to pay for her college tuition.

Thanks to the compassion of others, this lovely young woman got her life back!

Isn't it amazing what can be achieved when people join their efforts in showing mercy?

"Are you called to help others? Do it with all the strength and energy that God supplies so that God will be glorified through Jesus Christ—to Him be glory and power forever and ever. Amen."
(1 Peter 4:11 TLB)

"We are not cisterns made for hoarding; we are channels made for sharing." **(Rev. Billy Graham)**

Mercy Minute Volume 24, Script 56; adapted from story by Scott Harrison, staff photojournalist on the Anastasis;

June 24

Nemeth Uniform Braille System

Abraham Nemeth was born blind. He loved math, but, at that time, there wasn't a Braille code for numerical equations. So, instead, he studied psychology in college and grad school.

He had trouble finding a job and decided he'd be happier as an unemployed mathematician than as an unemployed psychologist. So, he earned a doctoral degree in mathematics and devised the Nemeth Code—the universal math and science writing system for the blind. And, at age 91, he invented the Nemeth Uniform Braille System to standardize Braille codes across academic disciplines. He said, *"I'm living proof that it's better to light a candle than to curse the darkness."*

Follow his example and light a candle as you make someone's life better by showing mercy.

"For God, who said, "Let light shine out of darkness," made his light shine in our hearts to give us the light of the knowledge of God's glory displayed in the face of Christ." **(2 Corinthians 4:6 NIV)**

Mercy Minute Volume 48, Script 59; adapted from "Best Math Tool," Reader's Digest, *June/July 2010;*

June 25

Curing with Love

Sophie and Auriette have children who received free orthopedic surgeries onboard our hospital ship in Madagascar. Eunice, a volunteer writer, asked them, "What is your favorite memory of being on the ship?"

"To my surprise, they both had the same answer … a delightful answer. Their favorite memory was the way the Mercy Ships staff took care of them.

They deeply appreciated that everything we did was laced with love. The way we try to make them smile. The way we give coloring books to children during recovery time. The way we play and laugh and engage with them. Auriette worded it this way: 'You cure with love.'"

Yes, a dose of God's love accompanies every act of kindness we show to one another.

"Little children (believers, dear ones), let us not love [merely in theory] with word or with tongue [giving lip service to compassion], but in action and in truth [in practice and in sincerity, because practical acts of love are more than words]."
(1 John 3:18 AMP)

"There are many in the world who are dying for a piece of bread, but there are many more dying for a little love." **(Mother Teresa)**

Mercy Minute Volume 69, Script 52; from interview of Auriette and Sophie by Eunice Hiew, staff writer, 2014-15 AFM *Madagascar Field Service;*

June 26

Richard's Cleft Lip

Somewhere in the world—every 3 minutes—a baby is born with a cleft lip or palate. In developed countries, cleft lips are easily repaired. But Richard was born in Benin, a poor country in West Africa. Medical help was not available.

So, Richard grew up in a dark world of isolation. He said, *"I felt ashamed. I stayed in my room a lot."*

One day, when Richard was 17 years old, he heard that a hospital ship had arrived in Benin. Could it help him?

And the answer was YES. A two-hour surgery not only repaired his lip ... it repaired his life.

Richard's new life was a gift of mercy—from the compassionate hearts of volunteers and supporters.

"I bless the holy name of God with all my heart. Yes, I will bless the Lord and not forget the glorious things He does for me. He forgives all my sins. He heals me. He ransoms me from hell. He surrounds me with loving-kindness and tender mercies. He fills my life with good things! My youth is renewed like the eagle's!"

(Psalm 103:1-3 TLB)

Mercy Minute Volume 40, Script 36; from patient story by Richard Brock, staff writer, 2009 AFM *Benin Field Service;*

June 27

Wright's Law

Jeffrey Wright teaches physics at a high school in Kentucky. He's famous for wacky experiments. But there's one particularly powerful lesson.

Each year, Wright tells about his special-needs son. Adam has a rare genetic disease called Joubert Syndrome. He doesn't speak and can't control his body's movements.

Wright began to teach Adam sign language. And, one day, his son signed, "I love you."

Wright tells his students, *"That's when I knew the reason of* why *things work—it's because of love. So, in this great big universe, somebody cares about you a lot. If we care about each other . . . that's where we go from here."*

Yes, our purpose is to reflect God's love and mercy to others. Prove you care by showing kindness to someone today.

"But we Christians have no veil over our faces; we can be mirrors that brightly reflect the glory of the Lord. And as the Spirit of the Lord works within us, we become more and more like Him."
(2 Corinthians 3:18 TLB)

Mercy Minute Volume 55, Script 32; adapted from "Laws of Physics Can't Trump the Bonds of Love," by Tara Parker-Pope; NYTimes.com, 12/24/12; and "Wright's Law," by Zach Conkle; YouTube video; 12/28/12;

June 28

Prince Eddie's Wedding Ring

Prince Eddie had a problem. He wanted to wear his wedding ring—the symbol of his commitment to his wife Millicent. But his hands had been burned when he was a child. He couldn't straighten his fingers.

But one day, Prince heard that the *Africa Mercy* was docked in Benin, West Africa. Volunteer surgeons provided a free surgery onboard the hospital ship.

Now, his fingers are straight, and he can wear his wedding ring. He said, *"I can wear my wedding ring, and I am so excited! I am so grateful for the work of Mercy Ships."*

Prince Eddie's ring is a symbol of commitment … and a symbol of mercy. Make a commitment to make kindness and mercy a daily priority.

***"Commit everything you do to the Lord. Trust Him to help you do it, and He will."* (Psalm 37:5 TLB)**

***"The good you do today may be forgotten tomorrow. Do good anyway. Give the world the best you have, and it may never be enough. Give your best anyway. For you see, in the end, it is between you and God."* (Mother Teresa)**

Mercy Minute Volume 40, Script 43; from patient interview by staff writer, Megan Petock; 2009 AFM *Benin Field Service;*

June 29

Ward Warriors

A volunteer onboard our hospital ship wrote her description of what she calls "ward warriors":

"The word warrior *often conjures up images of flashing swords and war-painted faces—you know, like in the movie 'Braveheart.'*

But, the volunteers onboard the Africa Mercy *are some of the Bravest Hearts I've ever seen!*

One time, some hospital chaplains—including one with a guitar—came in and started singing happy songs. It worked on the child I was sitting next to. He just smiled and smiled.

The nurses employ a variety of preferred weapons in eliminating boredom—toys, balloons, funny facial expressions and imaginative antics.

Thank you, ward warriors, for being our patients' heroes."

Yes, anyone who shows mercy is a hero. And you can be a "brave heart" by showing mercy to someone today.

"The Lord is my strength and my shield; my heart trusts in Him, and He helps me. My heart leaps for joy, and with my song I praise Him." **(Psalm 28:7 NIV)**

Mercy Minute Volume 69, Script 58; by Eunice Hiew, staff writer; personal observation; 2014-15 AFM *Madagascar Field Service;*

June 30

Never Too Late to Read

Ed Bray served in World War II. He earned many medals, including two purple hearts. But his toughest obstacle was not being able to read. Ed determined to read one book before he died. Over the years, many people had tried unsuccessfully to teach him. Then he contacted Professor Tobi Thompson at Northeastern State University in Oklahoma. They began with weekly talks and graduated to flash cards. Finally, at the age of 90, Ed read his first book—a biography of George Washington.

Professor Thompson said, *"It gave me goose bumps—and it still does."*

It just proves you're never too old to learn . . . or to help someone else achieve their goal. Yes, sometimes mercy requires patience and persistence. I encourage you to be persistent in showing mercy to others.

***"We want each of you to show this same diligence to the very end, so that what you hope for may be fully realized."* (Hebrews 6:11 NIV)**

***"Scripture is filled with examples of men and women whom God used late in life, often with great impact—men and women who refused to use old age as an excuse to ignore what God wanted them to do."* (Rev. Billy Graham)**

Mercy Minute Volume 55, Script 38; based on "World War II Veteran Learns to Read," by Steve Hartman; http://wtvr.com/2013/04/22/ed-bray-world-war-vet-learns-to-read/;

JULY

"Let us not become weary in doing good, for at the proper time we will reap a harvest if we do not give up. Therefore, as we have opportunity, let us do good to all people, especially to those who belong to the family of believers."
(Galatians 6:9-10 NIV)

July 1

Serving Africa

Africa is a beautiful continent full of beautiful people—people with giant dreams and giant hearts. And the volunteers onboard our Mercy Ship discover that serving Africa changes them:

"I studied in Zambia. I wanted to return to Africa because of the people I met there. They showed me how to love God and love others …

And I am becoming a better person in Benin. The reason for this is because of my patients and because of the day-crew. Every day I see their love for one another. Every day I see their joy. Every day I see their belief in a big God.

Every day stereotypes are broken, fear is broken, apathy is broken. In the end, all that is left is love."

Devote yourself to serving others … and you will be changed in the process.

"We don't yet see things clearly. We're squinting in a fog, peering through a mist. But it won't be long before the weather clears and the sun shines bright! We'll see it all then, see it all as clearly as God sees us, knowing Him directly just as He knows us! But for right now, until that completeness, we have three things to do to lead us toward that consummation: trust steadily in God, hope unswervingly, love extravagantly. And the best of the three is love."
(1 Corinthians 13:12-13 MSG)

Mercy Minute Volume 70, Script 5; by Anna Psiaki, staff writer; from Kirsten Eller's personal blog; used with permission; 2016-2017 AFM *Benin Field Service;*

July 2

A Cure for Depression

Marion was battling depression and could barely drag herself out of bed.

Her counselor wisely said, *"One surefire way to feel better is to find someone needy and help them."*

So, Marion, a trained artist, volunteered to visit hospital patients. On her first day, she knocked on a patient's door. She glanced at the posted information: Coy Pritchett, age 20; condition: kidney complications, quadriplegic, depression. Opening the door, she said, *"Hi, I'm Marion. Would you like to paint a picture?"*

"Shoot, yeah!" Coy answered. And so began a relationship that blossomed into friendship. Coy painted with a brush held in his teeth as Marion held the canvas.

And Marion? Yes, she defeated depression by helping someone else.

You can brighten someone's life—and probably your own—by helping someone today.

"In everything I showed you that by working hard in this manner you must help the weak and remember the words of the Lord Jesus, that He Himself said, 'It is more blessed to give than to receive.'"
(Acts 20:35 NASB)

⚓ In 1983, the *Anastasis* conducted outreaches to Fiji, Tonga and Samoa after Tropical Cyclone Oscar.

Mercy Minute Volume 65, Script 2; by Larry Mast, staff writer; adapted from Guideposts *July 2001, by Marion Bond West;*

July 3

An Exciting Day for Rajo

The first day patients board the *Africa Mercy* is an exciting day! But those first moments can be overwhelming for patients.

Take Rajo, for example. His clubbed foot limited his mobility. He clung to his daddy's arms while Nurse Jenica greeted him. But, when he gave a little wave, Jenica knew Rajo wasn't *that* shy.

And she was right! As the two played hide and seek, Rajo ran to Jenica with his arms lifted high, waiting to be picked up.

Later that evening, Jenica thought, *"I hope, Rajo, that you feel the unconditional, limitless love that I have for you, this ship has for you, and people all over the world have for you and God has for you."*

And that's what mercy is all about … unconditional love.

"This is how God showed His love among us: He sent his one and only Son into the world that we might live through Him. This is love: not that we loved God, but that He loved us and sent His Son as an atoning sacrifice for our sins. Dear friends, since God so loved us, we also ought to love one another." **(1 John 4:9-10 NIV)**

Mercy Minute Volume 62, Script 38; by Tanya Sierra, staff writer; from crew interview; 2014-2015 AFM Madagascar Field Service;

July 4

Staff Sergeant Salvatore Guinta

It was nighttime in the Afghanistan mountains in 2007. Suddenly, Taliban fighters poured a wall of machine-gun and rifle fire into the American army platoon.

Staff Sgt. Sal Giunta rushed forward, throwing grenades and firing to save trapped soldiers. Although two soldiers later died from their wounds, he helped save the platoon from annihilation.

Sal is the first living person since the Vietnam War to receive the Medal of Honor. He says, *"I didn't run through the fire to do anything heroic or brave. I did what I believe anyone would have done."*

You see, putting your life on the line to help others is a stunning act of mercy. Take a moment on this Fourth of July to let a member of our military—or their families—know that you are thankful for their service.

***"Do nothing from selfishness or empty conceit, but with humility of mind regard one another as more important than yourselves; do not merely look out for your own personal interests, but also for the interests of others."* (Philippians 2:3-4 NASB)**

***"Those who are happiest are those who do the most for others."* (Booker T. Washington)**

Mercy Minute Volume 52, Script 14; by Nancy Predaina, Special Project Writer/Editor; from www.desmoinesregister.com 9/11/2010; www.arkansasonline.com 9/10/2010;

July 5

Falling in Love

A volunteer nurse onboard our hospital ship shared a personal love story:

"It happened. I swore it wouldn't. … I fell in love on the love boat.

It took only one snuggle, both arms wrapped around my neck, and his little stitched-up nose against my shoulder. I melted. I've started calling him 'my baby.' I hold him and rock him—even while he's still attached to IVs and monitors.

His name is David. He is a true miracle. Part of his brain formed outside his skull. But now, after surgery, it's repaired.

When I watch him, a new tenderness fills my heart. It begins to flood with prayers … for his future. Then my heart turns to worship."

Allow God to flood your heart with love as you show mercy to others today.

"For the Lord your God has arrived to live among you. He is a mighty Savior. He will give you victory. He will rejoice over you with great gladness; He will love you and not accuse you. Is that a joyous choir I hear? No, it is the Lord himself exulting over you in happy song." **(Zephaniah 3:17-18 TLB)**

Mercy Minute Volume 70, Script 60; by Anna Psiaki, staff writer; from personal blog of volunteer Angela Cuccia; used with permission; 2016-2017 AFM *Benin Field Service;*

July 6

The Class of 2032

Marty Burbank has had a successful career and absolutely loves sailing. So, he and his wife decided to buy their dream boat.

Mrs. Burbank grew up in South Korea. With her aunt's help, she became a first-generation college graduate. The Burbanks often donated notebooks and food to the Rio Vista Elementary School in Anaheim, California.

And they decided to give up their dream boat. Instead, they're going to pay the college tuition for the 26 kindergarteners at the school—at a cost of about $1 million! Mrs. Burbank says, *"I got a lot of help, and now I'm helping others."*

What a sacrificial gift of mercy for the graduating class of 2032!

Acts of kindness—big or small—are sacrificial gifts, and God will bless you for them.

"Give, and it will be given to you. A good measure, pressed down, shaken together and running over, will be poured into your lap. For with the measure you use, it will be measured to you."
(Luke 6:37-38 NIV)

"The most obvious lesson in Christ's teaching is that there is no happiness in having or getting anything, but only in giving."
(Henry Drummond)

Mercy Minute Volume 64, Script 45; http://www.dailykos.com/story/2016/2/8/1481773/-Couple-forgo-buying-dream-boat-and-decide-to-put-entire-kindergarten-class-through-college

July 7

The Indoor Parade

Fresh air and exercise are important to the patients recovering on the *Africa Mercy*. But what do you do when the rainy season drowns your play time? You host an indoor parade, of course!

During our Madagascar field service, patients and nurses lined the hallways on rainy days. They had balloons and music. They danced, and they sang in both English and Malagasy. For an hour, Deck 3 was filled with laughter, smiles and joyful noise. But, most importantly, nurses and patients just enjoyed the time of relaxation and friendship.

One boy with bandaged head and arms shouted, "*This is fun*!" And he was right!

Sometimes mercy involves a few balloons, music and a lot of fun. Show mercy by bringing joy into someone's life today.

"He has given me a new song to sing, of praises to our God. Now many will hear of the glorious things He did for me, and stand in awe before the Lord, and put their trust in Him."
(Psalm 40:3 TLB)

⚓ On July 7, 1978, a down payment of $100,000 USD was made to purchase the *Victoria*, an Italian-built ocean liner, which became the *Anastasis*. Exactly 4 years later, the ship made its first sail.

Mercy Minute Volume 62, Script 23; by Tanya Sierra, staff writer; from crew interview; 2014-2015 AFM *Madagascar Field Service;*

July 8

The Nameless Girl

She had an "X" instead of a first name. Mercy Ships volunteer nurse Sue Clynes checked the medical notes. It was true. The Malagasy girl receiving a free surgery for cleft lip and palate was known only by her family name … for her entire 12 years of life! The Malagasy translator said it was because she was born with a major facial disfigurement.

Sue wondered how the girl must feel—approaching womanhood, but without a name.

Well, the girl would soon have a new face. So Sue thought, *"What if we ask her family if she can also have a new name?"*

That's how the nameless girl became known as Chara … meaning *"beautiful."*

You know, you can supply what's missing in the lives of others by showing mercy and making them feel beautiful.

"You'll get a brand-new name straight from the mouth of God. You'll be a stunning crown in the palm of God's hand, a jeweled gold cup held high in the hand of your God. No more will anyone call you Rejected …" **(Isaiah 62:2-4 MSG)**

Mercy Minute Volume 62, Script 27; by Sharon Walls, staff writer; from crew interview; 2015-16 AFM *Madagascar Field Service;*

July 9

Baby Number 7357

Dr. Bruce Shephard decided to become an obstetrician because they bring life. He opened his own practice so that he could get to know his patients. And so that, when it was time, he would be the one to deliver their babies. He was constantly on-call. He slept with a walkie-talkie, then a pager, then his cell phone. At least once every week, he was awakened by a baby who wouldn't wait.

His office walls are covered with children's photos. He brought each of them into the world.

Finally, at age 72, Dr. Shephard decided to retire. He delivered his last baby, number 7357, and said, "*Welcome to the world, Angel.*"

What a legacy of compassion! You can build your legacy of mercy by helping someone today.

> ***"One generation shall praise Your works to another, and shall declare Your mighty and remarkable acts."*** **(Psalm 145:4 AMP)**

Mercy Minute Volume 66, Script 45; "After a Lifetime of Labor and Sleepless Nights, a Tampa Doctor Decides to Deliver His Last Baby, No. 7357," by Lane DeGregory; 7/1/16; www.tampabay.com

July 10
God Smiled

Becky Bynum has served with Mercy Ships for more than 25 years. She makes sure our hospital ship has the medical supplies it needs. She describes her reaction to a sermon on commitment that changed her life:

"I stood up and said, 'God, I want to be one hundred percent committed to You. I will go where You call me, and will do what You call me to do.' I reminded God that I really did not like to travel, and I did not like to talk, and most certainly I did not do microphones. God must have smiled."

Yes, I imagine God often smiles—or maybe even laughs—when we plan our lives while He has something else in mind. Now you go, allow God to direct you to show mercy to someone today.

***"Many plans are in a man's mind, but it is the Lord's purpose for him that will stand (be carried out)."* (Proverbs 19:21 AMP)**

Mercy Minute Volume 64, Script 1;by Nancy Predaina, Special Project Writer/Editor; from "A Surrendered Life," The Spirit Today, *January 2016;*

July 11

No Longer Left Behind

Sandrins watched her sisters leave for school. She desperately wanted to go with them, but her clubbed foot meant she was often left behind. In Madagascar, orthopedic care is out of reach for the poorest of the poor.

But good news arrived. Our hospital ship offering free surgeries had arrived. Sandrins' mother carried her eight-year-old daughter on her back to the patient screening. And they heard the words that would change Sandrins' life forever, *"This is a surgery we can do."*

The little girl asked her mother, *"Do you mean if this man fixes my foot I can return to school?"* Her mother smiled warmly and nodded.

And that's when Sandrins knew she would no longer be left behind.

You and I need to make sure no one is left behind in receiving mercy.

***"Let us not become weary in doing good, for at the proper time we will reap a harvest if we do not give up. Therefore, as we have opportunity, let us do good to all people …"* (Galatians 6:9-10 NIV)**

***"I'm a little pencil in the hand of a writing God, who is sending a love letter to the world."* (Mother Teresa)**

Mercy Minute Volume 62, Script 50;by Tanya Sierra, staff writer; personal observation / patient interview; 2014-2015 AFM *Madagascar Field Service;*

July 12

Families for AIDS Orphans

Again and again the plight of South Africa's AIDS orphans replayed in Yvonne Greig's mind. And God's mercy-seed was planted.

And it grew into a village … the Ingane Yami children's village. The name translated from Zulu means "my child." Each little brick house has a Mamma whose heart is as big as Africa. Up to six small children are placed into her tender, Godly care … for their entire childhood.

Yvonne believes demonstrating God's mercy transforms nations. She says, *"Imagine if everyone just did one thing and sustained it—we could change the world we live in."*

Follow Yvonne's example and find that "one thing" you can do to show God's mercy to someone today.

"*A father to the fatherless, a defender of widows, is God in His holy dwelling.*" (Psalm 68:5 NIV)

Mercy Minute Volume 62, Script 14;by Sharon Walls, staff writer; site visit and interview with Pastor Yvonne Greig; 8/23/15 in Kloof, SA; http://inganeyami.com; 2015-16 AFM *Madagascar Field Service;*

July 13

Mariette's Birthday

Birthdays are special days. But spending your birthday in a hospital can be a bit of a downer … unless you're onboard our hospital ship, the *Africa Mercy*!

Thirteen-year-old Mariette wasn't excited about spending her birthday in a hospital. She was recovering from surgery to repair her feet.

But she was in for a big surprise. The nurses decided to host an impromptu party out on the deck just for her! Balloons, streamers and music transformed the deck into a delightful party place. One nurse even baked Mariette's favorite dessert—chocolate cake with sprinkles.

A grinning Mariette, said, "*Thank you*!"

You know, mercy is always decorated with sprinkles of love. Give someone a reason to celebrate by showing mercy today.

***"This is the day which the Lord has made; let us rejoice and be glad in it."* (Psalm 118:24 NASB)**

Mercy Minute Volume 62, Script 55; by Tanya Sierra, staff writer; personal observation; 2014-2015 AFM *Madagascar Field Service;*

July 14

Blitz Survivor Has Sight Restored

The time was World War II. John Gray was on duty as a firewatcher in Glasgow, Scotland, when the air raid sirens sounded. A devastating bombing raid killed twelve hundred people. John was pulled from the rubble with terrible injuries, including the loss of sight in one eye.

Then, 66 years later, John developed severe macular degeneration in his healthy eye. His sight couldn't be saved. But Dr. Ian Bryce was determined to help. He looked at John's war-injured eye and discovered that the retina was still intact. So, he removed scar tissue and inserted an artificial lens. Now John sees out of an eye that had been blind since 1941! He says his surgeon deserves a knighthood.

You may not receive a knighthood, but you will receive God's blessing as you show kindness to others.

"A generous person will prosper; whoever refreshes others will be refreshed." **(Proverbs 11:25 NIV)**

Mercy Minute Volume 33, Script 47; by Nancy Predaina, Special Project Writer/Editor; from "Blitz Survivor Has Sight Restored," http://news.bbc.co.uk 4/7/08;

July 15

A Celebration of Sight

The intense African sun causes thick cataracts. Every week, blind patients receive free eye surgeries onboard our Mercy Ship where we celebrate restored sight . . . and hope . . . and life. I'd like to describe one of these celebrations that I attended:

Can you imagine over 100 people—after years of darkness—celebrating the return of their sight? As the drums began to beat, the excitement intensified. People sang with their hands raised in praise to Jesus.

One of the joyous patients was a Muslim mullah. As I watched him sing and praise God, my heart was stirred. What a special moment!

That special moment—and many more—are made possible by compassionate hearts ... people just like you!

***"So, chosen by God for this new life of love, dress in the wardrobe God picked out for you: compassion, kindness, humility, quiet strength, discipline."* (Colossians 3:12 MSG)**

***"Let no one ever come to you without leaving better and happier. Be the living expression of God's kindness: kindness in your face, kindness in your eyes, kindness in your smile."* (Mother Teresa)**

Mercy Minute Volume 39, Script 28; by Nancy Predaina, Special Project Writer/Editor; from personal account of Don Stephens, 2009 Field Service to Benin;

July 16

Mercy Plays Softball

Teams were playing for a spot in the softball league's playoffs. Sara, from Western Oregon, had never hit a homerun in 4 years of college play. But today, she hit the ball out of the park!

As she rounded first base, Sara missed the bag. As she reversed direction, a tendon in her knee snapped. She collapsed, weeping.

And that's when mercy showed up! Rules prevented Sara's team from helping her. But two opposing team members carried her around the bases. Everyone cheered.

Sara's team won, but the opposing team didn't regret what they did. One player said, *"In the end, it's not about winning. It's about this girl—she needed help."*

When others need help, mercy shows up! I challenge you to show up for someone who needs help.

***"Be devoted to one another with [authentic] brotherly affection [as members of one family], give preference to one another in honor; never lagging behind in diligence; aglow in the Spirit, enthusiastically serving the Lord ..."* (Romans 12:10-11 AMP)**

Mercy Minute Volume 33, Script 51; by Nancy Predaina, Special Project Writer/Editor; from sports.aol.com 5/1/08 and fromthepasture.blogspot.com 5/6/08

July 17
Sambany

A benign tumor grew on Sambany's face for 36 years. It weighed over 16 pounds and was the size of two extra heads.

Then he heard a radio announcement that a hospital ship was coming to Madagascar. They removed tumors for free!

Sambany struggled with his weakness. Five people took turns carrying him on their backs for two days . . . but he made it.

The Mercy Ships medical team explained the risks. Sambany said, "*I know I might die in surgery, but I already feel dead inside. I choose to have surgery.*"

When Sambany looked in a mirror after the surgery, he said, "*I like it. I am happy.*" An incredible transformation—thanks to mercy.

> ***"Do not conform to the pattern of this world, but be transformed by the renewing of your mind. Then you will be able to test and approve what God's will is—His good, pleasing and perfect will."***
> **(Romans 12:2 NIV)**

⚓ Sambany's surgery took over half a day. Our crew, our "living blood bank," literally poured life into him. The blood of seventeen people from six nations now runs through his veins.

Mercy Minute Volume 60, Script 51; by Nancy Predaina, Special Project Writer/Editor; from Patient Story by Eunice Hiew, staff writer; 2014-2015 AFM *Madagascar Field Service*

July 18

Max's Second Chance

Max is 39 years old and lives in West Africa. For ten years, he suffered with tumors on his face. People viewed this as demon possession or worse. He lost his job, and his wife and children left him.

Then Max heard about the arrival of our Mercy Ship. He knew it was his only hope. Mercy Ship surgeons told Max they could remove the tumors, but there was a risk of possible paralysis to his face. Max decided to have the surgery anyway.

When Max awoke from the surgery, he discovered there were no more tumors ... and no paralysis! After losing everything, Max had been given a second chance. He reunited with his wife and children and was able to seek new work.

As we show mercy and kindness to others, we are giving them a second chance … a chance for hope and happiness.

"It is because of the Lord's lovingkindnesses that we are not consumed, because His [tender] compassions never fail. They are new every morning; great and beyond measure is Your faithfulness." **(Lamentations 3:21-23 AMP)**

Mercy Minute Volume 34, Script 17; by Beth Herndon, staff member; from patient story "Max: Life Begins Again," by Claire Boot; Benin, 2004-2005 ANA *Benin Field Service*

July 19

Quick Thinking on a Train Track

Chris Ihle parked his motorcycle in front of his office. He noticed a car with disabled-person tags stalled on the railroad tracks. An elderly man in a neck brace was turning the key and hitting the gas. Then he heard the train whistle!

Chris ducked under the crossing gates and shouted at the man to put the car in neutral. He could hear the train's brakes squealing. He wedged his boots against the tracks and shoved. Finally, the car rolled off the tracks. Chris flattened himself against the side of the car as the train roared past.

Chris staggered back to work and poured himself a cup of coffee. He said, "*There's a time to talk, and there's a time to act.*"

Now you decide to act and show mercy to someone today.

> ***"For God did not give us a spirit of timidity or cowardice or fear, but [He has given us a spirit] of power and of love and of sound judgment and personal discipline [abilities that result in a calm, well-balanced mind and self-control]."*** **(2 Timothy 1:7 AMP)**

Mercy Minute Volume 60, Script 47; from "Quick Thinking Saves a Couple Stalled in a Train's Way," by Nick Heil; Reader's Digest, *November 2014;*

July 20

A Remarkable Mercy Team

Bethany serves as a Ward Nurse onboard our hospital ship. She describes a very special celebration of mercy:

"The entire team of nurses and day-crew gathered to celebrate what had happened the past ten months.

One of our day-crew explained that when you walk into our ward, you are hit with the 'air-conditioning of peace and the hand of love.'

When you choose to respect one another, when you apply your time and energy to serving the 'least of these,' and when you do it as a living 'thank-you' to God . . . the result is the team I saw as I looked around."

Yes, showing mercy—the "air-conditioning of peace and the hand of love"—creates an amazing bond.

"The King will answer and say to them, 'I assure you and most solemnly say to you, to the extent that you did it for one of these brothers of Mine, even the least of them, you did it for Me.'"
(Matthew 25:40 AMP)

"I see Jesus in every human being. I say to myself, 'This is hungry Jesus, I must feed him. This is sick Jesus. This one has leprosy or gangrene; I must wash him and tend to him.' I serve because I love Jesus." **(Mother Teresa)**

Mercy Minute Volume 60, Script 42; by Catherine Murphy, staff writer; from story submitted by Bethany Salmonson, Ward Nurse General Team Leader, 2013-14 AFM *Congo Field Service;*

July 21

Fredia

Six-month-old Fredia is as feisty as they come! Her mama struggles day in and day out to feed her. But the baby's feistiness isn't the problem. A cleft lip and palate are to blame. The infant girl dangerously kept losing weight.

Then Mercy Ships arrived in Madagascar. Fredia's desperate mother came to our hospital ship, the *Africa Mercy*, for help.

Fredia was placed in the infant feeding program so she'd be strong enough for surgery. Nurse Brenda Sossou sums up the program in one sentence: "*We take babies, and we fatten them up.*"

And it worked! Fredia gained weight, and a free surgery repaired her lip and palate. Now she'll have the strength to show off her feistiness.

Love and compassion always make a difference. Be a difference-maker by showing kindness to others.

***"It is God himself who has made us what we are and given us new lives from Christ Jesus; and long ages ago He planned that we should spend these lives in helping others."* (Ephesians 2:10 TLB)**

Mercy Minute Volume 60, Script 58; by Tanya Sierra, staff writer; from patient interview; 2014-2015 AFM *Madagascar Field Service;*

July 22

From a Dump to Harvard

Justus was nine years old and orphaned by ethnic genocide. He lived in a burned-out car in a garbage dump in Rwanda, scavenging for food and clothes. He says, *"It was a really dark time, because I couldn't see a future. I couldn't see how life could be better."*

But then Clare, the founder of a charity called *Esther's Aid*, visited the dump. All the other children ran away, but Justus faced her and announced, *"I want to go to school."*

And he got his wish! Clare moved him into her charity's orphanage. He made straight A's in school and became a student at Harvard.

All because of a meeting with Clare . . . a meeting with mercy.

How can you use kindness and mercy to make life better for someone?

***"What no eye has seen, what no ear has heard, and what no human mind has conceived—the things God has prepared for those who love him—"* (1 Corinthians 2:9 NIV)**

Mercy Minute Volume 60, Script 39; from "From a Rwandan Dump to the Halls of Harvard," by Ian Thomas Jansen-Lonnquist; New York Times, *October 22, 2014;*

July 23

The Gangway

A crew member describes the mission of Mercy Ships from an unusual perspective . . . the gangway of our hospital ship:

"I connect the big, white hospital ship to the people it serves. Every journey of transformation begins with me.

Forty-three steps up . . . courageous steps of hope. They include physical pain and discomfort and usually emotional scars. I can feel their weight.

Inside they receive a free surgery. They are loved.

Then—forty-three steps down. I can feel the extra bounce in their steps, filled with excitement and anticipation of what's to come . . . excitement for the new life that awaits them!"

What a wonderful description of mercy! And your acts of kindness can be the bridge that connects hurting people to hope and joy.

"Whether you turn to the right or to the left, your ears will hear a voice behind you, saying, 'This is the way; walk in it.'"
(Isaiah 30:21 NIV)

Mercy Minute Volume 60, Script 24; by Nancy Predaina, Special Project Writer/Editor; from Weekly Scoop-Week of October 20 from AFM *Communications Team, 10/27/14;*

July 24

Nike Flyease

Matthew Walzer, a 16-year-old with cerebral palsy, posted a letter on social media. He said he was going to college in a couple of years and couldn't tie his own shoes.

So, Tobie Hatfield, a designer for Nike, started thinking about shoe design that would help many people with disabilities.

Tobie found out that Matthew was a great fan of LeBron James, so he designed a basketball athletic shoe called the Nike Flyease. It had a wraparound zipper system that could be fastened with one hand.

Matthew says, *"I'll never forget putting them on. I felt this wave of independence I never got to experience before."*

Can a pair of basketball shoes be a gift of mercy? Absolutely! I challenge you to find a creative way to meet a need.

"But whoever has the world's goods (adequate resources), and sees his brother in need, but has no compassion for him, how does the love of God live in him?" **(1 John 3:17 AMP)**

Mercy Minute Volume 62, Script 20; by Nancy Predaina, Special Project Writer/Editor; from "Nike Flyease Story," www.youtube.com;

July 25

Dan Hier

At the seasoned age of 65, most people think of slowing down … but NOT Dan Hier! He volunteered for seven consecutive summer projects on our former Mercy Ship, the *Anastasis*. With toolkit in hand, he helped with massive renovation jobs.

He attacked his jobs with gusto, wise-cracking all the way, pencil behind ear, silver hair askew. His strength left youths embarrassed. His humor lightened the hard work. His unshakeable zeal cheered all who were working with him.

Dan died suddenly of a heart attack while working at home in Michigan. He is one of many unsung heroes in Mercy Ships—having lived a life of mercy.

Follow Dan's example and use YOUR God-given skills to show mercy to others.

"Now God gives us many kinds of special abilities, but it is the same Holy Spirit who is the source of them all. There are different kinds of service to God, but it is the same Lord we are serving. There are many ways in which God works in our lives, but it is the same God who does the work in and through all of us who are His." **(1 Corinthians 12:4-6 TLB)**

"Even if you're on the right track, you'll get run over if you just sit there." **(Mother Teresa)**

Mercy Minute Volume 62, Script 34; by Larry Mast, staff writer; from March 15-21, 2000 Anastasis *weekly report by Paula Kirby;*

July 26

HOPE Center Bonfire

In each field service, we remodel a building in town for the HOPE (Hospital Out-Patient Extension) Center. Here patients gain strength before surgery or stay for follow-up treatments after surgery. Crewmember Leah described a special night:

"We had a bonfire at the Hope Center. We introduced our patients to a great American treat—s'mores!

The night was full of beaming smiles, plenty of dancing, and the music of many voices—young, old, and in-between.

Looking up at the wispy clouded night, I thanked the Lord for the journeys that brought each of these glowing faces to this campfire, and I thanked Him that I could be a part of it."

Isn't it wonderful that God allows us to be part of "journeys of mercy" as He gives us opportunities to help others?

***"Give to the one who asks you, and do not turn away from the one who wants to borrow from you."* (Matthew 5:42 NIV)**

Mercy Minute Volume 60, Script 56; by Catherine Murphy, staff writer; from story submitted by Leah Ferguson, HOPE Center Coordinator, 2013-14 AFM Congo Field Service;

July 27

Community Help for Kindame

Carl Luther, an alumni of Mercy Ships, is now a missionary doctor in Papua, New Guinea. A patient named Kindame had a large abscess in her abdomen. So, he sent her to the closest surgeon, three hours away. But the surgeon couldn't do the surgery because Kindame's blood count was too low, and the hospital didn't have the blood supply she needed.

So a community of missionaries came to her rescue. Seven of them, who had the needed blood type, donated blood. Others provided much-needed financial help.

Kindame had the surgery and recovered quickly. Dr. Luther says, *"God's people came together to make a difference. I am thankful that I can celebrate alongside Kindame's family."*

What a wonderful community of mercy! Join with others in your community to help those in need.

> ***"Instead, we will lovingly follow the truth at all times—speaking truly, dealing truly, living truly—and so become more and more in every way like Christ who is the Head of His body, the Church. Under His direction, the whole body is fitted together perfectly, and each part in its own special way helps the other parts, so that the whole body is healthy and growing and full of love."***
> **(Ephesians 4:16 TLB)**

Mercy Minute Volume 62, Script 24; by Nancy Predaina, Special Project Writer/Editor; from "Luther Log," newsletter from Carl and Carol Luther, June 2015;

July 28

Blessed in Return

Long-term Mercy Ships volunteers go through our training program called OnBoarding. It includes a field project in Africa. One group painted an orphanage in Sierra Leone, where 40 handicapped children lived and attended school.

The children were excited about helping the painters. A twelve-year-old boy named Abu climbed out of his wheelchair onto his knees. He held a bowl of paint on his head for several hours to help a painter.

One child said, "*We want to help. This is* **our** *house.*"

The team wanted to bless the children by helping. But they were blessed by the children's sincere desire to participate.

Yes, mercy is often double-sided—blessing the giver and the receiver.

"The one who blesses others is abundantly blessed; those who help others are helped." **(Proverbs 11:25 MSG)**

⚓ Our hospital ships include a fully accredited, kindergarten through 12th grade, academy for crew children.

Mercy Minute Volume 66, Script 35; by Nancy Predaina, Special Project Writer/Editor; from interview with Cassidy Habig, painter on project team, by Elaine Winn, staff writer; 2011 AFM Sierra Leone Field Service;

July 29

Leigh Changes Her Plan

Volunteer crew member Leigh Jackman shared a lesson she learned from a little four-year-old, Lingala-speaking girl in Congo:

"I thought I had everything planned out the day I went to the wards to read to the children. And then I met Jodelle. She crawled into my lap and began playing with my hair, chattering away in a language I don't know.

Everything changed. In fact, the story was never even read. I let go of my plan, and love happened in the most unplanned, unscripted way that it could have. And it was perfect. When you release control, the important things in life happen."

Yes, mercy often changes our plans in unexpected ways. But it's always perfect. Let mercy change your plans as you help someone today.

***"But let all who take refuge in You be glad; let them ever sing for joy. Spread Your protection over them, that those who love Your name may rejoice in You."* (Psalm 5:11 NIV)**

Mercy Minute Volume 66, Script 35; by Nancy Predaina, Special Project Writer/Editor; from personal experience shared by Leigh Jackman, Communications Manager, with Catherine Murphy, staff writer; 2013-14 AFM *Congo Field Service;*

July 30

Estella's Brilliant Bus

Estella Pyfrom retired from teaching and bought a custom-designed bus with 17 computer stations and high-speed Internet. On the side are the words "Have Knowledge, Will Travel" and "We bring learning to you."

And that's exactly what Estella's Brilliant Bus does—it takes educational opportunity to low-income families. It travels to schools, shelters and community centers throughout Palm Beach County, Florida.

It offers regular classes, tutoring sessions, computer lessons, and college preparatory assistance. Adults can receive help searching for jobs and affordable housing.

Estella says, "*We've got to keep rolling . . . and we are going to keep making a difference.*"

Yes, mercy always makes a difference. And you can make a difference by showing mercy to someone today.

***"Get wisdom—it's worth more than money; choose insight over income every time."* (Proverbs 16:16 MSG)**

Mercy Minute Volume 62, Script 31; by Nancy Predaina, Special Project Writer/Editor; from "'Brilliant Bus' Shrinking Digital Divide," by Danielle Berger, http://www.cnn.com/2013/04/04/us/cnnheroes-pyfrom-brilliant-bus/index.html

July 31

Saving Lives

Many Mercy Ships volunteers come from countries were medical care is widely available. They bring state-of-the-art medical care to patients who suffer from treatable medical conditions, patients who live in countries where medical care is very limited. Operating room nurse Michelle Anderson explains:

"They just happen to be born in a nation that doesn't have that available. And it's heartbreaking to think of little children dying from things that are so easily repaired in a western hospital. If you have the ability to help somebody, you should go and help them, so that they have that chance."

Yes, the world needs people who are willing to donate their time and skills to help. Make a commitment to use your talents to help others.

"Are you called to help others? Do it with all the strength and energy that God supplies so that God will be glorified through Jesus Christ—to Him be glory and power forever and ever. Amen." **(1 Peter 4:11 TLB)**

"There is a light in this world, a healing spirit more powerful than any darkness we may encounter. We sometimes lose sight of this force when there is suffering, too much pain. Then suddenly, the spirit will emerge through the lives of ordinary people who hear a call and answer in extraordinary ways." **(Mother Teresa)**

Mercy Minute Volume 60, Script 59; by Nancy Predaina, Special Project Writer/Editor; from crew interview by Nancy Predaina and by Ambassador Advertising Team; 2012 AFM *Guinea Field Service;*

August

"Finally, all of you, be like-minded, be sympathetic, love one another, be compassionate and humble."
(1 Peter 3:8 NIV)

August 1

A Symbol of Hope

I end every Mercy Minute radio broadcast with the phrase *"Bringing hope and healing to the world's forgotten poor."* Crewmember Dr. Bob Burlingame describes what that looks like:

"The Mercy Ship to me is just a symbol of hope. These people have really no hope, and when you hear them speak of having heard about the Mercy Ship and that possibly it could give them hope, give them surgical correction of their problem—their eyes light up, their hearts light up, they're joy-filled as they speak of what Mercy Ships represents to them. And, through that, I've really come to feel even more so that this is a just a great symbol of hope."

I couldn't have said it better myself! And when you show kindness to someone going through a difficult time, you give them hope for a better tomorrow.

***"Now may the God of hope fill you with all joy and peace in believing, so that you will abound in hope by the power of the Holy Spirit."* (Romans 15:13 NASB)**

Mercy Minute Volume 70, Script 15; by Nancy Predaina, Special Projects Writer/Editor; from interview with Dr. Bob Burlingame by AFM *Communications Team, 2016-17* AFM *Benin Field Service;*

August 2

I Dare You to Stop Me

During the first Gulf War, thousands of Kurds fled Iraq into Turkey. They huddled in the high mountains in frigid winter weather, starving and freezing. They were forbidden by Turkish troops to move down the mountain to warmer climates.

A Kurdish woman came carrying a sick child. She asked permission to visit a medical clinic nearby. The soldiers refused to let her pass.

Then an American Ranger — a member of the US Army's elite fighting force — noticed her predicament. With M-16 in one hand, he scooped up the child in his other arm. His body language said to the soldiers, *"I dare you to stop me!"* The Turkish soldiers backed out of his way as he carried the child into the clinic.

Be bold! Be daring in showing mercy on somcone's behalf today.

***"Have I not commanded you? Be strong and courageous. Do not be afraid; do not be discouraged, for the Lord your God will be with you wherever you go."* (Joshua 1:9 NIV)**

⚓ Captain Hal Burton and Engineer Bill Horn were the first technical crew for the *Anastasis*, the first Mercy Ship.

Mercy Minute Volume 23, Script 30; by Larry Mast, staff writer; from Rebel With a Cause, *by Franklin Graham*

August 3

Celestine Sings

The crew onboard our hospital ship includes both medical and non-medical personnel. HR Facilitator, Elza, shares an experience:

"Celestine was sitting in the admissions tent on the dock. I said 'Hi' to her papa and then took her hand and walked her to the edge of the dock to look at the fish. I picked her up, and her little bowed legs fit snug around my waist. She sang to me in French, while twisting my hair in her little fingers.

I hear often about how much we love our patients. What a wonderful thing it is to be reminded how much our patients love us!"

Yes, mercy is born from love and inspires love in return. Let mercy flow from your heart of love … and you will be blessed when you receive love in return.

"For though we have never yet seen God, when we love each other God lives in us, and His love within us grows ever stronger." **(1 John 4:12 TLB)**

"Being a Christian is more than just an instantaneous conversion—it is a daily process whereby you grow to be more and more like Christ." **(Billy Graham)**

Mercy Minute Volume 58, Script 44; by Nancy Predaina, Special Projects Writer/Editor; from story submitted by Elza Varga, AFM *HR Facilitator, to Catherine Murphy,* AFM *staff writer; 2013-14* AFM *Congo Field Service;*

August 4

President Reagan Helps

R.L. Alford and his wife Hilda never met President Reagan. But they did come face to face with his compassion.

The Alfords had only been married 10 months when they had a serious car accident. Hilda was never again able to walk or use her arms. Some years later, they needed a house to accommodate Hilda's deteriorating condition . . . but they couldn't afford it.

President Reagan heard their story, called the couple, and sent two personal checks to help out. His gift sparked a national response, and the Alfords were able to build their house.

President Reagan said, *"We can't help everyone, but everyone can help someone."*

The Alfords will always cherish the memory of a president who took time to help. And you can create a cherished memory by your act of kindness to someone today.

"Remember those who led you, who spoke the word of God to you; and considering the result of their conduct, imitate their faith."
(Hebrews 13:7 NASB)

Mercy Minute Volume 58, Script 46; by Nancy Predaina, Special Projects Writer/Editor; from "A Local Couple Remembers Ronald Reagan's Compassion," by Hermelinda Vargas, June 9, 2004, http://www.wjhg.com/news/headlines/820512.html

August 5

Dana Perino Visits the Africa Mercy

Fox News anchor, Dana Perino, visited the *Africa Mercy* in Congo. She shared these thoughts with staff writer, Catherine Murphy:

"Today, about fifty patients went through another round of screening and tests, with most being scheduled for a follow-up visit or surgery. Some will need to take medicines before surgery. Others need to gain some weight before their procedures can be done.

Everyone—housekeepers, cooks, teachers, doctors, nurses—were preparing for Sunday when patients will start arriving for their pre-ops. Some of them may never have seen a medical doctor. If they had, they'd been told nothing could be done. But, here, they'll be secure on this ship of mercy that is just, frankly, really hard to describe."

Yes, mercy is often indescribable! And you can choose to show indescribable mercy to someone today.

"And in their prayers for you their hearts will go out to you, because of the surpassing grace God has given you. Thanks be to God for His indescribable gift!" **(2 Corinthians 9:14-15 NIV)**

"Prayer in action is love; love in action is service."
(Mother Teresa)

Mercy Minute Volume 58, Script 32; by Nancy Predaina, Special Projects Writer/Editor; from Material submitted by Dana Perino to Catherine Murphy, Director of Digital Marketing; **

August 6

Solo Flight Gone Wrong

Seventeen-year-old McKenzie Morgan left Laurel, Montana, in a Cessna 172 for her first solo flight with three stops along the way. But, on the last leg, she accidentally transposed the zero in the GPS heading.

Suddenly, she found herself trapped in a box canyon. Strong winds caught the plane, causing it to stall and crash. McKenzie had only a sprained knee, but her survival chances were slim.

Then, in the middle of nowhere, an unlikely angel appeared—a hunter with a sprained ankle and an injured horse. He ignored his own pain to walk down the canyon and rescue McKenzie. *NBC Dateline's* report said, *"It was like two needles finding each other in a very large haystack."*

Yes, anyone can be an angel of mercy anywhere.

***"He will not let your foot slip—He who watches over you will not slumber ... The Lord will keep you from all harm—He will watch over your life ..."* (Psalm 121:3, 7 NIV)**

Mercy Minute Volume 61, Script 8; by Nancy Predaina, Special Projects Writer/Editor; from "Billings Teen Recounts Surviving Plane Crash," by Eddie Gregg, Billings Gazette, *8/21/13, AND "Hunters Come to Rescue of Montana Teen,"by OutdoorAly www.montanaoutdoor.com August 2013, AND NBC Dateline "Into the Wild," 8/25/14;*

August 7

Tani Learns about Beauty

Tani was 11 years old and knew all about pain. When she was only one year old, a fire destroyed the right side of her face. Her appearance was shocking, but her heart was pure gold. Her infectious laughter melted your heart.

It didn't take long for Tani to get close to the Mercy Ships crew members. She loved the way they accepted her, and some of the nurses taught her English.

One day, they were talking about beauty. They said, *"Beauty is in the eye of the beholder. Tani you are beautiful!"*

Soon Tani was marching the hallways of the hospital ship, announcing to the world, *"I AM BEAUTIFUL!"*

You see, eyes of mercy see everyone as beautiful. Do you want to give a great gift of mercy today? Make someone feel unconditionally loved and accepted.

"In this act we see what real love is: it is not our love for God but His love for us when He sent His Son to satisfy God's anger against our sins. Dear friends, since God loved us as much as that, we surely ought to love each other too."
(1 John 4:10-11 TLB)

Mercy Minute Volume 49, Script 26; by Nicole Pribbernow, staff writer; from interview with patient; 2012 AFM *Field Service to Togo;*

August 8
Utah Flood

Drenching rains in Utah turned the creek near Rolf and Renae Ludwig's home into a river. They grabbed flashlights and food and then took their five children to higher ground. The next morning, they watched the flood destroy their home.

Meanwhile, 40 miles away, Jeremy Johnson was recruited by the county sheriff to use his private helicopter for search and rescue. Johnson flew through the turbulent weather to rescue the entire Ludwig family. Renae said, *"He was like a brother, reaching out to us when we needed it the most."*

The following weekend Jeremy gave rides to people wanting to witness the flood damage, asking for donations. He gave the entire $20,000 to the Ludwigs.

You see, mercy reaches out to people in need. Now you go and show mercy to someone today.

***"Do not withhold good from those to whom it is due, when it is in your power to act."* (Proverbs 3:27 NIV)**

⚓ Four First Ladies from Central American countries visited the *Caribbean Mercy* in Honduras in 2004 to discuss children's health issues.

Mercy Minute Volume 24, Script 33; from "Out of the Flood," by Gail Wescott, Reader's Digest, *August 2005;*

August 9

A Multinational Army

Volunteer surgeon Dr. Mark Shrime shared these thoughts about a patient:

"I met a two-year-old boy who had a tumor in his mouth. He went to surgery, where we took out a mass the size of my fist—ridiculously large for a two-year-old.

As he was wheeled into surgery, a small, multinational army welcomed this child—two anesthesiologists, one intensive care physician, one anesthetic assistant, two nurse anesthetists, three surgeons, and three OR nurses. We were from the US, the UK, the Netherlands, Switzerland, and Congo.

This is surgery. It's not just scalpels and suction; it's infrastructure. And, while it's hard to build, it can be built . . . and help patients along the way."

Mercy takes all of us, and we can all find a way to use our talents to change lives.

"Therefore, my dear brothers and sisters, stand firm. Let nothing move you. Always give yourselves fully to the work of the Lord, because you know that your labor in the Lord is not in vain."
(1 Corinthians 15:58 NIV)

Mercy Minute Volume 58, Script 22; by Catherine Murphy, staff writer; from story submitted by Dr. Mark Shrime to Catherine Murphy, staff writer; 2013-14 AFM Congo Field Service;

August 10
Joseph Jones

Joseph Jones' 32 years of life had been tragic. During Liberia's civil war, rebel soldiers killed his family and friends. To make matters worse, Joseph had a large tumor on his neck.

But he couldn't afford a hospital. For 20 years he prayed that a hospital would come to him. He told everyone in his village that someday it would happen. So he wasn't surprised when he heard on the radio that a Mercy Ship was coming. It was filled with surgeons providing free surgeries.

After the doctors successfully removed the tumor, Joseph headed home. He said, *"I will tell them all God answered my prayers."*

Just imagine! Sometimes God uses our acts of kindness to answer someone's prayer.

"But He listened! He heard my prayer! He paid attention to it!"
(Psalm 66:19 TLB)

Mercy Minute Volume 24, Script 16; by Nancy Predaina, Special Projects Writer/Editor; from onamercyship.com, website of Scott Harrison, staff photojournalist; 2005-06 Anastasis *Liberia Field Service*

August 11

Jackson Kaguri

Jackson Kaguri received an Ivy League education and was planning to buy a house in Indiana. But then he made a visit back home to Uganda.

The next morning there were long lines of grandmothers begging him for help. Their own children had died. They were raising their grandchildren. Some of those children had HIV/AIDS.

Kaguri said, "*These women had seen me grow up . . . what was I supposed to do?*"

So, he and his wife used their life savings to build the Nyaka School, brick by brick. Fifty-six AIDS orphans were the first students. Today there are two schools with almost 600 students who receive free education and healthcare.

You know, mercy is often what happens while we're making other plans.

"If, however, you are [really] fulfilling the royal law according to the Scripture, 'You shall love your neighbor as yourself [that is, if you have an unselfish concern for others and do things for their benefit]' you are doing well." **(James 2:8 AMP)**

"The true neighbor will risk his position, his prestige, and even his life for the welfare of others." **(Martin Luther King Jr.)**

Mercy Minute Volume 56, Script 17; by Nancy Predaina, Special Projects Writer/Editor; from "Cashing in the American Dream to Help AIDS Orphans," http://www.cnn.com; 6/21/12;

August 12

Ravette's Cheerleaders

Ravette is an 11-year-old orthopedic patient. She suffered from a deformity that caused her knees to bend backward. It was difficult for her to walk or sit, and she couldn't go to school. She received free corrective surgery onboard our hospital ship. A crew member described an encounter with Ravette:

"Ravette is still in casts, but she's learning to walk again. This morning she hobbled into the common area we call the café. She quickly snagged everyone's attention.

That's when the clapping started. Each table she walked past gave a little cheer.

I've never seen a child with a smile as big as hers was today."

Yes, Ravette had her very own cheerleaders. And one way to show mercy to others is to be their encouraging voice … their cheerleader.

***"Do not let any unwholesome talk come out of your mouths, but only what is helpful for building others up according to their needs, that it may benefit those who listen."* (Ephesians 4:29 NIV)**

Mercy Minute Volume 56, Script 33; by Catherine Murphy, staff writer; from My Life Acquatic, blog of Catherine Murphy, AFM *staff writer, November 2013; 2013-2014* AFM *Congo Field Service; used with permission;*

August 13

Freed from Revenge

Yousif and his wife Alia were Christians living in a Muslim area in Iraq. Their neighbors began throwing rocks at their church. And, the couple and their three children escaped just ahead of an armed mob.

The Muslim neighbors expected Yousif to return and take some kind of revenge. He did return, but he did something unexpected. He worked with a medical mission called Partners International to turn the church into a greatly needed medical and dental clinic.

What a powerful example of mercy! Lewis Smedes said, "To forgive is to set a prisoner free and discover that the prisoner was you." And, in this case, forgiveness freed Yousif to share about the love of Jesus.

Jesus gave us an amazing model for forgiveness. If you have someone in your life that you need to forgive, please do so … you will free that person and yourself.

***"Your heavenly Father will forgive you if you forgive those who sin against you; but if you refuse to forgive them, He will not forgive you."* (Matthew 6:14-15 TLB)**

Mercy Minute Volume 56, Script 44; by Larry Mast, staff writer; from Partners International, Winter Magazine, *Page 5;*

August 14

Elizabeth's Hospitality

Obstetric fistula is a childbirth injury caused by obstructed labor. It's common in countries with little or no healthcare. Often women are left incontinent and abandoned.

One woman traveled miles from her home in up-country Congo to our hospital ship. She was also blind. After her free surgery, she didn't have anyone to come get her or to take care of her.

Now, Elizabeth is one of the local African day-crew we hire to help in various roles. She took the woman home to live with her indefinitely or until a family member decided to help. Ward Nurse Bethany said, *"It reminds me of Jesus' words: 'what you do unto the least of these, you do to me.'"*

Yes, following the 2000-year-old model of Jesus is all about serving others.

"Watch what God does, and then you do it, like children who learn proper behavior from their parents. Mostly what God does is love you. Keep company with Him and learn a life of love. Observe how Christ loved us. His love was not cautious but extravagant ... Love like that." **(Ephesians 5:1-2 MSG)**

Mercy Minute Volume 56, Script 23; by Catherine Murphy, staff writer; from Presentation by Bethany Salmonson, Ward Nurse, Community Meeting, October 2013; 2013-14 AFM *Congo Field Service;*

August 15

Angels in the Water

Mike McClure waded out into Sarasota Bay in Florida to enjoy some fishing. The low tide made it possible to walk 100 yards from shore.

Near sunset, he decided to head back in a more direct path. But the bay suddenly became very deep with a strong current. His waders rapidly filled with water, pulling him under.

Three college girls at the New College of Florida campus saw his predicament. They swam to his rescue. By the time they reached him, he'd managed to free himself from the waders but was losing consciousness. Mike says, *"I looked over my shoulder, and these three little angel faces were looking at me. It was almost mystical."*

Yes, mercy is a miraculous gift! And you can be the "angel" who gives the gift of mercy to someone today.

***"For He will give His angels charge concerning you, to guard you in all your ways."* (Psalm 91:11 NASB)**

⚓ On two occasions in 2013, CBS *60 Minutes* aired a 12-minute segment highlighting Mercy Ships. This produced a flood of positive response in donations and volunteer applications.

Mercy Minute Volume 56, Script 61; from "Angels in the Water," by Jason Kersten, Reader's Digest, *August 2009;*

August 16

A Blood Donor Named Jesus

Mercy Ships nurse Rosie Timms shared a heartwarming story:

"I got to know the family that I gave blood to. They were just absolutely amazed that I would give blood to this child of theirs that had been deformed, and, I think, kind of rejected by the family. And the mother was just amazed. In fact, she made a comment, 'Well, now, you gave your blood to her, so now she's your daughter.'

It was a great opportunity for me to talk about Jesus, who really shed His blood to give us eternal life."

Rosie's right! Jesus is the most amazing blood donor ever! Let's tell others about Him!

"... just think how much more surely the blood of Christ will transform our lives and hearts. His sacrifice frees us from the worry of having to obey the old rules and makes us want to serve the living God. For by the help of the eternal Holy Spirit, Christ willingly gave Himself to God to die for our sins—He being perfect, without a single sin or fault." **(Hebrews 9:14 TLB)**

Mercy Minute Volume 55, Script 50; by Nancy Predaina, Special Projects Writer/Editor; from interview by Nancy Predaina and by Ambassador Team; 2012 AFM Guinea Field Service;

August 17

Giselle

Giselle is a remarkable young woman from Argentina. She decided to spend her "gap" year with Mercy Ships before she started medical school. And she described her favorite thing onboard the hospital ship:

"The hospital on Sunday mornings is Heaven on earth. The corridors of the Africa Mercy *fill up with the sound of bongos and joyful voices. People of all sizes, nationalities, and ages praise and worship the only God Almighty, who has the power to fill them with overwhelming joy.*

Some of them are patients with faces covered in bandages. Some are crew—nurses, doctors, and kitchen staff. Words are not enough to describe the beauty of these moments."

It IS beautiful to watch hearts joined in worship of the source of all mercy!

"Praise the Lord. Praise the Lord, my soul. I will praise the Lord all my life; I will sing praise to my God as long as I live." **(Psalm 146:1-2 NIV)**

"Like supernatural effervescence, praise will sometimes bubble up from the joy of simply knowing Christ. Praise like that is … delight. Pure pleasure!" **(Joni Eareckson Tada)**

Mercy Minute Volume 58, Script 16; by Grace Antonini, staff writer; from interview with Giselle Tellerin-Kuipers (ARG) by Grace Antonini; 2013-14 AFM *Congo Field Service;*

August 18

From Homeless to Homeless

Queen Street in Auckland, New Zealand, is full of interesting people—magicians, living statues, musicians ... and homeless people.

Often people avoid looking at the homeless. Sometimes they'll give a few coins. But one day a college student gave a homeless man a MacDonald's meal. You may be thinking, "*Well, that's nice, but it's not really that unusual.*"

What followed WAS unusual ... even extraordinary. The man who received the meal walked across the street and gave it to another homeless person. It reminds me of the biblical story of the widow who gave all she had. Now, that's amazing mercy!

What do you have to give to others? It may be time, skills, a listening ear, or money for a meal. But you can find a way to show amazing mercy to someone.

"'Really,' He remarked, 'this poor widow has given more than all the rest of them combined. For they have given a little of what they didn't need, but she, poor as she is, has given everything she has.'"
(Luke 21:3-4 TLB)

Mercy Minute Volume 58, Script 21; by Eunice Hiew, staff writer; from story heard by Eunice Hiew at Bible study in New Zealand, June 4, 2014;

August 19

Ama's Bible

Joanne Thibault volunteered onboard our hospital ship, the *Africa Mercy*. She shared a heartwarming story about a patient named Ama:

"We removed a very large invading tumor, and at the same time we realized that she had cataracts. So arrangements were made to have her cataracts removed. Well, the moment she knew that she had that appointment, she asked could we please give her a Bible.

It was an incredible moment when Ama did have her sight restored. She immediately opened her new Bible and started reading to her grandson. Amazing!"

What wonderful gifts of mercy—sight and God's Word!

"These things that were written in the Scriptures so long ago are to teach us patience and to encourage us so that we will look forward expectantly to the time when God will conquer sin and death."
(Romans 15:4 TLB)

Mercy Minute Volume 58, Script 30; by Nancy Predaina, Special Projects Writer/Editor; from interview by Nancy Predaina and by Ambassador Team; 2012 AFM Guinea Field Service;

August 20

Mercy in Kosovo

In 1999, John Mason of Forestville, California, read a newspaper article about war-torn Kosovo. He thought, *"Who's going to help them?"*

John is a paramedic and former carpenter. He decided to get involved. So, he took vacation time, packed his tools and clothes, and set off for Kosovo.

Winter was fast approaching. Government bureaucracy prevented donated money and supplies from getting to the people.

In a marathon of meetings and pleading with officials, John finally got the supplies to the people, and hundreds of houses were repaired and rebuilt before winter.

You see, one person, plus ten weeks of effort, plus a determined compassionate heart equaled a great amount of mercy!

Donate your time and your mercy to answer the question, *"Who's going to help them?"*

> ***"But if someone who is supposed to be a Christian has money enough to live well, and sees a brother in need, and won't help him—how can God's love be within him?"* (1 John 3:17 TLB)**

> ***"If we always helped one another, no one would need luck."* (Sophocles)**

Mercy Minute Volume 64, Script 37; by Larry Mast, staff writer; from Guideposts, *July 2001, page 19, "To Light One Candle;"*

August 21

Taking Time for Judlin

Seven-year-old Judlin has a smile that lights up a room. As a toddler, he experienced a traumatic brain injury. That's a difficult injury to recover from, especially in a developing country like Madagascar with limited access to doctors and hospitals. Judlin had many physical challenges, including decreased muscle tone in his legs.

Mercy Ships corrected Judlin's crouched gait with physical therapy. But there was one other thing that Nurse Pat decided to address—Judlin still wore diapers. Nurse Pat worked with Judlin and his mom. Within weeks, Judlin was toilet-trained.

Outpatient Leader Natalie Bullock said, *"Pat took the time. She gave that boy love and a chance."*

You know, sometimes mercy and love are spelled T-I-M-E.

***"As long as it is day, we must do the works of Him who sent me. Night is coming, when no one can work."* (John 9:4 NIV)**

Mercy Minute Volume 64, Script 42; by Tanya Sierra, staff writer; from crew interview; 2014-2015 AFM *Madagascar Field Service;*

August 22
Natache

Many women in Africa are injured in childbirth. It's called obstetric fistula or vesico-vaginal fistula (VVF). It usually results in a stillborn baby, incontinence, and social isolation. However, a free surgery onboard our hospital ship restores hope. Crew member Tracey Wall explains:

"We got to know one of the VVF women named Natache. We printed off some of the pictures we had with her. I put stickers on the back of them with verses from the Bible. You would have thought we'd given her diamond rings! As the translator read the verses, Natache choked up at the realization that she was loved.

The story of these women is an amazing window into the heart of God. We got to take a peek, and we were blown away!"

Letting others know how much God loves them is a wonderful act of mercy.

***"But You, Lord, are a compassionate and gracious God, slow to anger, abounding in love and faithfulness."* (Psalm 86:15 NIV)**

***"All [God's] glory and beauty come from within, and there He delights to dwell. His visits there are frequent, His conversation sweet, His comforts refreshing. His peace passing all understanding."* (Thomas à Kempis)**

Mercy Minute Volume 62, Script 21; by Catherine Murphy, staff writer; from story submitted by Tracey Wall, Crew Physician Assistant, to Catherine Murphy, staff writer; 2013-2014 AFM *Congo Field Service;*

August 23

Mercy in Iraq

Many families in Iraq fled from ISIS militants, escaping with little but the clothes on their backs. Samaritan's Purse set up hundreds of tents for them in northern Iraq. Samaritan's Purse provided food, blankets, and shelter … and they shared the hope of the gospel.

Eman is a widow with two daughters. Islamic militia came to her home and asked her husband Tarik if he was a Christian. He bravely answered, "*Yes, I am a Christian.*" The men cut Tarik's head off right in front of Eman. She and her daughters fled from their home and lived in a tent provided by Samaritan's Purse.

A merciful heart does its best to alleviate suffering—even when faced with the terror of a ruthless enemy like Isis.

Show mercy today by joining me in praying for Christians who are persecuted like never before in history.

***"Continue to remember those in prison as if you were together with them in prison, and those who are mistreated as if you yourselves were suffering."* (Hebrews 13:3 NIV)**

Mercy Minute Volume 63, Script 24; by Larry Mast, staff writer; from www.samaritanspurse.org October 17, 2014 and August 19, 2014;

August 24

Molly and Sabrina

Many volunteers onboard our hospital ship, the *Africa Mercy*, find that certain patients touch their hearts in special ways. Volunteer nurse Molly tells us about such a patient:

"Sabrina is in her thirties and had a burn to her neck and face. She was selling fruit, and someone threw acid on her. The wounds got infected and weren't healing well. I got to do her dressing changes.

She started telling me her life story. She lost her three-year-old child, then she had her accident, and her husband left her. She had felt cast out for a long time.

The community of patients on the ship surrounded her and supported her. We saw an amazing change in her."

Yes, encouragement is a restorative act of mercy. Ask the Lord to guide you to someone who needs to hear an encouraging word.

> ***"Now glory be to God, who by His mighty power at work within us is able to do far more than we would ever dare to ask or even dream of—infinitely beyond our highest prayers, desires, thoughts, or hopes."* (Ephesians 3:20 TLB)**

Mercy Minute Volume 63, Script 23; by Nancy Predaina, Special Projects Writer/Editor; from interview with volunteer nurse Molly Gacetta by Tanya Sierra, staff writer; 2015-16 AFM Madagascar Field Service;

August 25

Mighty Moms of Walter Reed

There's a book called *Unbreakable Bonds: The Mighty Moms and Wounded Warriors of Walter Reed.* It's about faithful moms who care for their adult children wounded in military service. Some have spent *years* living with their children at Walter Reed National Military Medical Center.

Stacy Fidler's son Mark stepped on a land mine in Afghanistan. She appreciates the support of other moms, saying, "*We share the good things and the bad things.*"

Most of these women have given up their jobs in order to be full-time caretakers and advocates for their children.

Yes, these mighty moms are great examples of mighty love and mighty mercy.

"See what great love the Father has lavished on us, that we should be called children of God! And that is what we are!"
(1 John 3:1 NIV)

Mercy Minute Volume 63, Script 39; by Nancy Predaina, Special Projects Writer/Editor; from "The Mighty Moms of Walter Reed," http://www.foxnews.com/politics/2014/11/29/

August 26

Baby Rescue Center

Many crew members on our hospital ship find ways to show mercy in their spare time. Volunteer Shelly Grivette described how she spent weekends in Guinea, West Africa:

"What is worth driving for an hour and a half from the ship, dodging potholes, pedestrians, and stray animals? That's easy—it's the Baby Rescue Center in the village of Kobaya.

When we finally arrive at the Rescue Center, we have one primary job—holding babies!

I am drawn to Daniel, an 18-month old boy with disabilities. He needs to be held. I watch the children lift their tiny arms, wanting to be loved. The Baby Rescue Center is the highlight of my week!"

Make mercy the highlight of your week as you help someone today.

***"For even the Son of Man did not come to be served, but to serve, and to give His life as a ransom for many."* (Mark 10:45 NIV)**

***"A living, loving God can and does make His presence felt, can and does speak to us in the silence of our hearts, can and does warm and caress us till we no longer doubt that He is near, that He is here."* (Brennan Manning)**

Mercy Minute Volume 63, Script 37; by Larry Mast, staff writer; from Shelly Grivette, Mercy Ministries Coordinator, Jan 30, 2013;

August 27

Gentle Mercy

Mercy Ships volunteers entered an 8-foot square structure, home to a young bedridden woman in a poor African village. She'd had a stroke and lived with her mother, who also faced physical challenges.

They asked the young woman, *"Would you like to go outside in the sunlight?"* She nodded yes. They carefully lifted her into a wheelchair, and she enjoyed fresh air while her mother changed the bedding.

One volunteer gently massaged the young woman's arm to coax the muscles from their contorted state. Then they boiled water, gave her a bath, helped her into clean clothes, and carefully eased her back into her fresh bed. She was smiling.

Sometimes a gentle touch is a wonderful act of mercy. Find a simple, gentle way to show mercy to someone today.

"But the wisdom that comes from heaven is first of all pure and full of quiet gentleness. Then it is peace-loving and courteous. It allows discussion and is willing to yield to others; it is full of mercy and good deeds. It is wholehearted and straightforward and sincere."
(James 3:17 TLB)

Mercy Minute Volume 68, Script 39; by Windsor Marchesi, staff writer; from personal experience with Onboarding Field Practice (home visit with Physical Therapist Stefanie Neeb); 2016-2017) AFM *Benin Field Service;*

August 28

Parties for Needy Kids

Megan Yunn was helping with an after-school program for underserved kids. A little girl named Beverly told her she'd never had her own birthday party … or even a slice of birthday cake.

Megan was stunned and created a charity and called it *Beverly's Birthdays*. It provides birthday parties to homeless children in the greater Pittsburgh area. It works with 43 agencies, including homeless shelters, and residential treatment facilities.

Each party includes gifts, cupcakes and entertainment. But it's about more than just presents. Megan says, *"It's about a child knowing there's someone out there who really cares for them."*

What a great example of a merciful heart that sees a need and then does something about it! Stay alert for the opportunity to show mercy in your community.

"But whatever is good and perfect comes to us from God, the Creator of all light, and He shines forever without change or shadow." **(James 1:17 TLB)**

⚓ The *Africa Mercy's* first field service was in Liberia, a country devastated by a decade-long brutal civil war.

Mercy Minute Volume 63, Script 36; by Nancy Predaina, Special Projects Writer/Editor; from "Make a Wish!" by Kellie B. Gormly; Family Circle; *October 2015; ©2015 Mercy Ships, All Rights Reserved*

August 29

A Typical Ship's Day

Volunteer nurse Emily Kacsmar described her day onboard the *Africa Mercy*—onboard our hospital ship in Madagascar:

"I wake up in my six-berth cabin. And I will typically make my own coffee in a French press. If I have the day off, I can go into town, walk around markets, go to the beach, or eat in a local restaurant.

If I'm working, I take my 30-second commute down the hall to the hospital floor. The nurses pray before each shift. I care for my patients, sing songs, paint nails, provide nursing care, administer medications, learn Malagasy words, and find ways to show my patients how much I love them."

That sounds like a good day to me! In fact, any day filled with mercy is a great day!

> ***"His compassion never ends. It is only the Lord's mercies that have kept us from complete destruction. Great is His faithfulness; His loving-kindness begins afresh each day."***
> **(Lamentations 3:22-23 TLB)**

Mercy Minute Volume 63, Script 47; by Nancy Predaina, Special Projects Writer/Editor; from media interview with Emily Kacsmar by Pauline Rick, US Public Relations Coordinator; 2014-15 AFM *Madagascar Field Service;*

August 30

Robots and Land Mines

Helen Greiner loves computers and inventing things. She's the co-founder of *iRobot*. Her company developed Roomba, a vacuuming robot. Now she's using that technology in a very unusual way.

Troops in Afghanistan had a problem. Fleeing Taliban fighters left stashes of weapons in caves—booby-trapped with land mines. It was dangerous to send soldiers blindly into the caves. So, Helen developed the PackBot, a robot designed to clear land mines. The troops gave the robots nicknames. Helen says, *"A Marine brought in Scooby Doo, his blown-up PackBot. Only the head had survived. The Marine credited Scooby Doo with saving him and his buddies several times in 17 missions."*

You see, our creativity is a gift from God, and we can use it to find amazing ways to help others.

"... and He has filled him with the Spirit of God, with wisdom, with understanding, with knowledge and with all kinds of skills—to make artistic designs for work in gold, silver and bronze ..."
(Exodus 35:31-32 NIV)

Mercy Minute Volume 34, Script 56; by Nancy Predaina, Special Projects Writer/Editor; from "The Bot Master," Reader's Digest, *September 2008;*

August 31

Forgiveness in Royesville

Mercy Ships volunteers Jean-Claude and Anastasie wanted to start a community farm in the Royesville area—a group of twenty Muslim villages in rural Liberia. To introduce the project, they invited the villagers to a meal.

But the people refused to sit together. Hatred, anger, and resentment from Liberia's long civil war divided them. So, Jean-Claude asked, *"Where shall we eat? We do not belong to your village."*

Finally, one of the chiefs stood and said, *"God has brought these people to help us. We must work together."* People asked for and offered forgiveness. Walls were broken down. And now they are working, sweating, and laughing together. And, yes, they're even studying scriptures together.

You see, forgiveness is a transforming act of mercy! Transform a life by offering forgiveness or requesting forgiveness.

"Do not judge, and you will not be judged. Do not condemn, and you will not be condemned. Forgive, and you will be forgiven."
(Luke 6:37-38 NIV)

Mercy Minute Volume 34, Script 56; by Nancy Predaina, Special Projects Writer/Editor; from interview with Ken Winebark, October 2008;

SEPTEMBER

"Dear friends, let us love one another, for love comes from God. Everyone who loves has been born of God and knows God. Whoever does not love does not know God, because God is love." (Galatians 6:9-10 NIV)

September 1

Wilma Rudolph

Wilma Rudolph was the 20th of 22 children. She was born prematurely in 1940 and weighed only 4 ½ pounds. Most of her childhood was spent in bed—with scarlet fever, whooping cough, measles . . . and polio. But her family was determined she could be a "normal kid." Her siblings massaged her legs. And, once a week, her mother took her 90 miles roundtrip for therapy. And it worked! She got rid of her leg braces and became a high school basketball star. At the 1960 Olympics, Wilma became the first American woman to win three gold medals in one Olympics. She encouraged young athletes, saying, ".... *the triumph can't be had without the struggle.*"

And you can be a mercy-giver when you follow Wilma's example and encourage others who are struggling.

"Since we have such a huge crowd of men of faith watching us from the grandstands, let us strip off anything that slows us down or holds us back, and especially those sins that wrap themselves so tightly around our feet and trip us up; and let us run with patience the particular race that God has set before us." **(Hebrews 12:1 TLB)**

⚓ In 1986 Mercy Ships assisted victims of the earthquake in Mexico by sending medical, dental, construction and outreach teams.

Mercy Minute Volume 55, Script 57; by Nancy Predaina, Special Projects Writer/Editor; from "Rudolph Ran and World Went Wild," by M.B. Roberts. http://espn.go.com/sportscentury/features/00016444.html;

September 2

The Telephone Lady

In Sierra Leone, West Africa, it's not easy to find a job—especially if you're a woman. But there is a new "telephone lady" in one village.

Abi came to Mercy Ships for a free surgery to repair a childbirth injury and received an extra benefit! While she recovered from surgery, she learned basic math. She was taught how to operate a new payphone device. And she was given a phone to take home with her.

Now her neighbors come to Abi and pay to make their calls. Her new role as "telephone lady" gives her status and respect, as well as a small income. She's very thankful.

In the United States, we celebrate Labor Day. Be thankful for the job you have and dedicate it to the Lord.

"And let the [gracious] favor of the Lord our God be on us; confirm for us the work of our hands—yes, confirm the work of our hands."
(Psalm 90:17 AMP)

Mercy Minute Volume 32, Script 51; by Morgen Kleinknecht at the Aberdeen West African Fistula Centre; 9/12/07;

September 3

A Job at Greyston Bakery

Greyston Bakery in Yonkers, NY, makes wonderful brownies. But it also serves mercy. Every job applicant's name goes on a list. When a job becomes available, it's offered to the first person on the list.

A young man named Dion ended up in prison for selling drugs. When he got out of prison, he applied at Greyston Bakery. In a few weeks he got a call offering him a job. He went from apprentice to lead operator, to research and development, and finally was selected for supervisor training.

Dion says, *"I'm not rich, but I'm happy. When you give a person a job, you give that person a second chance in life."*

A merciful heart takes a chance on people. Take a chance and show mercy to someone today!

"Servants, do what you're told by your earthly masters. And don't just do the minimum that will get you by. Do your best. Work from the heart for your real Master, for God, confident that you'll get paid in full when you come into your inheritance. Keep in mind always that the ultimate Master you're serving is Christ."
(Colossians 3:23-24 MSG)

Mercy Minute Volume 64, Script 61; by Nancy Predaina, Special Projects Writer/Editor; from "The Bakery that Gave Him a Second Chance," www.youtube.com

September 4

Ama Is Back in Business

Ama is a seamstress in Sierra Leone, West Africa—but a facial tumor made it hard for her to work.

When Mercy Ships arrived, Ama sold her sewing machine to pay for a taxi to go to the patient screening. And she received a free surgery onboard our hospital ship to remove the tumor.

But now, how was she going to support her family? Crew member Elaine heard Ama's story—and she and her husband bought a new sewing machine for Ama.

A delighted Ama returned home with a new sewing machine. She immediately put her measuring tape around her neck. Elaine said, *"That meant she was back in business!"*

And YOU can help someone "get back in business" through your acts of kindness.

***"And God is able to bless you abundantly, so that in all things at all times, having all that you need, you will abound in every good work."* (2 Corinthians 9:8 NIV)**

***"A quiet morning with a loving God puts the events of the upcoming day into proper perspective."* (Janette Oke)**

Mercy Minute Volume 48, Script 58; by Catherine Cooper, staff writer; from conversation with Elaine B. Winn, October 4, 2011; 2011 AFM *Sierra Leone Field Service;*

September 5

Mailman Delivers Mercy

Sometimes our jobs provide unexpected opportunities for mercy …

Kurt Spaller was delivering mail one beautiful day in Florida. Halfway through his route, he saw smoke pouring out of an apartment complex. Kurt knew which units were occupied. He rushed in, pounded on doors, and helped people evacuate. The five-alarm fire singed the hair on his arms and legs.

A spokesman for the National Association of Letter Carriers described the incident as an example of *"the time-honored tradition of letter carriers . . . coming to the aid of people in danger along their postal routes."*

Make mercy a time-honored tradition in your life and in your work day.

"In everything I showed you that by working hard in this manner you must help the weak and remember the words of the Lord Jesus, that He Himself said, 'It is more blessed to give than to receive.'"
(Acts 20:35 NASB)

Mercy Minute Volume 36, Script 56; by Nancy Predaina, Special Projects Writer/Editor; adapted from "West Florida Letter Carrier Named 'Hero of the Year,'" www.nalc.org 8/20/2004;

September 6

100 Grandchildren and Counting

Carole Smalley had 100 grandchildren… give or take a dozen or so! Carole worked in the accounting office onboard a Mercy Ship in West Africa. Like many crewmembers who work in support positions, Carole looked for opportunities to get more directly involved after hours. While the Mercy Ship was in Liberia, Carole spent a lot of her free time at the Great Commission Orphanage.

Carole says, *"I didn't do much … just showed the kids a little attention. I handed out lots of smiles and hugs. They sat in my lap and braided my hair."* Carole did more than she knows. Before she left, the kids were calling her "grandma."

You can be a person of influence on an impressionable life by showing mercy and a hug to someone today.

"Pure and undefiled religion in the sight of our God and Father is this: to visit orphans and widows in their distress, and to keep oneself unstained by the world." **(James 1:27 NASB)**

Mercy Minute Volume 26, Script 7; by Mike Osborne, staff writer; interview with Carole Smalley, July 2006; 2005-06 Anastasis *Liberia Field Service;*

September 7

Not Finished Yet

Sometimes volunteers onboard our hospital ship *Africa Mercy* to decide to stay longer than they'd originally planned. One nurse explains:

"I wanted to use my nursing skills to help people in a land that I knew nothing about. I was going to volunteer for three months and not a day longer.

But the joke's on me. Three months wasn't enough. I didn't expect to be inspired by the souls I interact with every day. When asked what made me want to stay, I blurted out, 'Well, I just don't feel like I'm finished here yet.'

I'm excited to open my heart to new faces . . . as they have done for me."

You know, we're never finished in showing mercy because we're never finished in following the model of Jesus.

***"This is the kind of life you've been invited into, the kind of life Christ lived. He suffered everything that came His way so you would know that it could be done, and also know how to do it, step-by-step."* (1 Peter 2:21 MSG)**

Mercy Minute Volume 56, Script 52; by Grace Antonini, staff writer; from http://kpal5.blogspot.com 11/30/13 blog of Karen Palomba, volunteer nurse; 2013-14 AFM *Congo Field Service;*

September 8

Baby Anthony

Grace looked at her beautiful newborn boy, Anthony. Then she saw a cyst, about the size of a baseball, attached to Anthony's lower back. This defect is called a meningocele. If it isn't surgically corrected, life-threatening infections occur. Unfortunately, healthcare in much of West Africa is almost non-existent.

Grace's husband wanted to put the baby up for adoption. But Grace trusted God. Someone at the hospital said that our Mercy Ship could help. Grace took the baby to the *Africa Mercy*, and Dr. Bruce Steffes performed a free surgery for five-day-old Anthony. Grace told her husband, *"See what God can do. See my fine baby you wanted to give away?"*

God works through those who will dedicate their lives and skills to Him—people like you and me. We can make a difference by showing mercy.

"And we know that all that happens to us is working for our good if we love God and are fitting into His plans."
(Romans 8:28 TLB)

Mercy Minute Volume 33, Script 44; from "Surgery Saves Infant from Dangerous Birth Deformity," by Megan Petock, Mercy Ships volunteer; Philadelphia Inquirer *4/13/08;; 2008* AFM *Liberia Field Service;*

September 9

Mbalu—a Merciful Grandmother

Here's a wonderful story told by a merciful grandmother in Sierra Leone, West Africa:

"My great-grandson Abdul was born with a cleft lip. He and his thirteen-year-old mother had nowhere to live, so I took them into my home.

We took Abdul to a screening to have his cleft lip repaired by the volunteer surgeons on the Africa Mercy. *He was accepted as a patient, but his mother wasn't old enough to be admitted as his caregiver. I said, 'I will be the caregiver ... and his mother can come, too.'*

Now my three-month-old great-grandson has a beautiful mouth!"

Mbalu is a wise grandmother who has learned the value of mercy and love. That's a wonderful legacy for her family. Be an example of mercy to your family today.

"Children's children are a crown to the aged, and parents are the pride of their children." **(Proverbs 17:6 NIV)**

Mercy Minute Volume 48, Script 62; by Elaine B. Winn, staff writer; from Interview with Mbalu Bangura, AFM 2011 Sierra Leone Field Service;

September 10

$20 from Myles

Army Sgt. Andy Eckert died in Iraq, just five weeks after his son Myles was born. Myles built his idea of his father from other people's memories and his own imagination.

One day, eight-year-old Myles was thrilled to find a $20 bill on a restaurant parking lot. Just think what he could buy!

Then he saw Lt. Col. Frank Dailey in uniform. So, Myles wrapped the twenty dollars in a note that read, *"Dear Soldier, My dad was a soldier. He's in heaven now. I found this 20 dollars in the parking lot. We like to pay it forward in my family. It's your lucky day! Thank you for your service."*

Yes, Myles and his mother are both big believers in mercy!

***"Give as freely as you have received!"* (Matthew 10:8 TLB)**

***"Good character is the best tombstone. Those who loved you and were helped by you will remember you when forget-me-nots have withered. Carve your name on hearts, not on marble."* (Charles Spurgeon)**

Mercy Minute Volume 56, Script 15; by Nancy Predaina, Special Projects Writer/Editor; from "On the Road," CBS News, by Steve Hartman; 2/28/14;

September 11

Fenosoa and His Grandpa

Fenosoa lives in his grandpa's hut even though his parents are in the same village. Why? His grandpa, Papa Denis, says, *"Because he loves me."*

Fenosoa was born with a cyst on his side. For five years it grew along with the little boy, sometimes making him lose his balance.

One day, Papa Denis heard on the radio that Mercy Ships was providing free surgeries in Madagascar. So the 86-year-old grandpa and his pint-sized grandson walked for five days to get to the Mercy Ship … and the free surgery Fenosoa desperately needed.

Papa Denis said they would take it easy after the young boy's recovery—they would take six days to go home, instead of five.

You know, grandparents are very special mercy-givers.

"'As for me,' God says, 'this is My covenant with them: My Spirit that I've placed upon you and the words that I've given you to speak, they're not going to leave your mouths nor the mouths of your children nor the mouths of your grandchildren. You will keep repeating these words and won't ever stop.' God's orders."
(Isaiah 59:21 MSG)

Mercy Minute Volume 64, Script 65; by Sharon Walls, staff writer; from interview with patient; 2015-16 AFM *Madagascar Field Service;*

September 12

Hospice Blankets

Acts of mercy often inspire more mercy. Linda, from Indiana, shares a great example:

"Mom spent her last months in hospice care. The kind nurses gave her Valentines, a Halloween pumpkin and candy, homemade pies, and a lap quilt. Every item made her feel loved. Their willingness to answer my questions during this hard time made me feel loved, too.

Mom's gone now, but I wanted to give back some of the kindness we'd received. My mother taught me to sew at age five. As my way to honor Mom, I decided to make lap quilts for the hospice. I know each blanket will mean a great deal to both patients and family members."

The best way to follow the model of Jesus is to serve others. Think of some ways to show mercy … and make people feel loved.

"Anyone wanting to be a leader among you must be your servant. And if you want to be right at the top, you must serve like a slave. Your attitude must be like My own, for I, the Messiah, did not come to be served, but to serve, and to give My life as a ransom for many."
(Matthew 20:26-28 TLB)

Mercy Minute Volume 56, Script 19; by Larry Mast, staff writer; from Guideposts, *January 2013,*

September 13

Big Brother Trenton

Lindsay Cochran has been in a wheelchair since she was two years old. She was born with Spinal Muscular Atrophy which prevents her from walking. But she was also born with a great blessing—a wonderful big brother and best friend named Trenton.

Trenton is her greatest defender and ally. It makes her feel good when he runs the 5K race every year to raise funds to fight her illness. He believes his life would have been different without her. He says, *"She's my best friend. I would take a bullet for her."*

And Lindsay is certain that it's much easier to go through life with a big brother like Trenton.

Yes, mercy and love always make it much easier to go through life.

"So, chosen by God for this new life of love, dress in the wardrobe God picked out for you: compassion, kindness, humility, quiet strength, discipline. Be even-tempered, content with second place, quick to forgive an offense. Forgive as quickly and completely as the Master forgave you. And regardless of what else you put on, wear love. It's your basic, all-purpose garment. Never be without it."

(Colossians 3:12-14 MSG)

Mercy Minute Volume 56, Script 39; by Nancy Predaina, Special Projects Writer/Editor; from http://www.breakingchristiannews.com/articles/display_art_pf.html?ID=13180;

September 14

Our Vision Statement

At Mercy Ships, we use hospital ships to transform individuals and serve nations, one at a time. Listen as a crew member eloquently explains this vision statement:

"Think of all the patients . . . of all the places they come from . . . and how love is going to affect each of those lives. It's going to spread throughout the country.

As we share those simple little acts of love every day, the patients get transformed—and that's how a nation gets transformed. That excites me and reminds me that we are part of something so much bigger than we realize."

Yes, as we follow the model of Jesus, people experience physical, emotional, and spiritual transformation. It IS exciting! What is YOUR vision statement—may it include Mercy!

"Don't copy the behavior and customs of this world, but be a new and different person with a fresh newness in all you do and think. Then you will learn from your own experience how His ways will really satisfy you." **(Romans 12:2 TLB)**

"Be such a person and live such a life, that if every one were such as you, and every life a life such as yours, this earth would be God's paradise." **(Phillips Brooks)**

Mercy Minute Volume 56, Script 38; by Catherine Murphy, staff writer; from presentation by Kirstie Randall, Ward Supervisor, Community Meeting, October 2013; 2013-14 AFM *Congo Field Service;*

September 15

Diana's Eyesight Restored

Diana was just 12-years-old and blind from cataracts. She fumbled her way aboard the *Africa Mercy*. She had grown up in severe poverty. There were only two eye surgeons in her entire country. And Diana's family couldn't afford the necessary surgery to remove the cataracts.

But Diana's mother prayed for a miracle … and she got an answer! Our *Africa Mercy* came to Liberia with a volunteer eye-surgery team. After the 20-minute eye surgery, which cost her family nothing, Diana opened her eyes and clapped for joy. For the first time in many years, she could see beautiful colors!

The next day, she walked down the gangway, with her sight—and her hope—restored. You see, acts of mercy color life with hope.

"And we are sure of this, that He will listen to us whenever we ask Him for anything in line with His will. And if we really know He is listening when we talk to Him and make our requests, then we can be sure that He will answer us."

(1 John 5:14-15 TLB)

Mercy Minute Volume 34, Script 7; by Nancy Predaina, Special Projects Writer/Editor; from Direct Mail Letter from Mercy Ships 5/9/08;

September 16

Val Sprinkles Love and Mercy

Life was difficult for Hope and Grant when they moved to Auckland, New Zealand. It wasn't easy raising children on limited income while taking classes and family so far away.

Then they met Val—a tractor-driving property manager whose husband had abandoned her. She came to the rescue and became Hope and Grant's family for 5½ years.

Val helped in so many ways—babysitting, washing dishes, unblocking the toilet, and even disposing of mice.

Hope says, "It's a very mundane story, in some ways. But it's a very real story of kindness."

You see, Val didn't cure diseases or end poverty. But she sprinkled love and mercy into the hungry hearts of a young family—and that made all the difference!

I challenge you to find a way to sprinkle love and mercy into someone's life.

"God is not unjust; He will not forget your work and the love you have shown Him as you have helped His people and continue to help them." **(Hebrews 6:10 NIV)**

Mercy Minute Volume 58, Script 1; by Eunice Hiew, staff writer; from interview with Hope; June, 2014;

September 17

Ravette

Ravette lived her eleven years of life in Congo with a deformity known as "backward-bending knee." She struggled to walk. She couldn't attend school.

When Ravette came to our hospital ship, her legs were placed in special casts to gradually stretch them. Then, she had a free surgery to straighten them.

Hobbling around the wards with her crutches, Ravette created smiles and laughter. Gradually, casts and braces would come off until she could walk without assistance.

She was very clear about her future plans, saying, *"I want to find a job in an office working on a computer. I will be a boss!"*

And everyone on our hospital ship believed her!

Yes, mercy was putting Ravette on the path to a brighter future. You can brighten someone's future through your acts of kindness.

"Trust in the Lord with all your heart and do not lean on your own understanding. In all your ways acknowledge Him, and He will make your paths straight." **(Proverbs 3:5-6 NASB)**

"Give yourself fully to God. He will use you to accomplish great things on the condition that you believe much more in His love than in your own weakness." **(Mother Teresa)**

Mercy Minute Volume 56, Script 14; by Eunice Hiew, staff writer; from interview with Hope; June, 2014;

September 18

Photos of Baby Sophia

Baby Sophia passed away six weeks after her birth. Her dad, Nathan Steffel, posted a photo of the infant and this request on Reddit, a social networking site:

"My daughter recently passed away after a long battle in the children's hospital. Since she was in the hospital her whole life, we never were able to get a photo without all her medical tubes. Can someone remove the tubes from this photo?"

The response from electronic artists was overwhelming! Nathan received condolences in the form of hundreds of PhotoShopped versions of the photo, drawings and paintings of beautiful little Sophia.

What a beautiful outpouring of sympathy, love and mercy to bring a bit of joy into the midst of a heartbreaking tragedy!

***"He will wipe every tear from their eyes. There will be no more death or mourning or crying or pain, for the old order of things has passed away."* (Revelation 21:4 NIV)**

⚓ The *Anastasis* carried relief goods to Jamaica in 1988 after Hurricane Gilbert.

Mercy Minute Volume 58, Script 33; by Nancy Predaina, Special Projects Writer/Editor; from "Father Asked Strangers to PhotoShop Photo," www.boredpanda.com;

September 19

Welcome Home, Vernel

Clementine is a hospital chaplain on our hospital ship, the *Africa Mercy*. She shared a special moment with a young patient who had a free surgery to repair a cleft lip:

"Vernel had been rejected by his community and teased by his peers. His welcome home celebration was remarkable. His family cooked, and his mother and aunties danced around the village. His entire community praised God that Vernel had been healed. They accepted him with open arms. It was a wonderful blessing to see the joy of Vernel's family when they saw their child restored."

The wonderful crew onboard our hospital ship follow the model of Jesus as they use their talents to provide physical healing. But there is often an emotional and spiritual healing that also takes place when you show kindness to others.

***"Come to Me, all you who are weary and burdened, and I will give you rest. Take My yoke upon you and learn from Me, for I am gentle and humble in heart, and you will find rest for your souls. For My yoke is easy and My burden is light."* (Matthew 11:28-30 NIV)**

Mercy Minute Volume 58, Script 37; by Catherine Murphy, staff writer; from story submitted by Clementine Tengue to Catherine Murphy; 2013-14 AFM *Congo Field Service;*

September 20

An Emergency Scooter

Hurricane Sandy slammed into the East Coast in October 2012. Roads were almost impassable in the town of Little Ferry. So, Jennifer Kaufman used her little silver Vespa as an instrument of mercy. The small scooter became an emergency vehicle.

She went to inaccessible areas, carrying food, clothing, and blankets. She helped people clean out ruined homes. And she located gas stations with available fuel and relayed the information to local reporters.

Jennifer is modest about her efforts, saying, *"There were so many people doing exactly what I was doing. I was just doing it on a scooter."*

A merciful heart always finds a way to help—maybe even on a scooter. Find creative ways to show mercy to others.

"... Behold, I have given you a wise and discerning heart, so that there has been no one like you before you, nor shall one like you arise after you." **(1 Kings 3:12 NASB)**

Mercy Minute Volume 58, Script 17; from "Inspiring Stories: The Heroes of Hurricane Sandy: The Little Engine that Could," http://rd.com, 2012;

September 21

Small Things Matter

Listen as volunteer nurse, Becky Johns, shares an important discovery she made on the ward of our hospital ship, the *Africa Mercy*:

"A patient's small hand reaches toward my face and strokes my cheek. What have I done to deserve this affection? Nothing more than squatting down to his level on the floor and offering a smile.

I am learning that small things can make all the difference—dyeing head bandages different colors and drawing faces on balloons.

All the small things I have been called to do point to the One who is not small—the One who has not created insignificant people or insignificant tasks."

Remember that small things can add up to something miraculous when you decide to show mercy!

***"Do not despise this small beginning, for the eyes of the Lord rejoice to see the work begin ..."* (Zechariah 4:10 TLB)**

Mercy Minute Volume 58, Script 14; by Grace Antonini, staff writer; from 2/27/2014 blogpost of Becky Johns, ward nurse; 2013-14 AFM Congo Field Service;

September 22

Comfort for Mr. Wang

A team from our hospital ship, the *Africa Mercy*, regularly visited a prison in the Congo. On one visit, crewmember Serenety Liu from China went along.

A prisoner named Mr. Wang had killed a brutal ship captain who beat him daily. Mr. Wang was facing either life imprisonment or a death sentence.

He'd never heard about Jesus, so Serenety began a priceless ministry. Several visits later, with a Bible in Chinese firmly in his hand, Mr. Wang decided to follow Jesus.

A crew member said, *"God, in His divine mercy, saw Mr. Wang's hopelessness and sent Serenety to bring him hope and comfort."*

Yes, Mr. Wang learned about Jesus in his own language. Hope and comfort replaced despair—now that's mercy! Share the love and mercy of Jesus with someone today.

"But in your hearts revere Christ as Lord. Always be prepared to give an answer to everyone who asks you to give the reason for the hope that you have. But do this with gentleness and respect."
(1 Peter 3:15 NIV)

Mercy Minute Volume 58, Script 15; by Nancy Predaina, Special Projects Writer/Editor; from email from Kim Robinson, teacher in AFM *Academy, to Catherine Clarke Murphy, staff writer; May 16, 2014;* AFM *Congo Field Service;*

September 23

From POW to Ambassador

Pete Peterson was an American pilot in Vietnam, flying nightly raids to bomb enemy transportation routes. One night a missile hit his plane, and he was forced to eject. He spent the next six brutal years in the infamous prison known as the Hanoi Hilton.

Thirty years after his release, his country asked him to return to Vietnam . . . as the first U.S. ambassador since the war. Pete often visited schools and hospitals and discovered that many children died from accidental injury.

So, he began a program called Safe Vietnam. It implemented mandatory use of helmets for cyclists and offered swimming instruction.

Peterson says, *"My life was preserved to do something constructive."* What a great example of forgiveness and mercy!

***"But indeed for this very reason I have allowed you to live, in order to show you My power and in order that My name may be proclaimed throughout all the earth."* (Exodus 9:16 AMP)**

***"You can talk to God because God listens. Your voice matters in heaven. He takes you very seriously ... Even if you stammer or stumble, even if what you have to say impresses no one, it impresses God—and He listens."* (Max Lucado)**

Mercy Minute Volume 58, Script 65; by Nancy Predaina, Special Projects Writer/Editor; from "Pete Peterson: The Ex-POW Teaching Vietnam to Swim," by William Kramer, BBC New Magazine, www.bbc.com 3/22/13; AND "A Former POW Tours Vietnam as an Envoy of Reconciliation," by David Lamb, Los Angeles Times, *2/21/98;*

September 24

Rosa's Doubts

Rosa was in her last year of high school when the cataracts started. Suddenly, all her future plans came crashing down. Then she heard that Mercy Ships was coming to her country of Benin, West Africa. She could receive a free surgery!

She was so excited! But she was also scared … scared to get her hopes up. She dreamed of being able to see again, but could she handle a slammed door … a *NO*?

She gathered her courage, and went to the hospital ship. Weeks later, it was time for the operation. She trembled as she walked down the ship's halls.

But, just one day later, she opened her eyes. She could see again! Her secret hopes had become reality.

Don't let YOUR doubts stop you … make someone's hope a reality by showing mercy today.

***"I will give thanks and praise to You, for I am fearfully and wonderfully made; Wonderful are Your works, and my soul knows it very well."* (Psalm 139:14 AMP)**

Mercy Minute Volume 70, Script 52; by Anna Psiaki, staff writer; from patient interview; 2016-2017 AFM *Benin Field Service;*

September 25

Surgery for Kalkidan

Some years ago, Grace Wilson received an email she couldn't ignore. Missionary friends told her about four-year-old Kalkidan. The little Ethiopian girl had a rare colon disease. The medical care she needed to survive was not available in her country.

Now, Grace attended a very small 25-member church in Kentucky. She asked the congregation to help sponsor an operation for this little girl. And they enthusiastically responded. They raised enough money to fly Kalkidan and her father to the states. A free operation at Cincinnati's Children's Hospital saved the little girl's life.

Grace said, "*One person can make a difference, not just in our local community, but in the global community.*"

***"For we are God's fellow workers [His servants working together]; you are God's cultivated field [His garden, His vineyard], God's building."* (1 Corinthians 3:9 AMP)**

Mercy Minute Volume 60, Script 23; by Nancy Predaina, Special Projects Writer/Editor; from Today's Christian, *Sept/Oct. 2007;*

September 26

A Simple Story

Many crewmembers participate in Mercy Ministries during their free time. One group visited the Mercy Ships HOPE Center, our outpatient recovery center. Keith Brinkman shared a humorous response to a story:

"We were telling the story of Jesus walking on the water. We reinforced the message of trusting in Jesus with a craft project. The 15 children and about a dozen adults folded paper to make a boat, complete with a drinking straw mast and sail, blue paper for water, and Play-Doh for Jesus and Peter.

A very bright seven- year- old girl said, 'I think it's simpler to trust Jesus than to make Jesus.'"

"Out of the mouths of babes!" Show mercy to someone today … you may even get a chuckle out of it.

***"Our mouths were filled with laughter, our tongues with songs of joy. Then it was said among the nations, 'The Lord has done great things for them.'"* (Psalm 126:2 NIV)**

Mercy Minute Volume 62, Script 37; by Larry Mast, staff writer; from blog posted on Navigator (Mercy Ships intranet) by Keith Brinkman, 4/13/15;

September 27

Photographer Windy

Our Mercy Ships HOPE Center is a great place for patients to recover and learn new things. Just ask twelve year-old Windy! He received a free surgery onboard the *Africa Mercy* to treat burns he suffered as a young child. The communications team often visited him while he was rehabilitating his arm. They fell in love with his sweet spirit and bright smile.

Windy loved all the gadgets and gear they carried—especially their cameras. Photographer Katie Keegan spent time showing him how to take pictures. He learned to use different lenses and how to zoom in on shots.

Windy was thrilled. He said, *"I'm a photographer!"* And a dream was born—he hopes to someday become a photographer or videographer.

Sometimes acts of kindness give birth to new dreams of a bright future.

***"Now glory be to God, who by His mighty power at work within us is able to do far more than we would ever dare to ask or even dream of—infinitely beyond our highest prayers, desires, thoughts, or hopes."* (Ephesians 3:20 TLB)**

***"Since you get more joy out of giving joy to others, you should put a good deal of thought into the happiness that you are able to give."* (Eleanor Roosevelt)**

Mercy Minute Volume 63, Script 13; by Tanya Sierra, staff writer; from personal observation; 2014-2015 AFM *Madagascar Field Service;*

September 28

Nicholas Saves Grandpa

Twelve-year-old Nicholas Channer spent the day with his Grandpa working with the cows. As they started to leave, his grandfather couldn't unlock the car door. He was unable to speak.

Nicholas was terrified, but he acted quickly. He called his father and then managed to place his grandfather in the car. He drove the half mile to his house, where they were met by the ambulance. Nicholas' grandfather had suffered a severe stroke, but his grandson's quick action saved his life. Nicholas says, *"I didn't cry until they put him in the ambulance."*

Nicholas was honored as a Hometown Hero. And his grandpa was there to see him receive the award.

You see, mercy responds to cries for help and does whatever is necessary to help others.

***"Show respect to the aged; honor the presence of an elder; fear your God. I am God."* (Leviticus 19:32 MSG)**

Mercy Minute Volume 36, Script 60; by Nancy Predaina, Special Projects Writer/Editor; from "Boy Saves Grandpa," by Daniel Huffman, www.weatherforddemocrat.com 1/27/09;

September 29

Fatoumatou's Birthday Card

Mercy is abundant on our hospital ships, from crew to patients... and sometimes from patients to crew. Here's Fatoumatou's story:

"I think I'm in my forties. In my West African village, we don't count our years. When I was a child, something happened to my jaw. It would not open. Then Dr. Gary, a doctor on Mercy Ships, fixed my jaw. I am so happy!

Today is Dr. Gary's birthday. The nurse gave me a pretty piece of paper to make a card. I drew a big flower and then I wrote:

I love you.
I wish you grace.
I have found my smile again."

You can help others find their smiles again just by showing love and kindness to them.

"A cheerful heart brings a smile to your face; a sad heart makes it hard to get through the day. … A miserable heart means a miserable life; a cheerful heart fills the day with song."
(Proverbs 15: 13, 15 MSG)

⚓ Dr. Gary Parker is a skilled and gifted oral and maxillofacial surgeon who has served full-time with Mercy Ships since 1986. He met his wife onboard, and they raised their two children onboard. Dr. Parker is our Chief Medical Officer onboard the *Africa Mercy*.

Mercy Minute Volume 51, Script 14; by Nancy Predaina, Special Projects Writer/Editor; from blog by Ali Chandra, 04/30/2012 (used with permission);

September 30

Rainstorm Fish and Chips

A group of disadvantaged kids in the UK were enjoying a free, week-long respite vacation provided by a non-profit called CHICKS—Country Holidays for Inner City Kids.

An unexpected rainstorm sprang up just as they were leaving the aquarium in Plymouth. They'd planned to eat sack lunches outside. Instead, their leader Annie asked the owner of a nearby fish and chip shop if the children could shelter there.

The owner, Mitch Tonks, did a lot more than just say "yes." He served the whole group free fish and chips, followed by ice cream!

Respite leader Annie said, *"It is not very often that you come across such kindness and generosity. Mitch made 15 children feel very special."*

And you can make someone feel very special through an unexpected act of kindness.

***"Do not forget to show hospitality to strangers, for by so doing some people have shown hospitality to angels without knowing it."* (Hebrews 13:2 NIV)**

Mercy Minute Volume 60, Script 26; by Vicki Gregg, volunteer writer; from www.facebook.com/chickscharity August 2014;

October

"For we are God's workmanship, created in Christ Jesus to do good works, which God prepared in advance for us to do."
(Ephesians 2:10 NIV)

October 1

Assan and Allusan

Assan and Allusan lived in a camp filled with people left homeless from Liberia's civil war. But they couldn't see the sad conditions around them. You see, Assan and Allusan are two-year-old identical twins who were both born blind. The odds of that happening are one in nearly 400 million.

At the Mercy Ships patient screening, the boys' eyes rolled aimlessly in opposite directions. They were selected for free eye surgery onboard a Mercy Ship.

Finally, the exciting moment arrived. They could see for the very first time in their lives! Their eyes were tracking normally! Their small hands eagerly reached for the bright yellow balloons.

Imagine the joy of those two little boys, seeing well enough to play their first game of "tag" together!

Yes, mercy and joy are dance partners! You can bring joy into someone's life by showing mercy and kindness.

***"But God's not finished. He's waiting around to be gracious to you. He's gathering strength to show mercy to you. God takes the time to do everything right—everything. Those who wait around for Him are the lucky ones."* (Isaiah 30:18 MSG)**

Mercy Minute Volume 24, Script 4; by Nancy Predaina, Special Projects Writer/Editor; from onamercyship.com, website of Scott Harrison, photojournalist; 2005-06 Anastasis *Liberia Field Service;*

October 2

Baby Francina

Marta Chase volunteered as a nurse onboard our hospital ship. She described her experience of working with cleft lip babies:

"Baby Francina had severe bilateral cleft lip and palate. But with the help of the infant feeding program, she fattened up and was able to have surgery.

One of my favorite things about taking care of cleft lip babies is watching the baby's mother. Francina's mother was always by her side. Francina will probably never remember having a free surgery or being on the Mercy Ship. But her mother will forever remember the love that she and her daughter experienced here."

Mercy—whether you are the receiver or the giver—is always an unforgettable experience.

***"And the God of all grace, who called you to his eternal glory in Christ, after you have suffered a little while, will Himself restore you and make you strong, firm and steadfast."* (1 Peter 5:10 NIV)**

Mercy Minute Volume 62, Script 32; by Nancy Predaina, Special Projects Writer/Editor; from interview with Marta Chase, volunteer nurse, by Pauline Rick, U.S. Media Liaison; 2014-15 AFM Madagascar Field Service;

October 3

A Dog for James

A group called Assistance Dogs New Zealand trains service dogs for people with disabilities. And nine-year-old James Isaac is kept safe and calm by a devoted dog named Mahe.

You see, James has autism. His mother says, "*We couldn't even go to a cafe as a family. James would get very anxious. But when we got Mahe, James would just sit there waiting for us to finish our coffee.*"

When James had to go to the hospital for an MRI, Mahe was right by his side during the procedure and in the recovery room. He's the little boy's best friend.

You see, the organizations that train service animals and provide them to those who need them are mercy-givers. Just ask James!

There are countless ways to show mercy to others … choose one.

***"Finally, all of you, be like-minded, be sympathetic, love one another, be compassionate and humble."* (1 Peter 3:8 NIV)**

***"All the great things are simple: freedom; justice; honor; duty; hope; mercy."* (Sir Winston Churchill)**

Mercy Minute Volume 64, Script 34; by Nancy Predaina, Special Projects Writer/Editor; from http://www.huffingtonpost.com/entry/moving-photo-shows-service-dog-comforting-boy-with-autism-before-mri_us_56cf3507e4b03260bf75c325

October 4

Siara

Mercy Ships volunteer Mirjam first saw little Siara at a patient screening in the Congo. The one-year-old baby weighed just seven pounds and had a cleft lip and palate.

Siara's dad brought her to our hospital ship for a free operation. Mirjam loved watching him learn how to lovingly care for his baby daughter.

Before heading to surgery, Siara received a pre-op medication and fell asleep. Her dad cried as he kissed his child goodbye.

After surgery and recovery, little Siara went home ... weighing 18 ½ pounds and with a beautifully repaired face and mouth!

Mirjam says, *"I would have given the world to be there when Siara's mom saw her baby daughter."* Yes! And I would have, too!

Mercy is always a beautiful sight!

***"For us there is only one Lord, one faith, one baptism, and we all have the same God and Father who is over us all and in us all, and living through every part of us."* (Ephesians 4:5-6 MSG)**

Mercy Minute Volume 64, Script 5; by Catherine Murphy, staff writer; from Story submitted to Catherine Murphy by Mirjam Plomp, Screening Coordinator, 2013-14 AFM *Congo Field Service;*

October 5

Caring Neighbors

Being a good neighbor is an act of mercy. Joyce Fisher's neighbors in Florida found a simple way to show her that they care about her:

"Ever since my husband passed away a few years ago, someone has brought my newspaper up the walk and to my front door each morning. No one admits to doing it, and it may be more than one person! I'm so blessed with caring neighbors—something everyone should have and cherish."

Jesus said, *"All the commandments are summed up in these two ... love God and love your neighbor as yourself."*

Yes, being a good neighbor IS an act of mercy. Be creative and find a simple way to show your neighbors that you care about them.

"Each of us should please our neighbors for their good, to build them up." **(Romans 15:2 NIV)**

⚓ On October 5, 1978, the remainder of the $1 million USD purchase price for the *Anastasis* was paid. The ship was towed by tugs to the Bay of Elevsis in Greece to begin its renovation.

Mercy Minute Volume 64, Script 9; from "Your Kind Acts," Woman's Day Magazine; *February 2016;*

October 6

A Clear Vision

Donna watched a father walk towards the Mercy Ship eye care center with his young son. The son's cataract surgery was tomorrow, but she noticed the father walked like a man with dim vision as well. When she examined his eyes, he admitted that he had cataracts. He hadn't asked about a surgery for himself because his concern was for his son's sight. He thought he might take away his son's surgery slot if he mentioned his problem as well.

Donna scheduled both of them to have their free operations back-to-back. Father and son left the ship together the next day with clear vision.

You see, mercy is placing another's need before your own, trusting God to reward the sacrifice.

"Don't forget to do good and to share what you have with those in need, for such sacrifices are very pleasing to Him."
(Hebrews 13:16 TLB)

Mercy Minute Volume 24, Script 58; from Leslie Merzig, crew member; February 2006; 2005-06 Anastasis *Liberia Field Service;*

October 7

Moukimi

The first Mercy Ships patient in our first Congo field service was Africa's best-dressed six-year-old little boy named Moukimi. He and his grandmother traveled by train for two days from their village in the interior to Pointe Noire.

Moukimi received a free surgery to repair his cleft lip. Two weeks later, he returned for his last post-operative appointment. And his smile was as charming as his outfit.

His grandmother says, *"He's in good health, and he can laugh! I do not have the words for how happy I am."*

Then they headed back home—with plenty of stories about a hospital, a ship, and 400 volunteers who follow the model of Jesus.

And that's what we are all called to do—follow the model of Jesus by serving others.

"For, dear brothers, you have been given freedom: not freedom to do wrong, but freedom to love and serve each other." **(Galatians 5:13 TLB)**

"Do all the good you can and make as little fuss about it as possible." **(Charles Dickens)**

Mercy Minute Volume 55, Script 49; by Catherine Murphy, staff writer; from patient interview; 2013-14 AFM *Congo Field Service;*

October 8

Refugee Olympian

Yusra was a member of the first Olympic team of refugees. She and her sister left war-torn Syria in 2014. They joined 18 other passengers on a tiny boat made to hold 6 people. They were traveling across the Mediterranean Sea to Greece.

Suddenly the boat's motor stopped, and it almost capsized. Yusra says, *"Only 4 out of 20 knew how to swim. It would have been shameful if the people had drowned. I wasn't going to sit there."*

So Yusra, a championship swimmer, plus her sister and another woman jumped into the water and pushed the boat to shore.

I know of 19 people who would love to give a medal to Yusra!

And you can be an ambassador of hope as you show mercy to others.

"We are therefore Christ's ambassadors, as though God were making His appeal through us. We implore you on Christ's behalf: Be reconciled to God."
(2 Corinthians 5:20 NIV)

Mercy Minute Volume 65, Script 53; from "Olympic Refugee Team: Swimming Heroine," by Patrick Marche, https://www.rio2016.com

October 9

A View from PICU

A volunteer nurse described the view from the Pediatric Intensive Care Unit onboard our hospital ship:

"Once patients become 'walkie-talkies'—healthy enough to transition out of intensive care—I often wonder, 'Is she able to sleep through the night? Did he get that plate of mashed potatoes he was craving? Has she lost that hoarseness in her voice? Did he get to go back to school?'

When a family pays a visit back to our unit to say hello, it means the world to us. It's the extra reminder that we are in the business of happy endings."

Yes, we ARE in the business of happy endings … and so are you when you show kindness and mercy to others.

***"And we know that God causes all things to work together for good to those who love God, to those who are called according to His purpose."* (Romans 8:28 NASB)**

Mercy Minute Volume 55, Script 42; by Grace Antonini, staff writer; from http://kpal5.blogspot.com/2013/09/transformation.html, 9/30/2013; blog of Karyn Palomba, volunteer nurse; 2013-14 AFM *Congo Field Service;*

October 10

Djimon Friday

Djimon grinned as much as his face would allow. He was excited because he was scheduled for a free Mercy Ships surgery the next day.

A tumor obstructed his speech and eyesight. It had forced him to quit work. He'd gone through two unsuccessful surgeries. He decided to go to the Mercy Ship docked in the neighboring country of Benin, in spite of people telling him it was hopeless. He said, *"I believe I will get my healing. God who created me will protect my life.*

Dr. Gary Parker performed two free surgeries that enabled Djimon to return home to Nigeria a remarkably transformed man. He says, *"Look at me now. I am beautiful. God is working!"*

Yes, God **is** working. And He can make life beautiful when we show mercy to those He brings across our paths.

> ***"He has made everything beautiful in its time. He has also set eternity in the human heart; yet no one can fathom what God has done from beginning to end."*** **(Ecclesiastes 3:11 NIV)**

> ***"The best things are nearest ... the light in your eyes, flowers at your feet, duties at your hand, the path of God before you."*** **(Robert Louis Stevenson)**

Mercy Minute Volume 55, Script 42; by Nancy Predaina, Special Projects Writer/Editor; from onamercyship.com, website of Scott Harrison, photojournalist; 2005-06 Anastasis *Liberia Field Service;*

October 11

Coffee Shop Comfort

Barbara Danner was waiting in the drive-thru lane at Dutch Brothers Coffee Shop in Vancouver, Washington, when she witnessed amazing mercy. The car in front of her was occupied by a distressed young woman whose husband had passed away.

The drive-thru cashier offered to pray with her. Other employees stopped what they were doing to help.

Barbara snapped a photo and posted it to the Dutch Brothers Facebook page. Positive comments poured in. One woman wrote, *"When my parents were in a head-on collision, the amazing kids at Dutch Brothers loaded up a gift card for her so she would not have to worry about paying for coffee during her recovery which took a long time!"*

Follow the example of Dutch Brothers Coffee Shop and take time to show mercy to someone today.

"When God's children are in need, you be the one to help them out. And get into the habit of inviting guests home for dinner or, if they need lodging, for the night." **(Romans 12:13 TLB)**

Mercy Minute Volume 65, Script 59; by Nancy Predaina, Special Projects Writer/Editor; from http://www.goodnewsnetwork.org/coffee-shop-employees-console-widow-window-drive-thru/ 3/23/16;

October 12

Lucrech's Wish

Sometimes five-year-old Lucrech tries to tickle you or jump into your arms. He's ALWAYS been a lovable whirlwind of energy and smiles.

…until three years ago. He fell and plunged his little arm into a boiling pot over an open fire outside his parents' African hut. Without medical care, his parents watched helplessly as his arm painfully contracted and shriveled. His hand pulled up, fusing his fingers together.

But a free surgery onboard our hospital ship restored the mobility and the function in his hand. He says, *"I want to play ball and learn how to write!"*

And thanks to the mercy of compassionate volunteers, donors and crew, Lucrech will get his wish! Use your acts of kindness to make someone's wish come true.

"If you, then, though you are evil, know how to give good gifts to your children, how much more will your Father in heaven give good gifts to those who ask Him!" **(Matthew 7:11 NIV)**

Mercy Minute Volume 55, Script 15; by Grace Antonini, staff writer; from patient interview with Lucrech and Nadja; 2013-14 AFM Congo Field Service;

October 13

Nicolly Sees and Hears

Diana Pereira, from Brazil, shared a story of hope fulfilled:

"My daughter, Nicolly, was born deaf and blind. She couldn't look me in the eyes or hear me say, 'I love you.' Seven eye operations in Brazil failed to help.

One day I posted her story on Facebook. Over 30,000 people followed it! This led to an incredible free surgery at Bascom Palmer Eye Institute in Miami. The doctors also discovered the cause of Nicolly's deafness. Now she can see and hear!

My heart is full. Only God could have done this. My two-year-old daughter has become a reference for people who don't believe in miracles."

And the rest of this story is that doctors at Bascom plan to train eye doctors in Brazil. Now you go, join with others in showing mercy to someone today.

"Under His direction, the whole body is fitted together perfectly, and each part in its own special way helps the other parts, so that the whole body is healthy and growing and full of love."
(Ephesians 4:16 TLB)

Mercy Minute Volume 70, Script 17; by Larry Mast, staff writer; from Tyler Morning Telegraph, *April 28, 2016;*

October 14

Singing in the Ward

Far away in the Congo, a new crew member onboard our hospital ship sat down for a cup of tea. Suddenly, she felt the beat of drums from the deck below. She ran downstairs and found people in the ward dancing and singing.

A nurse laughed and explained *"We asked if they wanted to sing a song before bedtime, and that was 40 minutes ago!"*

Giggling children in hospital gowns wove around their mothers' legs. An old woman with a bandaged head raised her arms to the ceiling.

The crew member scooped up a little boy—bouncing him in rhythm to the earnest prayers and songs.

And she reveled in this lavish display of joy and love.

Yes, lavish mercy produces lavish joy and love. And you can create joyful moments by showing lavish mercy to others.

***"So overflowing is His kindness toward us that He took away all our sins through the blood of his Son, by whom we are saved; and He has showered down upon us the richness of His grace—for how well He understands us and knows what is best for us at all times."* (Ephesians 1:7-8 TLB)**

Mercy Minute Volume 55, Script 24; by Grace Antonini, staff writer; personal experience; 2013-14 AFM *Congo Field Service;*

October 15

No More Pain

Marie got a toothache… A BAD toothache. She was in a great deal of pain, but she couldn't afford to see a doctor. The problem continued for nearly 15 years. A lump the size of a *tomato* grew inside her mouth. She could do nothing about it, so she lived with the pain and took care of her children.

Then a Mercy Ship arrived in her hometown. Volunteer dentists from the ship set up a clinic to give free treatment to the people of Liberia. In a short procedure, a dentist from England removed four teeth and the tomato-sized lump free of charge. For the first time in years, Marie was free from the pain that had plagued her.

A procedure that we take for granted, changed her life … thanks to the mercy of compassionate volunteers. Let us all put our compassion into action and find a way to show mercy to someone today.

"Therefore, as God's chosen people, holy and dearly loved, clothe yourselves with compassion, kindness, humility, gentleness and patience. Bear with each other and forgive one another if any of you has a grievance against someone. Forgive as the Lord forgave you. And over all these virtues put on love, which binds them all together in perfect unity." **(Colossians 3:12-14 NIV)**

Mercy Minute Volume 24, Script 24; by Angie Hess, staff writer; interview with Dental Team; 2005-06 Anastasis *Liberia Field Service;*

October 16

Hot Water Heater Mercy

Phil Overton left a Home Depot store and walked to his pickup. He saw a man and woman struggling to get a large hot water heater into the trunk of their small compact car.

Phil said, "*Put that in my truck. I'll haul it to your home.*"

The man asked, "*Where do you live?*"

Phil replied, "*I live south of Houston, but it doesn't matter,*"

The man exclaimed, "*I live* north *of Houston—it's too far!*"

But Phil kindly insisted. When they arrived at the couple's home, the man asked what he owed Phil.

Phil answered, "*Nothing. Just remember the next time you see someone needing help—give him a hand.*"

You see, kindness is contagious, and God's mercy is new every morning.

***"The Lord's lovingkindnesses indeed never cease, for His compassions never fail. They are new every morning; great is Your faithfulness."* (Lamentations 3:22-23 NASB)**

⚓ *The Mercy Minute* radio program first aired on October 16, 2000.

Mercy Minute Volume 53, Script 27; by Larry Mast, staff writer; from story from Phil Overton, December 19, 2012;

October 17

Dress Ceremony

The best part about the medical care Mercy Ships provides is celebrating with the patients afterwards! Stephanie Fiduk serves as a volunteer nurse onboard the *Africa Mercy*. She works with women who receive free surgery for a childbirth injury called obstetric fistula. And she helps them celebrate!

"It's the most beautiful thing. Once they have that new life, we do a dress ceremony. So we give them a new dress symbolizing a renewed sense of self. And we give them a Bible and a mirror and soap—things to symbolize a renewal of themselves.

They sing and they dance and they tell their stories, and there's not a dry eye, for obvious reasons. It's beautiful."

You can give someone a reason to celebrate just by showing kindness.

"Therefore if anyone is in Christ, he is a new creature; the old things passed away; behold, new things have come."
(2 Corinthians 5:17 NASB)

Mercy Minute Volume 54, Script 52; by Nancy Predaina, Special Projects Writer/Editor; from Interview by Nancy Predaina and by Ambassador Team; 2012 AFM Guinea Field Service;

October 18

Prison Children in Nepal

Every morning Pushpa Basnet wakes up to the sounds of 40 children. All of them once lived in prisons in Nepal, one of the poorest countries in the world.

Space is limited in the few existing children's homes. So, incarcerated parents often have to either bring their children with them or let them live on the streets.

Since 2005, Pushpa has helped many of these children. She established the Butterfly Children's Home, a day care program, and a residential home for older children. She says, *"My mission is to make sure no child grows up behind prison walls."*

At Butterfly Home, everyone helps with household chores . . . while being showered with love by Pushpa.

Make it your mission to shower others with God's love and mercy.

"I will make them and the places around My hill a blessing. And I will cause showers to come down in their season; they will be showers of blessing." **(Ezekiel 34:26 NASB)**

Mercy Minute Volume 52, Script 44; from "Pulling Children Out of Nepal's Prisons," by Kathleen Toner, www.cnn.com; 3/15/12;

October 19

Applause for Jaka

Five-year-old Jaka was spinning—around and around, smiling face, arms out. Suddenly, she stumbled into the cooking fire. Boiling water spilled over her shoulders, arms and back.

For months, little Jaka laid on her stomach, suffering unimaginable pain. The skin on her left arm and shoulder contracted, causing her arm to stick to her side.

Then Jaka received a free surgery onboard our hospital ship. Now her future is as bright as her smile. Who knows? Maybe she'll follow the example of Ellen Johnson Sirleaf of Liberia and become president of her country one day.

But, in the meantime, what is this giggling nine-year-old most excited about? *"Clapping!"* she says.

Yes, that's a happy ending worthy of applause! Create a happy ending by showing mercy to someone today.

"Come, everyone, and clap for joy! Shout triumphant praises to the Lord!" **(Psalm 47:1 TLB)**

Mercy Minute Volume 54, Script 16; by Catherine Clarke Murphy, staff writer; 2012-13 AFM *Guinea Field Service;*

October 20

The Effect of Jesus

A crewmember shared an interesting visit with a patient onboard our hospital ship:

"The patient had never seen electricity, running water, or a ship. I asked if she had heard about Jesus on the Mercy Ship. Her face broke into a big smile, she jumped up from her chair, and she nodded, 'Yes!' She reached over the table, hugged me and shook my shoulders. Then she grabbed the translator and shook and hugged him, too.

It would seem Jesus has had quite an effect on her! Which is credit to the love shown by the nurses, doctors, translators and chaplains."

Yes, when we demonstrate kindness by showing Jesus' love to others, it has quite a joyful effect!

***"For You, O Lord, have made me glad by what You have done, I will sing for joy at the works of Your hands."* (Psalm 92:4 NASB)**

***"How sad it is when someone comes to you looking for Jesus and all they see is you."* (Mother Teresa)**

Mercy Minute Volume 54, Script 50; by Nancy Predaina, Special Projects Writer/Editor; from newsletter from Rosie Timms, crew; 1/11/13;

October 21

Simple Mercy

Catherine came to a Mercy Ship in Liberia to receive free life-changing surgery. For years, she'd suffered from a serious health problem. After the surgery, she recovered onboard for several weeks. She received wonderful, compassionate care from the ship's nurses and doctors. Never in her life had she experienced such selfless mercy.

Catherine was so grateful to receive her free surgery on the hospital ship. It changed her life! But she was also thankful for the smaller, simpler things. She said, *"We didn't even have to get our own water."*

You see, mercy doesn't have to be publicized or dramatic. Even small things, when done with love, are very powerful! But it requires one ingredient… and that's YOU!

"Here is another of His illustrations: "The Kingdom of Heaven is like a tiny mustard seed planted in a field. It is the smallest of all seeds but becomes the largest of plants, and grows into a tree where birds can come and find shelter." **(Matthew 13:31-32 TLB)**

Mercy Minute Volume 24, Script 26; by Angie Hess, staff writer; from patient interview; 2005-06 Anastasis *Liberia Field Service;*

October 22

Chick-fil-A Helps Foster Children

The Chick-fil-A restaurants do much more than make a delicious chicken sandwich. In 1987, the chain's founder, Truett Cathy, decided to do something to help lost and abandoned children. So, he created WinShape Homes—foster homes dedicated to developing children physically, emotionally, and spiritually.

Chick-fil-A invests millions each year on these homes—providing everything from school to braces to vacations. The 14 foster homes are located in Georgia, Tennessee, and Alabama. Each home is Christ-centered and family-oriented, with two full-time parents.

Richard Yadkowski, who grew up in a WinShape foster home, says, *"It's neat that this isn't an institution—this is a family."*

Chick-fil-A is giving back in a special way. Find a way to share your blessings as you show mercy to others.

***"Father of orphans, champion of widows, is God in His holy house. God makes homes for the homeless ..."* (Psalm 68:6 MSG)**

Mercy Minute Volume 49, Script 256; by Nancy Predaina, Special Projects Writer/Editor; from "Children Are a Gift: Chick-fil-A Helps Foster Children," by Gillian Sheriday; www.cbs19 5/14/12; and http://homes.winshape.org/

October 23

Fun with Friends

Seven-year-old Yaya was an orthopedic patient in Guinea. When he was discharged from our hospital ship, he was heartbroken. He didn't want to leave his friends.

He went to the HOPE Center, our outpatient care center, and got a wonderful surprise—his special friend, Mafugie, was there!

Two months earlier, the two boys had been neighbors in the ward. They really had fun at the HOPE Center. They laughed and played games. In fact, they even managed to play soccer on crutches!

King Solomon said, *"As iron sharpens iron, so a friend sharpens a friend."* And friends just make life a lot more fun!

When you stop and think about it, friendship is a wonderful gift of mercy.

***"A true friend is always loyal, and a brother is born to help in time of need."* (Proverbs 17:17 TLB)**

***"Walking with a friend in the dark is better than walking alone in the light."* (Helen Keller)**

Mercy Minute Volume 54, Script 55; by Catherine Clarke Murphy, staff writer; from interview with Tori Hobson; 2013 AFM Guinea Field Service;

October 24

Justice AND Mercy

Hayden Carlo sighed when the lights of a police car flashed for him to pull over. He knew that his car registration sticker had expired.

As a struggling father of two, the 25-year-old Carlo decided to tell the truth to the officer from Plano, Texas. He said, "*There's no explanation, except that I don't have the money. It was either feed my kids or get the registration done.*"

The police officer handed Carlo a warning ticket. But when Carlo unfolded it, he discovered even more mercy—in the form of a $100 bill. Carlo says, "*He helped me out when I needed it. I'll never forget that man. He definitely restored my faith in God.*"

Justice accompanied by compassion is a powerful mixture. Follow the officer's example and surprise someone with an act of kindness.

"But He's already made it plain how to live, what to do, what God is looking for in men and women. It's quite simple: do what is fair and just to your neighbor, be compassionate and loyal in your love, and don't take yourself too seriously—take God seriously."
(Micah 6:8 MSG)

Mercy Minute Volume 52, Script 4; by Vicki Gregg, volunteer writer; from "Texas Cop Hands Out ticket—and $100 Bill," Yahoo News, 12/17/12;

October 25

A New Look

Amazing transformations are part of everyday life onboard our hospital ship, the *Africa Mercy*. Here's one crewmember's story:

"I had a wonderful day! I admitted a precious seven-year-old girl with a cleft lip. I showed her a photo in her chart and told her she could take it home so she could remember how she used to look. *Tears rolled down her face, and pretty soon her mother and I were also crying.*

Today was the last time she would look like that. An hour and a half surgery completely changed that. Tonight she looks like a new little girl who will be able to go to school and lead a normal life."

Yes, mercy transforms lives and gives hope for the future. When you show kindness to others, you change their lives for the better.

"And so we are transfigured much like the Messiah, our lives gradually becoming brighter and more beautiful as God enters our lives and we become like Him."
(2 Corinthians 3:18 MSG)

"Each of us is God's special work of art. Through us, He teaches and inspires, delights and encourages, informs and uplifts all those who view our lives." **(Joni Eareckson Tada)**

Mercy Minute Volume 53, Script 65; by Nancy Predaina, Special Projects Writer/Editor; from email newsletter from Rosie Timms; 9/27/12; 2012-13 AFM *Guinea Field Service;*

October 26

A Merciful Road Trip

One summer, a 21-year-old college student named Tyler Kellogg made an unusual road trip. He hit the road with the goal of bestowing random acts of kindness on 100 strangers.

He helped a man install a boat lift. He helped a policeman fix a downed barricade. He met a man who was crying because his wife had recently died. For three hours, they sat on the man's porch, as Tyler provided a listening ear and words of encouragement.

In 55 days, Tyler helped 115 strangers. He says, "*You don't have to be a billionaire to be a philanthropist. You just have to ask people, 'How can I help?'*"

So, I challenge you to keep that question in mind as you go through your days.

"Make sure you don't take things for granted and go slack in working for the common good; share what you have with others. God takes particular pleasure in acts of worship—a different kind of 'sacrifice'—that take place in kitchen and workplace and on the streets." **(Hebrews 13:16 MSG)**

Mercy Minute Volume 49, Script 4; from "Best Road Trip," Reader's Digest; *June/July 2010;*

October 27

Decorations of Mercy

Our hospital ship has an onboard Academy for crew children. In Guinea, a team of elementary students wanted to do something for the patients. And they came up with a great idea! They decided to decorate the Rehabilitation Tent, where Mercy Ships patients come for free orthopedic care.

The students got busy creating decorations out of paper and glue. Before long, they had plenty to fill the tent. Patients who came to the rehab tent entered a place of happiness and color. They were welcomed by cut-out stars, animals and balloons.

John Bunyan said, *"You have not lived today until you have done something for someone who can never repay you."* These young Mercy Ships students followed that advice in blessing others.

Find a way to decorate someone's life with mercy today.

"But when you do a kindness to someone, do it secretly—don't tell your left hand what your right hand is doing. And your Father, who knows all secrets, will reward you." **(Matthew 6:3-4 TLB)**

⚓ Originating from landlocked Switzerland, an all-volunteer team was recruited to restore the *Victoria*, an abandoned Italian passenger/cargo ship, transforming it into the first Mercy Ship.

Mercy Minute Volume 54, Script 63; by Catherine Clarke Murphy, staff writer; from interview with Tori Hobson by Catherine Murphy; 2012 AFM *Guinea Field Service;*

October 28

The Power of a Sticker

Imagine being a little three-year-old boy in Central Africa. Then imagine being carried onboard a huge white hospital ship, and someone takes you into a strange room with a big X-ray machine. That's pretty scary stuff!

Little Codjo was too young to realize how blessed he was to get a free surgery to repair his bowed legs. But he definitely understood pretty colors!

Well, Mercy Ships volunteer Radiographer Martha Henderson was well-prepared—not just with technical knowledge, but also with beautiful stickers. Mercy conquered fear.

The Greek storyteller Aesop said, *"No act of kindness, no matter how small, is ever wasted."* I think he would agree that colorful stickers make everything better!

Now you go, bless someone with an act of kindness … no matter how small!

"In everything I showed you that by working hard in this manner you must help the weak and remember the words of the Lord Jesus, that He Himself said, 'It is more blessed to give than to receive.'"
(Acts 20:35 NASB)

"Only a life lived for others is a life worthwhile."
(Albert Einstein)

Mercy Minute Volume 55, Script 8; by Nancy Predaina, Special Projects Writer/Editor; from "Weekly Scoop" (from AFM*), October 7, 2013; 2013-14* AFM *Congo Field Service;*

October 29

50 Acts of Mercy

Reagan Payne believes in helping others. When her grandfather passed away in 2008, she decided to honor him by completing 50 different volunteer projects by 2010.

She described each project on her blog. For example, she made instant potatoes for 1600 people. She recorded audio books for the blind, bottle-fed kittens at a shelter, and assembled care packages for soldiers.

For her 50th project, she cut off nine inches of her red hair and donated it to an organization that provides wigs for kids who have lost their hair.

Kirsten says, *"I wanted to show people how many ways there are to get involved."*

***"Let us not become weary in doing good, for at the proper time we will reap a harvest if we do not give up."* (Galatians 6:9 NIV)**

***"The greatest thing a man can do for his Heavenly Father is to be kind to some of His other children."* (Henry Drummond)**

Mercy Minute Volume 49, Script 62; adapted from "50 Ways to Lend a Hand," by Petra Guglielmetti, Reader's Digest, *June/July 2010;*

October 30

Abrahim and Amara

Abrahim hovered protectively over his ten-year -old brother Amara. They were onboard our hospital ship, the *Africa Mercy*, for a free surgery to repair Amara's severely burned hands.

After the surgery, Amara had to complete a number of exercises at home. The Mercy Ships Physiotherapy team was afraid that—like many children—he would forget to do them.

But, when Amara returned for his weekly check-up, a very proud Abrahim said, *"Every day I helped Amara with his exercises. I hope I have done well."*

A quick examination confirmed that he had done very well indeed! Amara's healing had progressed beautifully—thanks to his big brother and our Mercy Ships volunteers—and his hands were working correctly.

Abrahim was truly his brother's keeper and his mercy-giver. And you will be your brother's keeper when you show mercy to someone.

"Two can accomplish more than twice as much as one, for the results can be much better. If one falls, the other pulls him up; but if a man falls when he is alone, he's in trouble."
(Ecclesiastes 4:9-10 TLB)

Mercy Minute Volume 53, Script 60; by Joanne Thibault, staff writer; from interview with Amara; 2012-13 AFM *Guinea Field Service;*

October 31

A Therapet and a Toddler

Rocky is a 50-pound boxer who's been a Therapet, a therapeutic pet, for three years. His owner Wendy Clarke describes a merciful hospital visit:

"A nurse and mom were working with a fussy, squirming toddler. The nurse was trying to administer medication through steam inhalation. But the toddler kept pushing them away.

I asked if we should come back later, and they both said, 'NO!' I think they were quite frustrated.

The toddler petted Rocky and smiled—and breathed in the medicated steam without even noticing it. The room was filled with laughter and smiles.

What a difference we can make in others' lives in just a brief encounter!"

Wendy's absolutely right! And you can make a difference by showing mercy to someone today.

"And the peace of God, which surpasses all comprehension, will guard your hearts and your minds in Christ Jesus." **(Philippians 4:7 NASB)**

"The best and most beautiful things in the world cannot be seen or even touched. They must be felt with the heart." **(Helen Keller)**

Mercy Minute Volume 70, Script 61; by Nancy Predaina, Special Projects Writer/Editor; from story posted on Navigator (Mercy Ships intranet) by Wendy Clarke, 4/7/17;

NOVEMBER

"Enter His gates with thanksgiving and His courts with praise; give thanks to Him and praise His name."
(Psalm 100:4 NIV)

November 1

A Kaleidoscope of Celebration

On our hospital ships, we have a "Celebration of Sight" for patients whose sight has been restored through free cataract surgery. Here's an "eye witness" account by a crewmember:

"Soon the drums were out. The tent became a kaleidoscope of rotating colors as people clapped, danced, and sang. An older man, dressed in lime green from head to toe, was leading the charging—beaming at everyone from under the dark protective glasses that indicate a successful cataract surgery.

An elderly woman started to pray. I didn't understand the language, but I could feel the unbridled thankfulness for everything God had done. The real celebration of sight had begun."

Praise, prayer and celebration—all the result of mercy. You can give others a reason to celebrate by showing mercy to them.

"The Lord opens the eyes of the blind; the Lord raises up those who are bowed down; the Lord loves the righteous."
(Psalm 146:8 NASB)

Mercy Minute Volume 58, Script 53; by Catherine Clarke Murphy, staff writer; personal experience of Kyle Siemens, Media Liaison, submitted to Catherine Murphy; 2013-14 AFM Congo Field Service;

November 2

Hurricane Harvey Heroes

Hurricane Harvey ravaged the Houston area. But the hurricane also produced some amazing heroes. I'm going to name just a few of them:

Nick Sheridan and two other truck drivers drove nearly 200 miles with his big rig to rescue more than a thousand people stranded in floodwaters.

Realtor Stephanie Fry offered her own apartment to families who needed a place to stay.

Team Rubicon, a nonprofit made up of military veterans, helped people get to safety.

A photo was taken of a group of neighbors forming a human chain to rescue a man trapped in his flooded car.

Dr. Stephen Kimmel canoed through the flood waters to perform surgery on a 16-year-old boy.

And the list goes on and on … and so should we! You and I are called to show mercy to one another.

"Be merciful (responsive, compassionate, tender) just as your [heavenly] Father is merciful." **(Luke 6:36 AMP)**

⚓ The *Good Samaritan* embarked on her maiden voyage to Haiti in November 1985.

Mercy Minute Volume 70, Script 23; by Nancy Predaina, Special Projects Writer/Editor; from http://abcnews.go.com/US/incredible-acts-kindness-hurricane-harveys-wake/story?id=49511397

November 3

A Giant, Joyful Moment

Free cataract surgery is offered onboard our hospital ships. One patient caught volunteer Kirsten's attention:

"I couldn't help but stare. He had a smile etched on his face. The type of smile that gets stuck there ... the type of smile that comes from living a life of joy.

I thought about the years of darkness he has lived through. I thought about him walking up the gangway, into the unknown. I thought about the trust he had placed in a stranger's hand.

And I thought of how his life was going to change. In twenty minutes he was about to walk out of complete darkness, into astounding light. God is transforming years of struggle into a giant joyful moment. How incredibly beautiful!"

And it's incredibly beautiful when God allows us to use our acts of kindness to give joyful moments to His children.

"See how very much our Heavenly Father loves us, for He allows us to be called His children—think of it—and we really are! But since most people don't know God, naturally they don't understand that we are His children." **(1 John 3:1 TLB)**

Mercy Minute Volume 70, Script 63; by Anna Psiaki, staff writer; from personal blog of volunteer Kirsten Eller; used with permission; 2016-2017 AFM *Benin Field Service;*

November 4

No Price Tag on Serving

The crew members onboard our hospital ship find that serving the poor in Africa also helps them. Crew member Andrea Diallo explains:

"It reinforced what I know about God and what I really hope other people feel at some point in their life—which is that He loves us so much. That I got to have this treat and that I get to have this treat every single day ... it boggles my mind. It is amazing to me. You can't put a price tag on that."

And I agree! You can't put a price tag on serving others. It will change YOU in wonderful ways.

Amelia Earhart said, *"A single act of kindness throws out roots in all directions."* Yes, mercy is exactly like that ...

"Whoever goes hunting for what is right and kind finds life itself—glorious life!" **(Proverbs 21:21 MSG)**

"We will stand amazed to see the topside of the tapestry and how God beautifully embroidered each circumstance into a pattern for our good and His glory." **(Joni Eareckson Tada)**

Mercy Minute Volume 70, Script 64; by Nancy Predaina, Special Projects Writer/Editor; from interview with crew member Andrea Diallo by AFM *Communications Team; 2016-17* AFM *Benin Field Service;*

November 5

Kids Helping Kids

Mercy Ships received a check for $358.20 from St. Charles Elementary in St. Charles, Michigan. The kids came up with the creative idea of having a Leadership Safari Night. The fifth-grade classes had an Open-Air African Market, with all proceeds going to Mercy Ships.

The students had studied the continent of Africa and researched different charities in Africa. They discovered Mercy Ships and wanted to help African kids get free medical help.

The school follows the *7 Habits of Healthy Kids*, written by Stephen Covey. A letter from three of the teachers says, "*We have learned how giving to others makes us winners in our hearts.*"

Now THAT is great teaching! Follow the example of these elementary students and show mercy to others.

> ***"Let each one give [thoughtfully and with purpose] just as he has decided in his heart, not grudgingly or under compulsion, for God loves a cheerful giver [and delights in the one whose heart is in his gift]."* (2 Corinthians 9:7 AMP)**

Mercy Minute Volume 70, Script 27; by Nancy Predaina, Special Projects Writer/Editor; from letter sent to Mercy Ships Donor Services, 4/22/16;

November 6

Edith's Bears

Blessing Hospital in Quincy, Illinois, started a toy bear project about 25 years ago. Volunteers make stuffed bears for pediatric patients. One of those volunteers is Edith Kroencke.

Edith lives at the Curtis Creek Senior Living Center. She's been making bears for 12 years. She has a system. One day, she cuts the donated fabric. The next day she connects the pieces. Then she stuffs and closes the bears. Then she starts over on the next batch.

Edith is 99 years old and doesn't have any plans to stop. She says, "*I love it. It gives me a sense of accomplishment. It keeps my fingers busy.*"

And it puts BIG smiles on the faces of children at Blessing Hospital.

Ask God to show you how to put your hands to work to show mercy to bring joy to others.

***"And let the [gracious] favor of the Lord our God be on us; confirm for us the work of our hands—yes, confirm the work of our hands."* (Psalm 90:17 AMP)**

***"To appreciate beauty; to find the best in others; to give one's self; to leave the world a little better ... to know even one life has breathed easier because you have lived. ... This is to have succeeded."* (Ralph Waldo Emerson)**

Mercy Minute Volume 70, Script 41; by Nancy Predaina, Special Projects Writer/Editor; from http://www.whig.com/20170626/99-year-old-woman-has-made-more-than-1000-teddy-bears-for-kids-in-past-10-years#

November 7

A Broken Curse

Geovannie was still in her mother's womb when a man put a curse on her. So, when she was born with clubfeet and partial blindness, her mother was devastated and afraid. She dared to hope when she heard about possible treatment on our hospital ship.

Using a casting method known as Ponseti, in just a few months little Geovannie's feet were straightened! And an eye doctor gave her glasses to help her vision.

Geovannie's mom was overjoyed. Volunteer Marina says, "*She came to show me her daughter's new glasses. She was so grateful because she believed the spell was finally broken, and God has the victory!*"

Yes, God uses mercy-givers—like you—to break the chains of superstition and despair.

"Every word of God is tested and refined [like silver]; He is a shield to those who trust and take refuge in Him."
(Proverbs 30:5 AMP)

Mercy Minute Volume 70, Script 34; by Windsor Marchesi, staff writer; from interview with Marina Schmid; 2016-17 AFM *Benin Field Service 2016-2017;*

November 8

A Grandmother's Dance

Simon's grandmother sat beside the bed of her 12-year-old grandson. For years, his legs had been bowed. He couldn't run or skip. He could barely walk. Now, after a free surgery, casts covered his legs. Soon he would run and play like other children.

His 60-year-old grandmother says, *"We are farmers. We do not have anything."* But she has courage. She traveled for six hours to bring her grandson to our hospital ship.

During the hospital ward worship time, she dances for God like you wouldn't believe, moving with the energy of a 25-year-old! Just watching her, you feel happier. You forget your problems and just praise God.

I think Simon's grandmother has the right idea! Follow her example, put your problems aside, and praise God as you show mercy to others.

"Praise Him with the drums and dancing. Praise Him with stringed instruments and horns." **(Psalm 150:4 TLB)**

Mercy Minute Volume 70, Script 62; by Anna Psiaki, staff writer; from interview with Simon's grandmother by Anna Psiaki, staff writer; 2016-17 AFM *Benin Field Service;*

November 9

A Fireball Named Yasmine

The children onboard our hospital ship are just plain FUN! A crew member describes an especially lively little patient:

"Yasmine likes to give high-fives, but they're unlike any high-five you've ever experienced. This feisty four-year-old winds her arm back, locks eyes on her target—your defenseless palm—and swings with all her might, rarely missing!

By the time you've confirmed your arm is still attached, you realize she's already planning a second attack, giggling with a mischievous grin! So watch out ... once her bowed legs have been straightened from free surgery on the Africa Mercy, *there's no telling what this fireball might do!"*

And this little fireball DID get beautifully straightened legs—thanks to the compassion of volunteers and donors. I wonder what she's doing now!

"The city streets will be filled with boys and girls playing there."
(Zechariah 8:5 NIV)

"Children are the hands by which we take hold of heaven."
(Henry Ward Beecher)

Mercy Minute Volume 70, Script 24; by Nancy Predaina, Special Projects Writer/Editor; from Weekly Scoop, *12/19/16, by Windsor Marchesi, staff writer;*

November 10

Honor Flight

During World War II, 16 million people served in the United States Armed Forces. And 400,000 died. To honor them, a World War II Memorial was opened in 2004. But too many veterans would never get to see it.

So Earl Morse, a retired Air Force Captain, found additional pilots and donations and named his organization Honor Flight. In 2008, Honor Flight took 10,000 veterans to visit the memorial—at no cost to them!

Earl says, *"On the flight back, every one of those veterans has a personal realization of how revered, cherished, honored, and loved they are by this nation."*

Acts of mercy—including serving your country—are demonstrations of love. Tell a veteran how much you appreciate their service.

***"If I rise on the wings of the dawn, if I settle on the far side of the sea, even there Your hand will guide me, Your right hand will hold me fast."* (Psalm 139:9-10 NIV)**

Mercy Minute Volume 37, Script 11; by Nancy Predaina, Special Projects Writer/Editor; from "Honor Flight," by Renee Brincks, Humana Active Outlook Magazine, *Fall 2008;*

November 11

Hero Bennie Adkins

Smelling blood, the tiger stalked the small band of wounded American soldiers on a jungle hilltop. But the tiger was a good thing. The North Vietnamese were afraid and moved back. The American soldiers escaped, and army helicopters rescued them the next day.

But there was a two-day battle prior to their rescue. Sergeant First Class Bennie Adkins faced a mortar barrage even while wounded. The Army report says, *"He ran through exploding mortar rounds and dragged several comrades to safety."* He received 18 wounds during the 38-hour battle!

For heroism and acts of mercy, Adkins received the Medal of Honor at a White House ceremony.

You know, you're always a hero when you help others.

"For God did not give us a spirit of timidity or cowardice or fear, but [He has given us a spirit] of power and of love and of sound judgment and personal discipline [abilities that result in a calm, well-balanced mind and self-control]." **(2 Timothy 1:7 AMP)**

"When God is involved, anything can happen. God has a beautiful way of bringing good vibrations out of broken chords." **(Chuck Swindoll)**

Mercy Minute Volume 64, Script 16; by Larry Mast, staff writer; from "Despite Wounds, Medal of Honor Recipient Killed up to 175 Soldiers, Saved Soldiers," By Brad Lendon; www.cnn.com 9/15/14;

November 12

Afi Is Made Whole

Many of the patients who come to our hospital ship, the *Africa Mercy*, suffer emotional, as well as physical, pain. Here's Afi's story:

"I hid in the shadows of the Admissions Tent. Five years ago I had a seizure and fell face-first into a fire. Even my own children are afraid of me! People think I'm cursed.

Suddenly, a crew member walked up to me and placed her hand on my shoulder. She didn't look away! I said, 'No one has looked at me in the eyes in five years. But here, you look straight into me, you aren't afraid to touch me.'

She made me feel whole again."

The heartbeat of mercy is unconditional love and acceptance.

"The Lord appeared to us in the past, saying: 'I have loved you with an everlasting love; I have drawn you with unfailing kindness.'" **(Jeremiah 31:3 NIV)**

Mercy Minute Volume 49, Script 20; by Nicole Pribbernow, staff writer; from interview with Afi; 2012 AFM *Field Service to Togo;*

November 13

Alberta's Merciful Church

In Liberia, people earn less than $2 per day. But that doesn't stop mercy!

Mariah was cooking over an open fire. Her two-year-old granddaughter, Alberta, walked by the fire and fell down. The hot oil splashed on her, catching fire. Her left arm was burned into a frozen position.

For two years, Mariah searched for someone who could fix the child's arm. Then people at her church collected money to send them to Sierra Leone to our hospital ship called *Africa Mercy*. We fixed Alberta's arm in a free surgery! Mariah said, *"It's a miracle!"*

Yes, mercy is always miraculous. It doesn't require wealth. It only requires a kind and generous heart.

"If there is a poor man with you, one of your brothers, in any of your towns in your land which the Lord your God is giving you, you shall not harden your heart, nor close your hand from your poor brother; but you shall freely open your hand to him, and shall generously lend him sufficient for his need in whatever he lacks." **(Deuteronomy 15:7-8 NASB)**

"There is no exercise better for the heart than reaching down and lifting people up." **(John Andrew Holmes)**

Mercy Minute Volume 47, Script 61; by Elaine B. Winn, staff writer; from interview with Mariah Johnson, AFM 2011 Sierra Leone Field Service;

November 14

Jim Retires

A woman told this story of mercy involving her neighbor:

"My neighbor, Jim, had trouble deciding if he wanted to retire from the construction field ... until he ran into a younger man he'd worked with previously.

The young man had a wife and three children. He was finding it difficult to make ends meet, since he hadn't worked in some time.

The next morning, Jim went to the union office and submitted his retirement paperwork. As for his replacement? He gave them the name of the young man.

That was six years ago, and that young husband and father has been employed ever since."

You know, mercy is simply putting others ahead of yourself. And Jim is a great example of that! Put others first and show mercy to someone today.

> ***"For you, my brothers, were called to freedom; only do not let your freedom become an opportunity for the sinful nature (worldliness, selfishness), but through love serve and seek the best for one another."* (Galatians 5:13 AMP)**

Mercy Minute Volume 49, Script 20; from https://www.rd.com/truestories/inspiring/kindness-strangers/ by Miranda MacLean;

November 15

The Mirror

Mary lay in her hospital bed, holding a small mirror. The 14-year-old girl had received free surgery onboard our hospital ship. The volunteer surgeons had removed a disfiguring facial tumor.

The nurses were excited at her progress, and her mom beamed saying, *"She looks beautiful!"* Mary glanced at her reflection and smiled. But she needed time to take it all in.

After everyone left, she held the mirror and stared long and hard at her face. Who was this person? And inside she knew the answer—a girl with newfound hope and a future.

Desmond Tutu said, *"Hope is being able to see that there is light despite all of the darkness."* Reflect God's image as you show kindness to someone today.

"So God created man in His own image, in the image and likeness of God He created him; male and female He created them."
(Genesis 1:27 AMP)

Mercy Minute Volume 69, Script 11; by Windsor Marchesi, staff writer; personal observation; 2016-2017 AFM *Benin Field Service;*

November 16

The Prayer Blanket

Joseph received the daunting diagnosis of cancer. He was thankful that medical care was available, but he dreaded the treatments. A group of friends at the Nazarene Church in Longview, Texas, faithfully prayed for him. But they also wanted to give him a tangible reminder of their prayers.

So, they found a beautiful blanket that was decorated with a verse from one of Joseph's favorite hymns, "Blessed Assurance." Joseph said, *"Every time I get into my favorite chair, I pull the blanket over me, and I know that I am literally covered with prayer and love."*

Yes, praying for others and letting them know that we care is a wonderful act of mercy. And, as the hymn says, that is "a foretaste of glory divine!"

"Is anyone among you sick? Let them call the elders of the church to pray over them and anoint them with oil in the name of the Lord ... The prayer of a righteous person is powerful and effective."
(James 5:14, 16 NIV)

Mercy Minute Volume 56, Script 9; by Nancy Predaina, Special Projects Writer/Editor; personal experience of Joseph Predaina; 2013;

November 17

For God

Alusine developed a tumor on his jaw. He lost his business, his family, and all hope. Here's his story:

"One day I was in a taxi, and the driver said 'My brother, some people said the Mercy Ship can cure any sickness. Maybe they can help you.'

When I got there, they examined me, they made x-rays, but they didn't ask for a cent. Then they gave me my operation time. I asked the nurse, 'You will do the operation?'

She said, 'Yes.'

I said, 'For what?'

She said 'For God.'

I thought she didn't understand, so I asked, 'What will be the cost?'

The woman laughed. She said, 'We do this for God.' This surgery gave me back my life."

Yes, mercy is given freely—and it changes lives!

"He who did not spare His own Son, but delivered Him over for us all, how will He not also with Him freely give us all things?"
(Romans 8:32 NASB)

Mercy Minute Volume 48, Script 57; by Catherine Cooper, staff writer; from conversation with Alusine Kamara; 2011 AFM *Field Service to Sierra Leone;*

November 18

Seven Miles for Mercy

Clarence left a store and discovered he'd locked his keys and cellphone inside his car. A teenager rode by and asked if something was wrong.

Clarence explained. He added that even if he could call his wife, it wouldn't do any good. She couldn't bring him her key because they only owned one car.

The teenager handed Clarence his cellphone and said, *"Call your wife and tell her I'm coming to get her spare key."*

Clarence said, *"That's seven miles round trip!"*

The boy said, *"Don't worry about it."*

An hour later, he returned with the key. He refused any money, saying he needed the exercise.

Clarence says, *"Then, like a cowboy in the movies, he rode off into the sunset."*

What a great story of mercy! Follow this teen's example and help someone today.

"If one of you says to them, 'Go in peace; keep warm and well fed,' but does nothing about their physical needs, what good is it?"
(James 2:16 NIV)

Mercy Minute Volume 70, Script 29; from https://www.rd.com/true-stories/inspiring/kindness-strangers/ "Seven Miles for Me," by Clarence W. Stephens;

November 19

Finda's Merciful Bonus

A patient on our hospital ship received a free surgery … and an added bonus. Here's the story of Finda, a woman in Sierra Leone:

"I was in constant pain from an inflamed appendix. Then the Africa Mercy *arrived, and the volunteer surgeons provided my surgery for free!*

One day, while I was recovering, a young man entered the ward. He was a day-worker on the ship. I couldn't believe my eyes. He was Tamba, my sister's son. Our family got separated during the terrible civil war, and I hadn't seen him in 15 years!

I thank God that Mercy Ships brought us together."

Sometimes an act of compassion leads to unexpected moments of joy—merciful bonuses!

"The Lord replied: 'Look, and be amazed! You will be astounded at what I am about to do! For I am going to do something in your own lifetime that you will have to see to believe.'"
(Habakkuk 1:5 TLB)

Mercy Minute Volume 47, Script 52; by Elaine B. Winn, staff writer; from interview with Clementine Tengue, Tamba Sandi, and Finda Nyandemon, AFM *2011 Sierra Leone Field Service;*

November 20

Thankful for Opportunity

Traditional holidays can be quite different when serving onboard our hospital ship. Volunteer nurse Hannah Wysong shared a Thanksgiving memory:

"It was a crazy, beautiful international mix of my friends. We shared what we were thankful for. 'Opportunity' *was the one-word answer that left my lips.*

I have had the honor of leading the training program for local Congolese nurses. I have had my world view shaken. I have never had to decide if my money should be spent to get me to class on the big white ship or to provide lunch for my children.

Everyone deserves a chance to better themselves. I cannot explain the joy I feel knowing that I am in a position to pass on the gift of opportunity."

Yes, the opportunity to show mercy and kindness to others—that's what following the model of Jesus is all about.

"Right now, therefore, every time we get the chance, let us work for the benefit of all, starting with the people closest to us in the community of faith.'" **(Galatians 6:10 MSG)**

"No act of kindness, no matter how small, is ever wasted." **(Aesop)**

Mercy Minute Volume 61, Script 54; by Catherine Clarke Murphy, staff writer; from story from Hannah Wysong, volunteer nurse, submitted to Catherine Murphy; 2013-2014 AFM *Congo Field Service;*

November 21

Belinda's Thanksgiving

Belinda's mother owned and operated a small Tex-Mex eatery for 20 years. And through the two decades, she established a wonderful Thanksgiving tradition.

Every year at this holiday, Belinda's mom would cook for over 100 people in addition to her small family of three. She always described these dinners as her way of giving thanks for family, friends, and customers. Even though she was sharing, she always felt like she received the most! Everyone else was giving her so much more: companionship, friendship, and love.

What a wonderful memory and legacy for Belinda! And what a great expression of thanksgiving!

"You will be enriched in every way so that you can be generous on every occasion, and through us your generosity will result in thanksgiving to God." **(2 Corinthians 9:11 NIV)**

Mercy Minute Volume 29, Script 44; by Nancy Predaina, Special Projects Writer/Editor; from spreadthesharing.com "Giving Thanks" (Belinda-Texas);

November 22

A Thanksgiving Delivery

Tony Robbins is a best-selling author and a supporter of Feeding America. The organization provides millions of meals to hungry Americans. In an interview, Tony described a childhood memory:

"It was Thanksgiving, and we had no dinner. There was a knock at the door, and I answered to find a tall man holding a box of food, an uncooked turkey in a roasting pan at his feet. Well, that night we ate like kings.

When I was 17, I asked my church for the names of two families in need. I had saved enough money to buy groceries and deliver them anonymously."

You don't have to be rich to buy someone a meal, to offer them comfort and sustenance."

I agree with Tony. A great way to celebrate Thanksgiving is by helping those less fortunate in your community.

"Let them give thanks to the Lord for His unfailing love and His wonderful deeds for mankind, for He satisfies the thirsty and fills the hungry with good things." **(Psalm 107:8-9 NIV)**

⚓ The *Anastasis* carried its first animal cargo—sheep—from Gambia to Sierra Leone in November 2002 for a micro-enterprise project. The project was called "Mercy Sheep"!

Mercy Minute Volume 65, Script 54; from "The Kindness Project," Woman's Day Magazine; *September 2015;*

November 23

I Love You, Aunty

Ali Wilks served as a volunteer pediatric nurse onboard the *Africa Mercy*. Just before the ship left Liberia, she received a surprise visit from a former patient—six-year-old Harold. He and his mother had traveled several hours to see Ali one more time.

The little boy sat silently in Ali's lap with his head nestled against her neck. At the end of the visit, Ali knelt to give him one last hug. His arms went around her neck. And his mouth found her ear to whisper the only words he would say during the entire visit, *"I love you, Aunty."*

Gratitude and love motivate acts of mercy—which produce gratitude and love. It's a wonderful circle of thanksgiving.

***"Whatever you do [no matter what it is] in word or deed, do everything in the name of the Lord Jesus [and in dependence on Him], giving thanks to God the Father through Him."* (Colossians 3:17 AMP)**

***"Keep your eyes open to your mercies. The man who forgets to be thankful has fallen asleep in life."* (Robert Louis Stevenson)**

Mercy Minute Volume 37, Script 49; by Nancy Predaina, Special Projects Writer/Editor; from alirae.net/blog (Ali Wilks) November 24, 2009; used with permission;

November 24

A Lesson in Thankfulness

While on field service, Mercy Ships hires local African people for various tasks onboard our ships, including translating. They teach us a lot, as one crew member explains:

"I am constantly challenged by our day-crew from Benin. They trust God will provide everything. Every week on 'Thankful Thursday' the crew and local translators pray together. The crew might pray with a quiet voice, tentative. But the Day-Crew's prayers are loud. They thank God with voices so powerful they reverberate off the hospital walls. They thank God for good health, for a job, that they woke up this morning, that they are able to breathe, hear and see. I forget that all of these things are gifts from God. I'm learning how to thank God like my West African brothers and sisters."

I challenge you to follow the example of our day-crew—be bold and enthusiastic in praising God and showing mercy to others.

"Do not be anxious about anything, but in every situation, by prayer and petition, with thanksgiving, present your requests to God. And the peace of God, which transcends all understanding, will guard your hearts and your minds in Christ Jesus."
(Philippians 4:6-7 NIV)

⚓ On November 24, 1981, during the renovation of the *Anastasis*, fish started jumping out of the sea. We collected 8301. A rather dramatic lesson in provision!

Mercy Minute Volume 70, Script 33; by Anna Psiaki, staff writer; adapted from personal blog of Carron Meney, by Anna Psiaki, AFM *staff writer; used with permission; 2016-2017* AFM *Benin Field Service;*

November 25

Baby Buddies

If you want a fun volunteer job, I may have just the thing for you. Children's Healthcare of Atlanta, Georgia, pairs volunteers with premature babies who need cuddling. They're called Baby Buddies.

Volunteers spend up to four hours holding, rocking and reading to preemies in the neonatal intensive care unit. These babies often spend weeks or months in the hospital. Parents often have to return to work or take care of other children. Melinda is a Baby Buddy. She says, *"I think it does me more good than it does the babies. When they smile, it just warms my heart."*

If you don't live in Atlanta, check with hospitals in your area. They may have a similar program.

If you have a merciful heart and some extra time, find a way to volunteer in your community.

"For You formed my innermost parts; You knit me [together] in my mother's womb. I will give thanks and praise to You, for I am fearfully and wonderfully made; wonderful are Your works, and my soul knows it very well." **(Psalm 139:13-14 AMP)**

Mercy Minute Volume 70, Script 43; by Nancy Predaina, Special Projects Writer/Editor; from http://www.msn.com/en-us/news/good-news/these-nicu-volunteers-have-one-job-snuggle-babies/ar-BBD33I2?ocid=ientp

November 26

Lawson

Lawson was once a prominent soccer player in West Africa. But now he hid in his house—avoiding people who called him a "devil."

For four years, a large tumor had been growing in his mouth—slowly distorting his face and destroying his life. His wife left, leaving behind their three children.

Lawson was literally at the brink of death when our hospital ship, the *Africa Mercy*, arrived. It took three volunteer surgeons eight hours to remove the benign tumor and repair his face.

Lawson was unable to hold back tears of joy. He exclaimed, *"It's a miracle! My way was crooked . . . but now it's straight!"*

Yes, mercy straightens out the crooked places. You can smooth someone's path by showing kindness today.

"In all your ways know and acknowledge and recognize Him, and He will make your paths straight and smooth [removing obstacles that block your way]." **(Proverbs 3:6 AMP)**

"Wherever a man turns, he can find someone who needs him." **(Albert Schweitzer)**

Mercy Minute Volume 47, Script 35; by Elaine B. Winn, staff writer; from interview with patient; 2010 AFM *Togo Field Service;*

November 27

Forgiveness for Roswell McIntyre

A young man named Roswell McIntyre was drafted into the cavalry during the Civil War. He got scared and ran, and he was condemned to be shot for desertion.

Roswell's mother appealed to President Lincoln, but Lincoln's generals urged him to enforce discipline.

Lincoln prayed about it. Then he wrote: *"I have observed that it never does a boy much good to shoot him."*

He wrote a letter saying that Roswell would be readmitted into the cavalry. When he completed his enlistment, the desertion charges would be dropped.

This letter is displayed in the Library of Congress with a note saying: *"This letter was taken from the body of Roswell McIntyre, who died at the battle of Little Five Forks, Virginia."*

Follow President Lincoln's example and leave a legacy of mercy and forgiveness.

"Who is a God like You, who pardons sin and forgives the transgression of the remnant of His inheritance? You do not stay angry forever but delight to show mercy. You will again have compassion on us; You will tread our sins underfoot and hurl all our iniquities into the depths of the sea." **(Micah 7:18-19 NIV)**

Mercy Minute Volume 70, Script 51; http://www.welcomehomesoldier.com/permalink-61; "The Power of Forgiveness," by Steve Goodier;

November 28

Naomi Dances

A 14-year-old girl named Naomi came to our hospital ship in West Africa. She received a free surgery to repair a debilitating leg condition. A crew member tells the story:

"Naomi and her mom cried tears of joy when they realized Naomi would walk again. She'd spent eight years in a wheelchair. Now, surgery and rehab have changed all that! She's gone from taking her first steps, to walking down the gangway, and finally to dancing at her very own good-bye party!

Naomi said, 'I'm really happy I'll be going back to school NOT in a wheelchair! I can't wait to get back to doing things I love—like dancing and playing soccer."

Yes, the sky's the limit when mercy enters the picture! Let mercy enter someone's life through YOU!

"Great crowds came to Him, bringing the lame, the blind, the crippled, the mute and many others, and laid them at His feet; and He healed them. The people were amazed when they saw the mute speaking, the crippled made well, the lame walking and the blind seeing. And they praised the God of Israel." **(Matthew 15:30-31 NIV)**

"The most eloquent prayer is the prayer through hands that heal and bless." **(Rev. Billy Graham)**

Mercy Minute Volume 70, Script 30; by Nancy Predaina, Special Projects Writer/Editor; Adapted from Mercy Ships Weekly Scoop *by Windsor Marchesi, 6/12/17;*

November 29

Kathy Gives the Gift of Life

Sometimes, providing mercy is literally a life-saving act. Volunteer Kathy Long describes her first-hand experience:

"One night they made an overhead page for everybody with my blood type because we'd had a patient that had had surgery earlier in the day. She ended up taking eleven units of blood before they could stop the bleeding.

In the States, you pump out your little pint of blood. But having your blood taken right from your arm, right into the OR, and put into another person that you can go in and then talk to the next day—it puts a whole new meaning to say we give the gift of life."

You see, mercy saves lives—physically, emotionally, and spiritually. Consider being a blood donor—it's a great act of mercy.

"Share with the Lord's people who are in need."
(Romans 12:13 NIV)

Mercy Minute Volume 52, Script 29; by Nancy Predaina, Special Projects Writer/Editor; from interview with Kathy Long by Ambassador Team and Nancy Predaina; 2013 AFM *Guinea Field Service;*

November 30

Helping Fetene

Fetene has been a crossing guard at the Harvard Elementary School in Houston, Texas, for 10 years. The kids LOVE him! He's always positive, creating laughter and joy.

His life hasn't always been full of laughter and joy. He was a child soldier in Ethiopia, recruited at age 15. He stepped on a landmine, and his leg was blown off. Finally, he was granted political asylum to come to the United States.

Fetene's prosthetic leg was bothering him and needed some repairs. And the kids decided to help. They organized a bake sale and set up a GoFundMe campaign. And they surpassed their goal of $5500!

One parent said, *"He deserves this. He makes kids feel like he's their best friend."*

Follow these children's example and show mercy by helping someone today.

***"Feed the hungry! Help those in trouble! Then your light will shine out from the darkness, and the darkness around you shall be as bright as day."* (Isaiah 58:10 TLB)**

⚓ The HOPE Center is the Hospital Out-Patient Extension, a non-medical facility that supports the hospital onboard the ship. It is a place for extended recovery and frees up precious bed space in the ship's hospital ward.

Mercy Minute Volume 70, Script 47; by Nancy Predaina, Special Projects Writer/Editor; from http://abcnews.go.com/US/texas-school-community-surprises-beloved-crossing-guard-funds/story?id=43632659

December

"For to us a child is born, to us a son is given, and the government will be on His shoulders. And He will be called Wonderful Counselor, Mighty God, Everlasting Father, Prince of Peace." (Isaiah 9:6 NIV)

December 1

All of Us

Many wonderful volunteers work together to provide the free surgical care offered onboard our hospital ship. A crew member explains:

"How many people does it take to make Arnaud's bowed legs straight and strong? The answer: translators, family members, hospital supply workers, cleaning staff, nurses, doctors , and many more. And, as we celebrate Christmas on the Africa Mercy, *a lilting melody spreads over the dock. Patients and crew hold their flickering candles high, singing, 'O Holy night, the stars are brightly shining.' Christmas reminds us that we really* are *meant to hold our small flames up—creating a beautiful mosaic of compassion and mercy."*

Yes, it really does take all of us to make a difference! Join with others to show mercy during this Christmas season.

"Therefore the Lord Himself will give you a sign: Listen carefully, the virgin will conceive and give birth to a son, and she will call His name Immanuel (God with us)." **(Isaiah 7:14 AMP)**

"The great challenge left to us is to cut through all the glitz and glam of the season that has grown increasingly secular and commercial, and be reminded of the beauty of the One who is Christmas." **(Bill Crowder)**

Mercy Minute Volume 70, Script 8; by Nancy Predaina, Special Projects Writer/Editor; adapted from Mercy Ships Weekly Scoop, *12/19/16, by Windsor Marchesi, staff writer;*

December 2

New Life for Alusine

A dose of mercy has the power to transform lives. Alusine had a large tumor on his jaw. Here's his story:

"Because of this sickness, my life went to zero. I lost my wife, my children, and my business.

Then one day I was in a taxi. The driver said, 'The Mercy Ship is in Sierra Leone—maybe they can help you.'

When I got there, they made x-rays, they worked on me, but they didn't ask for a cent. The surgery changed my life completely. I will be able to work. I will get back my life."

Christmas is a wonderful time to remember God's mercy to all of us, and for us to show God's mercy to others.

***"The Word became flesh and blood, and moved into the neighborhood. We saw the glory with our own eyes, the one-of-a-kind glory, like Father, like Son, generous inside and out, true from start to finish."* (John 1:14 MSG)**

***"May we not 'spend' Christmas or 'observe' Christmas, but rather 'keep' it."* (Peter Marshall)**

Mercy Minute Volume 54, Script 1; by Nancy Predaina, Special Projects Writer/Editor; from patient interview by Catherine Cooper, staff writer; 2011 AFM *Sierra Leone Field Service;*

December 3

A Hanukkah Miracle

A boy in Australia loved his grandmother's stories about living in Latvia. She had a silver candy dish that had belonged to Jewish friends, the Slovins. But they'd disappeared during the Nazi invasion.

Her grandson decided to search for the Slovins. He finally located a surviving son living in Israel. He sent the silver dish by registered mail. When Mr. Slovin touched the dish, it instantly unlocked and healed his heart. You see, he'd never talked about the deaths of his parents and siblings.

So now at Hanukkah, Mr. Slovin's family listens to the story of their grandparents and an Australian angel—as candlelight sparkles on a small silver dish in the center of the table.

What a beautiful story of mercy!

> ***"But when the right time came, the time God decided on, He sent his Son, born of a woman, born as a Jew, to buy freedom for us who were slaves to the law so that He could adopt us as His very own sons."* (Galatians 4:4-5 TLB)**

> ***"We consider Christmas as the encounter, the great encounter, the historical encounter, the decisive encounter, between God and mankind. He who has faith knows this truly; let him rejoice."* (Pope Paul VI)**

Mercy Minute Volume 29, Script 56; from "A Chanukah Miracle," by Barbara Sofer; Woman's Day *12/5/06;*

December 4

A Changed Future

The free surgeries provided onboard our hospital ships change lives … and futures. Volunteer Matt Tveite explains:

"I think the patients that probably stand out most for me are the cleft lip children. I look at them, and they have no idea how their life is going to change. They have no idea the suffering that would be in front of them here in West Africa if they didn't have that lip fixed, and yet they come to us as early as two months old. It's going to be so satisfying to see that child—he has no idea what his future looks like and the change in his future."

I can't help thinking of another child … a child that changed **your** future and **my** future. And HE is the reason we celebrate Christmas!

"But you, Bethlehem, in the land of Judah, are by no means least among the rulers of Judah; for out of you will come a ruler who will shepherd my people Israel." **(Matthew 2:6 NIV)**

"At this Christmas when Christ comes, will He find a warm heart? Mark the season of Advent by loving and serving others with God's own love and concern." **(Mother Teresa)**

Mercy Minute Volume 70, Script 7; by Nancy Predaina, Special Projects Writer/Editor; from interview with crew member, Matt Tveite; 2016-17 AFM *Benin Field Service; ©2017 Mercy Ships, All Rights Reserved*

December 5

The Deere Still Runs

A 1938 John Deere tractor is a familiar site in Christmas parades in North Carolina. Some say, *"It's remarkable that the Deere still runs."*

But the really remarkable thing is the tractor's history. In the late 1930s, people in Davie County helped one another with harvest. They shared a steam-driven tractor. But one year, it exploded! Three people were killed and many injured.

James Orrell and his son John lived in a home without electricity or indoor plumbing. But they pinched pennies to buy a new 1938 John Deere tractor—one of the very first with rubber tires. And, every year, they helped their neighbors with harvest.

So, parade-goers aren't just seeing a piece of equipment—it's a reminder of hard work, faith in God, and helping one other.

Let's join together to turn back the clock to those values again!

"His mercy goes on from generation to generation, to all who reverence Him. How powerful is His mighty arm!"
(Luke 1:50-51 TLB)

"And when the Lord Jesus has become your Peace, remember, there is another thing: good will towards men. Do not try to keep Christmas without good will towards men." **(Charles Spurgeon)**

Mercy Minute Volume 70, Script 13; from https://www.rd.com/true-stories/inspiring/tractor-christmas-legacy/

December 6

Mary's Special Christmas

Mary was a cheerful 11-year-old. She was happy in spite of the fact that Mary had dealt with the devastating effects of noma—a horrifying disease that leaves gaping holes in the soft tissues of the mouth and face.

Then Mercy Ships came to Mary's hometown of Monrovia, Liberia. Volunteer surgeons performed free surgeries to reconstruct her face.

The little girl had to stay on the ship over the Christmas holiday. But Mary didn't mind. She enjoyed all the attention. Her nurse said, *"The most important thing we do is to show God's love."*

And that IS the most important thing *you* can do during this Christmas—show God's love to others.

"But when the kindness and love of God our Savior appeared, He saved us, not because of righteous things we had done, but because of His mercy. He saved us through the washing of rebirth and renewal by the Holy Spirit, whom He poured out on us generously through Jesus Christ our Savior..." **(Titus 3:4-6 NIV)**

⚓ In December 1990, the *Anastasis* arrived in Togo for its first African field service.

December 7

Pete's Time

The Easter Seals Rehabilitation Center in Evansville, Indiana, receives a special Christmas treat each year. They call it "Pete's time."

A man identified only as Pete calls and gives them a message with clues that sends the staff on search of the two-story building and grounds. The prize is Pete's donation for children with disabilities. One year, they found a small tin Christmas tree decorated with 30 crisp one hundred dollar bills. They always applaud, wave, and yell, *"Thank you, Pete!"* just in case he's watching.

Pete has given over $80,000 (and still counting) to the center. And his donation always comes with a note that promises, *"You will hear from me again."*

What a fun way to show mercy! Find a creative way to show mercy to someone this Christmas.

***"He who did not spare [even] His own Son, but gave Him up for us all, how will He not also, along with Him, graciously give us all things?"* (Romans 8:32 AMP)**

***"Look for Christ and you will find Him. And with Him, everything else."* (C.S. Lewis)**

Mercy Minute Volume 66, Script 1; from "Secret Santa" rd.com and http://www.tristatehomepage.com/news/anonymous-donor-pete-leaves-thousands-for-easter-seals;

December 8

Best Christmas Gift Ever

Prinscio was born with club feet. He learned to walk on the tops of his twisted feet. A dozen traditional healers in Madagascar gave his parents advice, but none of their methods worked.

When Prinscio was three, Mercy Ships came to his country. His feet were corrected by a series of eight casts, minor surgery, exercises, and night-time braces.

In spite of his deformity, Prinscio became a joyful little boy. He enthusiastically did his physiotherapy.

On December 22nd his final casts were removed. When his mom saw her little boy's beautiful straight feet, she exclaimed, *"This is the best Christmas gift ever!"*

You know, mercy is ALWAYS the perfect gift!

"My goal is that they may be encouraged in heart and united in love, so that they may have the full riches of complete understanding, in order that they may know the mystery of God, namely, Christ, in whom are hidden all the treasures of wisdom and knowledge." **(Colossians 2:2-3 NIV)**

"The Son of God became a man to enable men to become sons of God." **(C.S. Lewis)**

Mercy Minute Volume 66, Script 8; by Sharon Walls, staff writer; from patient story by Sharon Walls; 2015-16 AFM Madagascar Field Service;

December 9

Christmas Blessings

Marta Chase served as a volunteer nurse onboard our hospital ship. She compared the experience of Elsie, her niece in the U.S., with Francina, a baby in Madagascar. Both were born with cleft lips:

"Little Elsie will have surgery at about six weeks of age. Francina was over a year old by the time she got to have surgery.

Elsie's surgery is covered by insurance. The only way Francina could have surgery was if she received it for free.

I'm grateful for the ease of having surgery in the States. More than that, I'm grateful that, because of Mercy Ships, little ones like Francina get a chance that will change their lives forever."

Take a moment this Christmas to count your blessings … and share your blessings with others.

***"But God had mercy on me so that Christ Jesus could use me as an example to show everyone how patient He is with even the worst sinners, so that others will realize that they, too, can have everlasting life."* (1 Timothy 1:16 TLB)**

***"Faith is salted and peppered through everything at Christmas. And I love at least one night by the Christmas tree to sing and feel the quiet holiness of that time that's set apart to celebrate love, friendship, and God's gift of the Christ child."* (Amy Grant)**

Mercy Minute Volume 62, Script 1; by Nancy Predaina, Special Projects Writer/Editor; from interview with Marta Chase, volunteer nurse, by Pauline Rick, U.S. Media Liaison; 2014-15 AFM *Madagascar Field Service;*

December 10

The Happy Factory

Charlie and Donna Cooley decided to take up toy-making when they retired in 1995. At first, they made toys for their grandkids. But then they donated some extras to a children's hospital … and that changed everything. Donna says, *"We realized we'd found a way to use our free time for good."*

Word quickly spread, and requests for toys and donations poured in. Now The Happy Factory has donated over a million toys to needy kids.

Charlie passed away in 2011, but Donna continues the work, helped by over 50 volunteers. They make about 100 toy cars every day. Each one is given to a sick or underprivileged child.

That's the spirit of Christmas at work! Find a way to use your talents to brighten someone's Christmas.

***"On coming to the house, they saw the child with his mother Mary, and they bowed down and worshiped Him. Then they opened their treasures and presented Him with gifts of gold, frankincense and myrrh."* (Matthew 2:11 NIV)**

⚓ Christmas celebration onboard our Mercy Ships has an international flavor. We celebrate Santa Lucia with the Scandinavians. We have a Winter Wonderland Bazaar and cookie decorating. And on Christmas Eve, each crew member follows a Dutch custom by putting a shoe outside the cabin door to be filled with small gifts or treats from other crew members.

Mercy Minute Volume 66, Script 3; by Nancy Predaina, Special Projects Writer/Editor; from "Santa's Workshop," Woman's Day Magazine, *Dec 2015/Jan 2016;*

December 11

Jesus Helps Atasse

Eight-year-old Atasse received a free surgery onboard our hospital ship in the Republic of Congo to correct his misshapen feet. His grandmother described her gratitude:

"Did I feel that Jesus had a part in my grandson's care? Oh, yes—but let me say it louder! Jesus has played a big role in the healing of my grandchild! He walks normally now like other children. You know, I never expected that. Now he's going to school, something he could not do before. Alleluia! I am one grateful grandma!"

Christmas is all about the birth of Jesus—the incarnation of God's love and mercy, which is His great gift to each and every one of us.

"Of the greatness of His government and peace there will be no end. He will reign on David's throne and over his kingdom, establishing and upholding it with justice and righteousness from that time on and forever. The zeal of the Lord Almighty will accomplish this." **(Isaiah 9:7 NIV)**

"You can never truly enjoy Christmas until you can look up into the Father's face and tell Him you have received His Christmas gift." **(John R. Rice)**

Mercy Minute Volume 62, Script 7; by Catherine Clarke Murphy, staff writer; from patient interview; 2011-12 AFM Congo Field Service;

December 12

Angels for Kids

Sometimes personal tragedy inspires acts of mercy. Here's Shanyn's story:

"I lost both of my parents at a young age. So I know how hard it can be to celebrate the holidays without family. When I was 19, I organized a Christmas party for kids in group homes. In 2009, I founded a nonprofit, the Angels for Kids Foundation. I host Christmas events every year for homeless and underprivileged children. I talk to social workers to find out what each child really wants for Christmas.

As soon as they open that one present they wanted, their smiles are endless. The best part is that they will remember that someone cared enough to make their holidays special."

Yes, mercy and love create wonderful Christmas memories.

"But the angel said to them, 'Do not be afraid; for behold, I bring you good news of great joy which will be for all the people; for today in the city of David there has been born for you a Savior, who is Christ the Lord." **(Luke 2:10-11 NASB)**

"Believers, look up! Take courage! The angels are nearer than you think." **(Rev. Billy Graham)**

Mercy Minute Volume 58, Script 10; by Nancy Predaina, Special Projects Writer/Editor; from "Making a Difference," Woman's Day, *December 2012, and http://www.angelsforkidsamherst.com/;*

December 13

A Christmas Miracle for Harris

Harris sat on a wooden canoe, getting ready for his daily fishing trip. With any luck, he'd catch five or six fish to sell.

Harris was weighed down by an enormous tumor on the side of his face. It had been growing for 13 of his 34 years, forcing him into isolation. It was just a few days before Christmas.

A Mercy Ships photographer happened to stop at a rice store. He heard some men talking about a man with an enormous tumor. So, he searched until he found Harris. The photographer told Harris about a Mercy Ship that could take away the tumor, free of charge!

And that's exactly what happened—Harris had his own Christmas miracle!

And YOU can be a Christmas miracle to others by showing mercy and kindness to them.

***"So they hurried off and found Mary and Joseph, and the baby, who was lying in the manger. When they had seen Him, they spread the word concerning what had been told them about this child, and all who heard it were amazed at what the shepherds said to them."* (Luke 2:16-18 NIV)**

***"Jesus was God and man in one person, that God and man might be happy together again."* (George Whitefield)**

Mercy Minute Volume 29, Script 61; by Nancy Predaina, Special Projects Writer/Editor; from onamercyship.org website of Scott Harrison, staff photojournalist;

December 14

A Necklace of Mercy

Catherine Murphy, a Mercy Ships crewmember, shared this wonderful story:

"When Marie's home was looted during Congo's civil war, she lost a very special necklace. I shared her story on Facebook. A man in England named Eamonn O'Reilly wrote to me. He said he wanted to replace Marie's necklace.

Now Eamonn's daughter Emily happens to be a nurse with Mercy Ships. We delivered the necklace to a delighted Marie. Thanks to Eamonn's thoughtfulness and generosity, there is a woman in Congo who's probably still smiling from ear to ear!

I'm reminded that we have the power to create happy endings out of sad beginnings."

Now you go, celebrate Christmas by adding thoughtfulness, generosity . . . and mercy . . . to YOUR Christmas gift list.

"For God so [greatly] loved and dearly prized the world, that He [even] gave His [One and] only begotten Son, so that whoever believes and trusts in Him [as Savior] shall not perish, but have eternal life." **(John 3:16 AMP)**

Mercy Minute Volume 58, Script 7; from blogpost by Catherine Clarke Murphy, staff writer; 2013-14 AFM Congo Field Service;

December 15

A Christmas Tablecloth

Long ago, a young pastor came to a poor, run-down church in Europe. There was a big hole in the plaster wall behind the altar. How could he fix it before Christmas?

The answer came at a benefit auction. He bought a 15-foot beautiful gold and ivory tablecloth for $6.50 and used it to cover the hole.

On Christmas Eve, a war refugee entered the church to get warm. Suddenly, she recognized the tablecloth and exclaimed, *"My husband had the cloth made especially for me in Brussels!"* She showed the pastor the monogrammed initials on it.

A coincidence? Maybe. But I like to think of it as a small, bright miracle in a season in which we celebrate the greatest miracle. Celebrate Christmas by giving the miracle of mercy to someone today.

"And Mary said: 'My soul glorifies the Lord and my spirit rejoices in God my Savior, for He has been mindful of the humble state of His servant.'" **(Luke 1:46-48 NIV)**

⚓ Drawing upon over 40 years of organizational experience, the Mercy Ships International Board signed a contract on December 15, 2013, to construct a purpose-built hospital ship, the *Global Mercy*, which is the newest member of the Mercy Ships fleet.

Mercy Minute Volume 58, Script 6; from "The Gold and Ivory Tablecloth," http://www.rd.com; Reader's Digest, *2012;*

December 16

The Nativity Set

There are so many wonderful symbols associated with Christmas—stars, angels, nativity sets. Sometimes it's easy to forget that many people have never heard the beautiful story that goes with the symbols. Crewmember Dianna Cash, who served as a chaplain onboard our hospital ship, explained:

"In the Ship Shop you can buy beautiful locally-made soapstone nativity sets. Today a crewmate told me that she was able to explain the Christmas story with one of the hand-carved scenes. This was significant because she shared this with a Congolese day-crew who had NEVER heard the story.

It blew me away to be reminded that some have never heard the wonderful news of Christmas."

Yes, when you see a nativity set this Christmas, whisper a prayer for those who have not heard about the amazing love of Jesus.

"While they were there, the days were completed for her to give birth. And she gave birth to her firstborn son; and she wrapped Him in cloths, and laid Him in a manger, because there was no room for them in the inn." **(Luke 2:6-7 NASB)**

"The Almighty appeared on earth as a helpless human baby, needing to be fed and changed and taught to talk like any other child. The more you think about it, the more staggering it gets. Nothing in fiction is so fantastic as this truth of the Incarnation." **(J.I. Packer)**

Mercy Minute Volume 58, Script 8; by Catherine Clarke Murphy, staff writer; from story from Dianna Cash, PCG/Chaplain (USA), 2013-14 AFM Congo Field Service;

December 17

A Pilot's Mercy

It was December 1943. Young Charles Brown was on his first combat mission. His B-17 bomber had been severely crippled by enemy fire. And just three feet from his plane's wingtip was a German fighter. Ace pilot, Franz Stigler, needed one more kill to win The Knight's Cross for valor.

But Stigler didn't pull the trigger. He nodded at Charlie, and then escorted the wounded bomber home, saluted, and headed back to Germany.

The two men reconnected many years later and became friends. Stigler gave Charlie a book with this inscription: *"In 1940, I lost my only brother as a night fighter. On the 20th of December, four days before Christmas, I had the chance to save a B-17 from her destruction ... The pilot, Charlie Brown, is for me, as precious as was my brother."*

Now that's mercy!

"Now to the King of the ages [eternal], immortal, invisible, the only God, be honor and glory forever and ever. Amen."
(1 Timothy 1:17 AMP)

"Best of all, Christmas means a spirit of love, a time when the love of God and the love of our fellow men should prevail over all hatred and bitterness, a time when our thoughts and deeds and the spirit of our lives manifest the presence of God."
(George F. McDougall)

Mercy Minute Volume 62, Script 9; from "Two Enemies Discover a 'Higher Call' in Battle," by John Blake; www.cnn.com

December 18

A Malagasy Christmas, Part 1

Mercy Ships volunteer Rosie Timms spent Christmas onboard our hospital ship in Madagascar. She shared some memories in a newsletter:

"Since we have 33 nations onboard, you can bet we have many traditions. The Norwegians and 'wanna be' Norwegians put on a Santa Lucia celebration.

Another highlight was when the patients, caregivers and staff gathered on the dock for a candlelight Christmas carol sing. Some sang in English, some in Malagasy ... but it was beautiful. There was such a sweet spirit of unity among us."

Yes, celebrating the wonder of Christmas creates a common ground that brings people together in a joy-filled spirit of unity. Join with others in celebrating Christmas ... and mercy.

> ***"At once the angel was joined by a huge angelic choir singing God's praises: Glory to God in the heavenly heights, peace to all men and women on earth who please him."*** **(Luke 2:13-14 MSG)**

⚓ On December 18, 2015, our newest ship, the *Global Mercy*, was officially born, as the first block came to rest on the dry dock blocks. This keel-laying ceremony was marked by much joy and thankfulness.

Mercy Minute Volume 62, Script 4; by Nancy Predaina, Special Projects Writer/Editor; from E-Newsletter from Rosie Timms, 2014-15 AFM *Madagascar Field Service;*

December 19

A Malagasy Christmas, Part 2

Mercy Ships volunteer Rosie Timms thought spending Christmas onboard our hospital ship might be lonely. But she was surprised:

"The highlight was ward service on Christmas Day. I gathered up a new volunteer from Switzerland who looked a little lost. I said, 'Come on, this is the best part of Mercy Ships,' and I was right.

There was only a guitar to lead the singing. They went from one song to another ... no songleader, no sheet music. It was the usual group with casts on their legs, hospital gowns flapping, children toddling ... all with joy written all over their faces.

So pure and simple ... I am sure it will put a smile on Jesus' face."

And that is Christmas ... pure, simple love from God to us—in the form of a baby boy.

***"He tends His flock like a shepherd: He gathers the lambs in His arms and carries them close to His heart; He gently leads those that have young."* (Isaiah 40:11 NIV)**

***"Who can add to Christmas? The perfect motive is that God so loved the world. The perfect gift is that He gave His only Son. The only requirement is to believe in Him. The reward of faith is that you shall have everlasting life."* (Corrie Ten Boom)**

Mercy Minute Volume 62, Script 10; by Nancy Predaina, Special Projects Writer/Editor; from E-Newsletter from Rosie Timms, 2014-15 AFM *Madagascar Field Service;*

December 20

A Gift-Wrapped Dad

Army Sergeant Matt Wilder was in his fourth tour of duty in Iraq, with only six months left. So, it was unlikely he'd be home for Christmas. One of his two daughters said she wished he could be wrapped up and mailed home.

Then Matt found out he'd been accepted to flight school and would be coming home in early December. His wife Desiray thought, *"Wouldn't it be wonderful to surprise the girls at school?"*

At a school assembly, the girls stood in the middle of the gym, and an enormous gift-wrapped box was wheeled out. They ripped off the paper, out popped their father, still wearing his Army fatigues.

Now that's a great Christmas gift! If you know a military family, I encourage you to find a way to brighten their Christmas.

"You will tell His people how to find salvation through forgiveness of their sins. All this will be because the mercy of our God is very tender, and heaven's dawn is about to break upon us, to give light to those who sit in darkness and death's shadow, and to guide us to the path of peace." **(Luke 1:77-79 TLB)**

"Peace with God, peace with others, and peace in your own heart." **(Rick Warren)**

Mercy Minute Volume 62, Script 2; from "A Father's Surprise," Woman's Day, *12/1/2009;*

December 21

A Tender Moment of Mercy

They presented quite a contrast: a Mercy Ships volunteer eye surgeon—tall, slim, with a beard—and a little boy—just four years old, frightened, and blind from congenital cataracts. He had come to our Mercy Ship for a free surgery to restore his sight.

Very gently Dr. Fotios Kefalianakis carried the child into the operating room. As he placed the face mask carefully over the boy's mouth and nose, he sang a soft lullaby in French. The little boy went to sleep without struggling or crying. What a tender moment of mercy!

Isn't that what Christmas is all about—a tender moment of mercy. A moment when God sent His angels to proclaim, *"Fear not!"*

"After Jesus was born in Bethlehem in Judea, during the time of King Herod, Magi from the east came to Jerusalem and asked, ' Where is the One who has been born King of the Jews? We saw His star when it rose and have come to worship Him.'" **(Matthew 2:1-2 NIV)**

"The very purpose of Christ's coming into the world was that He might offer up His life as a sacrifice for the sins of men. He came to die. This is the heart of Christmas." **(Rev. Billy Graham)**

Mercy Minute Volume 62, Script 8; from Mercy Ships Weekly Scoop, *December 15, 2014; 2014-15* AFM *Madagascar Field Service;*

December 22

Riley's Christmas Bikes

One day, ten-year-old Riley Christensen was looking online for a bicycle … but she discovered Project Mobility. The organization provides specially engineered bicycles to people with disabilities. So, Riley decided to give bikes instead of receiving one.

Two days later, she sent a letter to 75 relatives and friends asking for donations. By Christmas, she had received $12,000—enough for *seven* specially engineered bicycles!

On Christmas Eve, Riley put on a Santa hat and personally delivered three of those bicycles. Riley said, *"This is the best Christmas I ever had. I want disabled kids to feel the wind in their faces."*

You see, the true joy of Christmas is not found in the gifts you receive, but in the gifts you give. Give the gift of mercy this Christmas!

***"The shepherds returned, glorifying and praising God for all the things they had heard and seen, which were just as they had been told."* (Luke 2:20 NIV)**

***"All the Christmas presents in the world are worth nothing without the presence of Christ."* (David Jeremiah)**

Mercy Minute Volume 54, Script 7; from "The Spirit of Giving," by Gary Sledge; Reader's Digest, *December 2010;*

December 23

A Miracle Christmas House

Kregg Grippo looked at the charred remains of the small house. His construction business was busy, and it was almost Christmas.

Just then elderly Mrs. Turek came out of the shed where she was living. He discovered she'd taught his aunt English when she immigrated to America. And he heard himself promising a new house—by Christmas.

Where would he find the workers and supplies? He got some men together and began to work. Word spread. A local TV station ran the story. Companies called to donate services and supplies.

And, sure enough, the house was finished on Christmas Eve! Kregg said, "*When you know there's something God wants you to do, take the first step—and trust Him for the rest.*"

God always wants us to show mercy, so get some people together and find a way to help someone this Christmas.

"'She will bear a Son; and you shall call His name Jesus, for He will save His people from their sins.' Now all this took place to fulfill what was spoken by the Lord through the prophet:" **(Matthew 1:21-22 NASB)**

"Christmas, my child, is love in action. Every time we love, every time we give, it's Christmas." **(Dale Evans)**

Mercy Minute Volume 29, Script 52; from "Last-Minute Miracle," Guideposts, *December 2005;*

December 24

Mercy Ships Night Before Christmas

'Twas the night before Christmas, when all through the ship
Not a patient was suffering, not even a bit;
The volunteer nurses handled everyone with great care,
Patients received love and smiles—they all saw their share!
The Africa Mercy *is no ordinary ship,*
And it's not a place for a simple day-trip;
It's a floating hospital, with doctors and nurses so hip,
They will even take care of your cleft lip!
Tumors and cataracts and teeth are all treated here,
Leaving patients grinning from ear to ear;
Baristas, writers, teachers and deckies, oh my!
This ship is so amazing, one could cry!
Volunteers and donors make it all possible,
This place is beyond phenomenal;
Bringing hope and healing is what we do,
But none of it is possible without donors like you;
Today we hold our patients extra tight,
As we exclaim from Africa:
"Merry Christmas to all, and to all a good night!"

Arahaba Tratry Krisimasy! (Merry Christmas in Malagasy!)

***"Now thanks be to God for His indescribable gift [which is precious beyond words]!"* (2 Corinthians 9:15 AMP)**

Mercy Minute Volume 42, Script 5; by Nancy Predaina, Special Projects Writer/Editor; from http:// aliinbenin.blogspot.com, 3/14/09, blog by Ali Herbert, OR nurse, 2009 AFM, *Benin Field Service; used with permission;*

December 25

Sleep in Heavenly Peace

A Mercy Ships staff member shares some Christmas thoughts:

"It's quiet in the children's orthopedic ward onboard our hospital ship. The beautiful African children are sleeping—living photos of innocence and trust, tiny hands curled gently on their pillows.

Are they dreaming of finally getting to go to school or play soccer and other wonderful games?

And what faces do they see in their dreams? The doctors, nurses, other crew? Perhaps people they've never met, people who gave so that they could have a chance at a good life? And behind those faces, do they see the loving face of Jesus?

And the words of the beautiful Christmas carol come to mind:
'Silent night, Holy Night,
All is calm, All is bright …
… Holy infant, So tender and mild,
Sleep in heavenly peace,
Sleep in heavenly peace.'"

From all of us at Mercy Ships, may you have a blessed and mercy-full Christmas.

"For a child will be born to us, a son will be given to us; and the government will rest on His shoulders; and His name will be called Wonderful Counselor, Mighty God, Eternal Father, Prince of Peace." **(Isaiah 9:6 NASB)**

"Once in our world, a stable had something in it that was bigger than our whole world." **(C.S. Lewis)**

Mercy Minute Volume 70, Script 11; by Nancy Predaina, Special Projects Writer/Editor; personal observations;

December 26

Daniel Gets New Shoes

Daniel was eight years old and had never walked! As an infant, his muscles and tendons didn't develop properly. He couldn't even stand.

Then our Mercy Ship arrived in West Africa. Volunteer surgeons released the muscles and tendons so Daniel could straighten his legs and stand. And he began intensive physical therapy. Each painful step was a fight, but he succeeded!

Inspired by Daniel's determination, a volunteer brought him a pair of barely-used tennis shoes. She bent down, slid the shoes on his feet, and laced them up. Daniel smiled brightly, saying, *"I love them."* Then he stood up and took a confident step in his "new" shoes.

You see, mercy gave Daniel new shoes, new steps, and a new life.

***"The steps of good men are directed by the Lord. He delights in each step they take."* (Psalm 37:23 TLB)**

***"Man has two great spiritual needs. One is for forgiveness. The other is for goodness."* (Rev. Billy Graham)**

Mercy Minute Volume 37, Script 62; by Carmen Radley, staff writer; personal observation; 2009 AFM *Benin Field Service;*

December 27

Bintou

Six-month-old Bintou had a white spot in her right eye. Her parents could barely afford daily rice, much less medical care. The spot grew and blinded her eye, while another spot appeared on her left eye. She lived in a world of shadows.

When Bintou was four, Mercy Ships arrived in Guinea, and her cataracts were removed free of charge! Then came the moment of suspended anticipation when the patches came off. Volunteer Kim Strauss reported, *"Bintou's father exclaimed over and over how we had given sight back to his beautiful daughter and hope to the entire family."*

Yes, the dark world that surrounded them had been conquered by mercy. And, now, Bintou's future is bright and clear.

You see, mercy always conquers the darkness. And you can bring light into the world by showing kindness to others.

***"Then Jesus again spoke to them, saying, 'I am the Light of the world; he who follows Me will not walk in the darkness, but will have the Light of life.'"* (John 8:12 NASB)**

Mercy Minute Volume 54, Script 14; by Joanne Thibault, staff writer; from patient interview; 2012-13 AFM *Guinea Field Service;*

December 28

Fanny Crosby

Fanny Crosby lost her eyesight when she was only 6 weeks old. But her faith in God inspired her to write more than 8,000 hymns during her 95 years.

A preacher once told Fanny it was a shame God hadn't given her the gift of sight. She disagreed and said, *"When I get to heaven, the first face that shall ever gladden my sight will be that of my Savior!"*

In spite of her own problems, she took time to think of others. In fact, Fanny Crosby dedicated her life to serving the poor. She often donated her income of $2 per song to mission work.

Fanny Crosby is a great example of a life dedicated to serving others … a life dedicated to mercy.

"Talk with each other much about the Lord, quoting psalms and hymns and singing sacred songs, making music in your hearts to the Lord." **(Psalm 5:19 TLB)**

Mercy Minute Volume 28, Script 38; from "Living by Faith, Not by Sight" by Joyce Williams; Reflecting God *devotional booklet; Word Action Publishing Company;*

December 29

Hasanatu's Reflection

A Mercy Ships volunteer nurse, Emily Seamon, describes a special moment with a patient:

"I was paged to the hospital ward because Hasanatu had woken up after her surgery. For the last 30 years, a benign tumor had grown on the side of her neck and head. Because of the absence of healthcare, she has had to live with it.

When Hasanatu saw herself in a mirror, tumor-free, she reached up and felt her face. After a few minutes, she understood—and through the tubes and gauze, she smiled.

So I come to you with good news out of Africa tonight—a woman named Hasanatu is smiling at her new reflection."

What an amazing moment of mercy! Ask God to help you provide moments of mercy for those around you.

"... to be made new in the attitude of your minds; and to put on the new self, created to be like God in true righteousness and holiness."
(Ephesians 4:23-24 NIV)

"Holiness does not consist in doing extraordinary things. It consists in accepting, with a smile, what Jesus sends us. It consists in accepting and following the will of God."
(Mother Teresa)

Mercy Minute Volume 52, Script 27; by Catherine Clarke Murphy, staff writer; from Catherine's blog, based on her interview with nurse Emily Seamon; used with permission;

December 30

Night Duty in Iraq

Air Force Chief Master Sergeant John Gebhardt served with a Medical Group in Iraq. A little girl about two years old arrived at John's hospital. Iraqi insurgents had executed the girl's entire family. She survived—even though she, too, had been shot in the head.

At night the little girl cried and moaned. Duty nurses discovered John was the only one who could comfort her. So during the worst episodes, John spent his nights sleeping in a chair, with the small child fast asleep on his shoulder.

A photo of the pair fast asleep helped John's wife through the long days until her soldier-husband came home.

And it was a beautiful picture of mercy. Don't rest until you show kindness to someone today.

***"In peace [and with a tranquil heart] I will both lie down and sleep, for You alone, O Lord, make me dwell in safety and confident trust."* (Psalm 4:8 AMP)**

***"Be at war with your vices, at peace with your neighbors, and let every new year find you a better man."* (Benjamin Franklin)**

Mercy Minute Volume 28, Script 24; by Larry Mast, staff writer; from email and photo from Terry Howlett;

December 31

Mama Victoria

Mama Victoria greets you with a broad gap-toothed smile. She started taking in orphans during Liberia's 14-year long civil war—after she lost her husband and while caring for five of her own children.

Mama Victoria did not have a permanent home, or food or money to care for the kids. But she believed it was the right thing to do. At one point, she was caring for 175 children.

The Mercy Ships crew gladly joined in and helped by raising money from friends at home and worked to build a better facility. In May of 2006, the children danced and sang a new song as the orphanage was dedicated. And God smiled.

You see, acts of mercy bring joy and music into the lives of others … and they make God smile.

> ***"The Lord bless you, and keep you; the Lord make His face shine on you, and be gracious to you; the Lord lift up His countenance on you, and give you peace."*** **(Numbers 6:24-26 NASB)**

⚓ A multinational crew from a wide spectrum of backgrounds continue to volunteer each year with Mercy Ships to "bring hope and healing to the world's forgotten poor."

Mercy Minute Volume 27, Script 34; by Nancy Predaina, Special Projects Writer/Editor; from Erin Blinn's blog on the Mercy Ships website, May 16, 2006; used with permission;

About the Authors

Don Stephens is the Founder of Mercy Ships. Recipient of various awards, Don speaks internationally and is the voice behind the *Mercy Minute*, a daily radio broadcast aired around the globe.

Nancy Predaina serves as Special Projects Writer/Editor at the Mercy Ships International Support Center and as coordinator for the *Mercy Minute* daily radio program. She is a published author.

Ships *of* Mercy

In Africa alone lack of access to surgery is a greater killer each year than HIV, typhoid and malaria put together. With 75% of the world's population living within 150km of a port city, Mercy Ships can reach people who live with little or no healthcare in some of the poorest parts of the world.

Celebrating 40 years of Mercy Ships, this is the story of how a Colorado farm boy built a navy, how a decrepit ocean liner became a hospital and how a boat-load of volunteers is literally changing the face of the world ... one person at a time.

The story of Don Stephens and his vision for Mercy Ships is simply breathtaking. His encounter with Mother Teresa shook his life to the core and I would challenge anyone not to be equally affected by reading Don's story here. - Gavin Calver

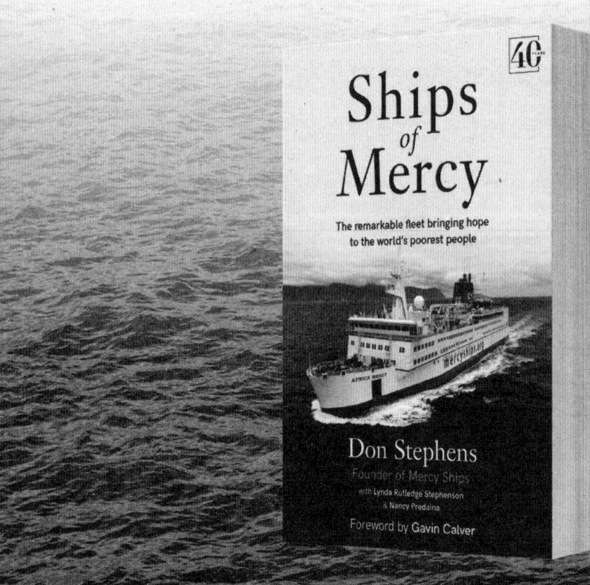

ISBN 978 1 473 68254 2